Sharon Creech

SHARON CREECH

PAMELA SISSI CARROLL

TEEN READS: STUDENT COMPANIONS TO YOUNG ADULT LITERATURE
JAMES B. BLASINGAME, SERIES EDITOR

GREENWOOD PRESS
WESTPORT, CONNECTICUT • LONDON

Library of Congress Cataloging-in-Publication Data

Carroll, Pamela S.
  Sharon Creech / Pamela Sissi Carroll.
      p. cm. — (Teen reads: student companions to young adult literature,
ISSN 1553-5096)
  Includes bibliographical references and index.
  ISBN-13: 978-0-313-33598-3 (alk. paper)
  1. Creech, Sharon. 2. Authors, American—20th century—Biography. 3. Young
adult fiction, American—History and criticism. I. Title.
  PS3553.R3373Z64 2007
  813′.54—dc22   2007021470

British Library Cataloguing in Publication Data is available.

Library of Congress Catalog Card Number: 2007021470
ISBN-13: 978-0-313-33598-3
ISSN: 1553-5096

First published in 2007

Greenwood Press, 88 Post Road West, Westport, CT 06881
An imprint of Greenwood Publishing Group, Inc.
www.greenwood.com

Printed in the United States of America

The paper used in this book complies with the
Permanent Paper Standard issued by the National
Information Standards Organization (Z39.48–1984).

10 9 8 7 6 5 4 3 2 1

for Lou Ann, Laura, and Ashley Lebovitz—
a trio of feisty ladies, full of love,
full of hope.

CONTENTS

SERIES FOREWORD

When young readers first find a book they love, the result is magical. A whole new universe opens up to them with possibilities as limitless as their own young imaginations. Finding a favorite author brings with it a powerful curiosity about that author as person and a thirst for more books from him or her. The Teen Reads series brings to young readers just the information they need to satisfy their curiosity and slake their thirst. Chapters about the authors' lives reveal to the young reader that this person was once young, too, with all the trials and tribulations of young people today. Sometimes, young readers will be surprised to find that their favorite author had a very difficult journey in life, and the admiration they hold for that author will grow even more with one wonderful benefit: the realization that challenges create the people we become, and adversity does not equal failure in life.

We have chosen six of the most popular and accomplished of authors who write for young adults: Joan Bauer, Sharon Creech, Chris Crutcher, Walter Dean Myers, Gary Paulsen, and Tamora Pierce. These six authors represent a priceless wealth of life experience, distilled through an author's heart and soul and poured out onto the page in stories of adventure, challenge, love, hardship, and triumph, some set in the Old West, some on another planet, and some right here and now. Each book in the Teen Reads series will delight young readers with connections between their favorite authors' books and the events in their lives that lead them to this vocation in life and sometimes even to the specific settings, characters, and events in their stories.

For each important novel or series of novels, readers will find synopses of the setting, characters, plots, themes, and literary techniques, along with interesting information that sheds light on how and why the author chose to write these books as he or she did. Using this series will help young readers to make connections with themselves, the world, and other books as they dig deeper in investigating their favorite authors and the books they have written. In addition, each book in this series will help to answer the foremost question on every reader's mind who is lucky enough to find joy in the work of a particular writer: "What else did this author write?"

James B. Blasingame

PREFACE

Why would you, a middle or high school student, or a teacher or parent of teens, want to read a book by Sharon Creech? What does Creech have to offer that a teenager is not likely to get by spending time, instead, in front of a computer, on a soccer field, at the mall, in a Key Club meeting, around a group of friends? The simple answer is that Sharon Creech's books offer hope. Through three-dimensional main characters who are middle and high school students themselves, and with situations that teenagers can imagine themselves struggling through—ranging from a lighthearted look at one teen's attempts to appreciate her oddly quiet, subtly smart cousin, to another's attempt to reconcile painful half-memories of the day her parents were killed with her new reality—Sharon Creech's subject, consistently, reliably, is hope.

There is power in books; as readers, we have the opportunity to examine our world while it is stopped in front of us on a page, and to think carefully about it. We can move in and out of the pages of a book, in and out of its situations, challenges, and revelations, and take its wisdom with us. Author for young adults Bruce Brooks explains the power of reading a book in terms of its demands on a reader: "Reading a work of literature takes everything that a human being has at his/her command; it stretches every muscle, fires every neuron, tests reaction time and mind-eye coordination, demands coherence of left brain and right. And—just to distinguish it from some kind of mental aerobics—it reaches and expands all levels of feeling, too" (*The ALAN Review*, Fall, 1988, 1).

Sharon Creech creates characters that readers are drawn to through their humanness. Among her characters, we find some who must retreat into solitude to discover themselves; some who long to leave ugly lives behind and join loving families; others who need companionship of siblings, friends, and loving adults in order to experience a sense of connection. Sharon Creech allows us to eavesdrop on them in the dens of mountain cabins, amidst the noisy confusion of urban classrooms, and in family kitchens. When we listen to the conversations, and join them, in our minds, we find hope.

This volume starts with the first book for teenagers that Creech published and moves chronologically, highlighting the most popular points on Creech's publication timeline. The books that are featured hold special appeal for pre-teen and teen readers for many reasons, including three important ones. First, the personalities and voices of Creech's main characters are clearly kids' personalities, with kids' voices. (Several of her novels, such as *Walk Two Moons*, *Ruby Holler*, and *Replay* feature main characters who are the age of middle school students. Others, including *Bloomability*, *The Wanderer*, and *Heartbeat,* feature slightly older main characters—those who are the age of high school students.) Second, the situations that grow into plots and sub-plots allow teen characters to prove themselves as thinkers and doers. Third, the literary forms that Creech employs, from the comedy of *Absolutely Normal Chaos*, to the poetic eloquence of *Love that Dog* and *Heartbeat*, and the drama that infuses *Replay*, provide literary variety and artistic quality.

The nine books presented in chapters three through eleven of this volume also appeal to teachers and adult readers who seek to present teen readers with literature that is not only topical and fresh, but also has high artistic integrity. Readers will notice several features within the collection of books discussed in this volume in which Creech's long career as a teacher of literature is linked to her work as a writer. As readers, we find many fingerprints of Creech the teacher: an emphasis on journal writing as a way to find out what we think and know; examples are the importance of using words precisely and carefully, and the fun of using the stories and language of classic literature as a lens through which to examine our ordinary, present lives. Readers will also find Creech's treatment of themes that are significant to teen readers, including these: relationships between friends, the significance of family and home, the importance of positive adults in the lives of teens. The fingerprints of Creech the teacher are discussed, in this volume, in each chapter that highlights a different one of her books.

Also discussed in each of the nine chapters on individual books are the fingerprints of Creech the artist, marks that are particularly evident in her well-drawn characters, familiar settings, and the frequent use of the journey as a motif. Creech is an artist who respects teen readers' emotions and their intelligence; that respect is apparent in each of her literary works.

Despite her success as a writer for teens, Sharon Creech also writes books that are popular among children and their parents: *Fishing in the Air* (2000) and *Granny Torrelli Makes Soup* (2003) are two. After becoming a grandmother, she added literature for infants to her repertoire, penning the delightful picture book, illustrated by David Diaz, *Who's that Baby? New Baby Songs* (2005). Creech sleuths will also find that Creech has published two novels for adults: *The Recital* (1990) and *Nickel Malley* (1991), both of which were released in England, using her married name, Sharon Rigg.

Another successful writer for young adults, Sue Ellen Bridgers, once noted that "My decision to write about people struggling to find meaning in life is a moral choice. It is the same choice millions of women make in their daily lives—a choice to nurture, to heal, to make decisions that reflect care rather than justice" (*The ALAN Review*, Fall, 1995, 3). Why would a teenager read a book by Sharon Creech? Because she treats young people with respect, with care instead of judgment or justice. In her novels, Creech acknowledges the difficulty of making good choices, of allowing others into our lives and trusting them, of claiming our own identities, of the power of sharing our dreams with other dreamers. And in her work, we always find the possibility of hope.

CHAPTER ONE

GETTING TO KNOW SHARON CREECH: THE WRITER, THE HUMAN BEING

O UR REASONS FOR wanting to know about the person who writes books that we enjoy are curious. On one hand, it should not matter to us, as readers, whether or not the person who creates characters that we are drawn to, invents scenes and situations that intrigue and energize us, and provides themes that leave us illuminated, confused, sad, and overjoyed, is someone we would like as a human as much as we like her as a writer, a person we would enjoy sitting with during an afternoon conversation or a casual evening meal. Whether or not the author gets along with his or her brothers and sisters, keeps pets, did well in school, was popular, athletic, bookish, aloof, or nerdy should not matter, since those personal traits may not have any direct impact on what we find in an author's literature. Yet somehow these things do matter to us as readers, don't they? We want to know that the person who is able to create characters who share so many of our traits—our self-consciousness, our problems, our goals, who brings to life settings that we want to visit, who causes us to reflect on our own attitudes about ourselves, others, the world we live in, and relationships among those, is a good person—a person we would respect, a person we would be happy to introduce to our family and friends. We want to know that an author whose books we read and enjoy is a person whom we would enjoy—and who would return the favor and enjoy us, as well. We want to be sure that we would have something in common with the author, and that we would have a good time spending time with him or her.

Sharon Creech, born on July 29, 1945, in Euclid, Ohio, a suburb of Cleveland, is an author whose books nudge us toward curiosity about the writer as a human being. We are eager to find out if the person matches up to the image we envision. After all, when reading several of Creech's novels, we can tell that she is a person who knows teens well, and who takes teens seriously. We can see in her books that she often draws on a positive sense of humor when she writes about thorny problems, and that she refuses to pretend that problems don't exist in teens' worlds. Is she really a human who believes in the talents and minds of teenagers?

What we find, when we get to know Sharon Creech the writer, is that she treats teenagers with the utmost respect and care. What we learn about Sharon Creech the human being, when we take a glance at her biography, is that her literary art reflects her experiences and attitudes toward teens, families, relationships, and the world. Sharon Creech the writer composes books that speak for Sharon Creech the human: through her literature, she offers us the gift of hopefulness, a sense that, like the characters she creates, we can find our place in the world, and that we matter, after all.

Creech's pedigree includes that of mother of a now-grown son and daughter and wife of the headmaster of Pennington School in Pennington, New Jersey. She is now a full-time writer, living in New Jersey, but the story that leads to the present has as many twists and turns as a trail in a country holler, or a highway alongside the Snake River.

BORN CREECH

Sharon Creech Rigg (Creech is her maiden name, and the one she uses when writing for children, teens, and young adults; Rigg is her married name, and the one she uses when writing for adults) grew up in a large, loud family that is similar to those she describes in several of her books, including *Absolutely Normal Chaos*, *Chasing Redbird*, and *Replay*. The second oldest of five children, she enjoyed playing outside, climbing trees, and visiting her cousins in their small-town homes in southern Ohio and northern Kentucky. In describing the visits with her father's family in those places, she writes energetically:

> For me, a suburban Cleveland girl, those hills and trees and creeks were heaven! I loved the cows, the horses, the chickens,

the fields, the barns, all of it. I loved climbing hills and trees and swimming in the creek. I don't know exactly why, but I have always been—and still am—drawn to rural locations and feel calmed by them. In this way, I am very much like Salamanca (*Walk Two Moons*), Zinny (*Chasing Redbird*), and Domenica (*Bloomability*). (personal correspondence, January 2, 2007)

Even in her Newbery Medal Acceptance Speech, which she delivered on June 25, 1995, in Chicago, Illinois, at the annual conference of the American Library Association, Creech remarks on her early, strong connection to the natural world. After saying that she grew up believing that her heritage includes American Indian blood, and that she "inhaled Indian myths" and "crept through the woods near our house, reenacting" the myths, she talks about her love of being outdoors:

I think I spent half of my childhood up a tree, for I had somehow got it in my mind that Indians climbed trees. And there in those trees—Oh! You could climb and climb, and you could reach a place where there was only you and the tree and the birds and the sky. It was a place where the sky was wide, and something in you—which was larger than you—was alive. (Creech, 1995, p. 421)

She further explains that the "wacky, funny" tone of *Absolutely Normal Chaos*, her first novel for teens, was "largely influenced by the remembered chaotic tone of my own family" (personal correspondence, January 2, 2007). She admits that there were times when she "felt like Zinny in *Chasing Redbird* and Leo in *Replay*—a bit lost in the shuffle" in a home that was "always full of our friends and our relatives: grandparents, aunts and uncles, cousins. It was like having our own tribe."

Creech points out that although *Absolutely Normal Chaos* presents a frenetic picture of a family, most of her books balance seriousness with humor, and "perhaps that combination is a more accurate reflection of my own younger self and my family.... I think that my young protagonists' relationships with siblings and with older people (grandparents, aunts, uncles, etc.) reflect my own relationships with my gentle, humorous relatives" (personal correspondence, January 2, 2007).

Teen readers who have annoying younger siblings may be encouraged to know, too, that Sharon Creech refers to her three younger brothers as "alternately funny and annoying" when describing them as children, but that she remains good friends with each of her siblings to this day; in fact, they spend two weeks together every year at a family retreat on Lake Chautauqua, in upstate New York.

Creech acknowledges that neither her childhood nor the adults who peopled it were perfect. Notice, though, the balance she provides when describing her parents' relationship with each other and with their children: "My parents both worked, and although sometimes they had a sparring relationship, we children always knew that they cared deeply for us. There was a lot of humor in our house, and noise, and just the right amount of discipline" (personal correspondence, January 2, 2007). In her Newbery Medal Acceptance Speech (1995), the author eloquently acknowledges her debt to her father, and to her lifelong appreciation for words:

> In 1980, when my children and I had been in England for nine months, my father had a stroke. Although he lived for six more years, the stroke left him paralyzed and unable to speak. Think of all the words we wanted to say to him, and all the words he must have wanted to say to us. Think of all those words locked up for six years, because his mind could neither accept nor deliver words.
>
> A month after he died in 1986, I started my first novel, and when I finished it, I wrote another, and another, and another. The words rushed out. The connection between my father's death and my flood of writing might be that I had been confronted with the dark wall of mortality: we don't have endless time to follow your dreams; but it might also be that I felt obligated to use the words that my father could not. (Creech, 1995, p. 420)

As readers of Creech's novels, we can quickly observe that family is important to the writer. When we have a glimpse of her biography, we see that family is even more important to Creech the human being.

CREECH AND SCHOOL: STUDENT, TEACHER, AND HEADMASTER'S WIFE

When in school, Sharon Creech was always interested in writing and reading. In one autobiographical essay, she describes her enthusiasm for words on a page:

> I don't remember the titles of books I read as a child, but I do remember the experience of reading—of drifting into the pages and living in someone else's world, the excitement of never knowing what lay ahead. I loved myths—American Indian myths, Creek myths, and the King Arthur legends—and I remember the lightning jolt of exhilaration when I read *Ivanhoe* as a teenager. These were all magical worlds, full of mystery and imagination: anything could happen, anything at all.
>
> To be a novelist: Oh! That seemed the most thrilling aspiration. To be able to create other worlds, to be able to explore mystery and myth—I couldn't imagine any better way to live—except, perhaps, to be a teacher, because teachers got to handle books all day long. (www.edupaperback.org, taken from H. W. Wilson Company, *Seventh Books of Junior Authors and Illustrators*, 1996)

She was not a child who dreamed about becoming a writer and a teacher but then moved to other ambitions. Her early ambitions continued to guide her. As a college student at Hiram College (Ohio), she took a writing course, and then went to graduate school at George Mason University outside of Washington, DC. There, she continued to build an interest in writing, taking a course with author John Gardner, and participating in workshops led by extraordinary contemporary writers including John Irving and James Dickey (www.cliffsnotes.com/WileyCDA?LitNote/id-98,pageNum51.html). While in graduate school, Creech immersed herself in the world of words. She worked at the Federal Theatre Project Archives and as an editorial assistant at the *Congressional Quarterly*. Although she loves words, she found the editing job unrewarding, since it relied on facts and politics, and her interest and instinct had always leaned toward telling stories that transcend facts. After ten years of marriage, and with two children, Rob and Karin, she and Rob Leuthy divorced. Creech sought a change of scenery and went to England, where she talked the headmaster of the Thorpe, Surrey, England campus of the American Grade School in Switzerland (TASIS) to hire her as a teacher of literature and to write for the school. Her teaching job was fortuitous for many reasons, not the least of which is that she began her new career at TASIS in England the same fall that another American from Ohio, Lyle Rigg, started there as assistant headmaster. The two met when Creech asked him for an ice cube for the typically ice-less soda she was drinking one day, and realized that, in addition to their Ohio roots, they had much in common. Three years later, they married. Rob and Karin went to school in England, and Creech continued to teach American and British literature. According to her husband, Lyle Rigg, it was not uncommon for Creech, like other teachers as TASIS, to have her students read about Canterbury, then "head off to Canterbury with her students, so that they could make the pilgrimage themselves. She'd offer *Hamlet*, and then off they would all go to Stratford-upon-Avon...." "Get them out into the world," Creech says, echoing the school's founder (Rigg, p. 427). The couple and Creech's children moved to Switzerland when Lyle took a position as headmaster of the American School in Switzerland (a school that appears, in a fictitious but clearly recognizable form, in Creech's *Bloomability*). After a few years in Switzerland, they returned to England, where he was a headmaster and she a teacher and writer, until they returned to the United States after eighteen years abroad.

CREECH AS AN AWARD-WINING WRITER

Lyle Rigg credits her receipt of the 1988 Billee Murray Denny Poetry Award, sponsored by Lincoln College in Illinois, given to Creech for her poem, "Cleansing" as the turning point that helped Creech accept the fact that she was meant to be a writer (Rigg, pp. 427–428). Creech could not have known then that just six years later, she would receive a telephone call to near-London from Philadelphia and would be told that she had been awarded the highest honor a writer of children's books can receive in the United States: the Newbery Medal, for her novel, *Walk Two Moons* (1994). The Medal came just four years after she published her first two novels, both of which are for adult readers: *Recital* (1990) and *Nickel Malley* (1991), both published under the name Sharon Rigg in England, where she lived at the time. When she received the phone call about the Newbery Medal, she was living in England and had just stepped outside to release a muffled scream, frustrated with what she was trying to accomplish in her next book.

In accepting the 1995 Newbery Medal, an effusive Creech told the audience that the news of the award brought her "disbelief, followed by overwhelming gratitude," and added that:

> I felt as if the eye of God had beamed down on me, and I'd better do everything I was told. In the days that followed, whenever the phone rang (and it rang constantly—constantly), I stared at it suspiciously; expecting that this caller would say, "Oops, sorry! We made a mistake, It wasn't *your* book." ... I'll be honest: I never dreamed a dream this big.
>
> When I first read articles referring to me as an "unknown," I was amused. It made me feel peculiar, as if I'd previously been invisible. But the articles were accurate: I was virtually unknown in the field of children's books in the States. An unknown has simple prayers: please let my books be published; please let readers know these books exist; please let me keep writing. What the Newbery does is answer all of these prayers. It calls attention not only to my books, but to other new books as well. It celebrates children's literature. What a grand thing this Newbery is! (Creech, 1995, pp. 418–419)

The awards have continued for Creech and her literary creations, tumbling like the waterfalls that spill from the rivers that cut through the mountains and hollers that she loves to inhabit in her experience-based fiction. In 2002, following the publication of her novel, *Ruby Holler*, she became the first American writer to win the coveted CILIP Carnegie Medal, which is thought of in the United States as the British equivalent of the Newbery Medal, and the first author ever to receive both the Newbery (1995) and the Carnegie medals. Previous recipients of the Carnegie Medal include C.S. Lewis and contemporary English author Philip Pullman. These paired honors place Creech in the brightest, sunniest pool of literary achievement for authors whose readers are young people.

When asked which young adult books she would praise by giving rave reviews, she responds with a twist of the question:

> The YA books I'd be likely to give outstanding review to are many (although I tend not to distinguish between YA and intermediate, or rather I tend to read books that cross those boundaries). It's easier for me to suggest writers who faithfully write great books: Karen Hesse, Katherine Paterson, Lois Lowry, Jerry Spinelli, Richard Peck, Philip Pullman, David Almond, Kate DiCamillo, oh there are so many! (Personal correspondence, January 2, 2007)

It is comforting, in an odd sense, that Sharon Creech admits that it is the bad reviews that she remembers, instead of the celebratory ones, since her confession is so similar to the way many of us respond to rewards and criticism, to our performance on a big test or at a recital or in a swim meet. I wonder if her tendency to focus on negative reviews applies to the letter she got from a young reader in which he stated, emphatically, "Your book wasn't that good, and you should have had a turtle in it, but I'm not saying you're a *horrible* writer"! The letters that included the line, "I thought I was going to explode into the ether if I didn't finish that book," and "I laughed so hard I thought my pants were going to fall off" are treasures that Creech must enjoy (personal correspondence, January 2, 2007). About listening to her critics, she says the following, again revealing her humility as a writer and her efforts to focus on her art instead of its rewards:

> Accolades are a bonus, but I don't sit around thinking about them. I feel *compelled* to write, so usually my mind is on the book-in-progress and how to solve its challenges. Every now and then, I try to "take stock," and appreciate the awards and accolades, but it doesn't feel comfortable; it feels as if I'm observing, from a distance, that Sharon Creech person, not *me*. (personal correspondence, January 2, 2007)

CREECH'S LIFE IN HER BOOKS

At her lively website, www.sharoncreech.com, Creech includes a "tidbit" and/or the inspiration for each of her children's and adolescent or young adult books. Most often, these tidbits and notes on inspiration point readers to links between Creech's literary art and her real life as a human. Following are examples, all extracted from Creech's own Web site:

Absolutely Normal Chaos (1990). Creech reveals that the address of Mary Lou Finney's house, 4059, was the address of the house where she grew up, in Euclid, Ohio. A photograph of the family home is posted on the Web site, with the house number vaguely visible. The inspiration was the result of homesickness: Creech, who had been living in England and Switzerland for about ten years, was lonely for her home and family in the United States. She decided to write an upbeat story about a family that was a lot like her own: "Writing the story was a way for me to feel as if my family were with me, right there in our little cottage in England" (www.sharoncreech.com/novels/03.asp).

Walk Two Moons (1994). Creech gives readers a hint of the story's inspiration, while protecting some of its mystery. She says that she started the book as a sequel to *Absolutely Normal Chaos*, with Mary Lou as a primary character. The novel changed substantially, though, after she read a fortune cookie fortune that was buried in the bottom of her purse. The message commanded, "Don't judge a man until you've walked two moons in his moccasins." With that, she determined that the story would be about a character who has to walk in someone else's shoes—and Sal became the main character; her journey was to retrace her mother's final adventure.

Chasing Redbird (1997). This novel required Creech to do research on hiking trails so that she could make Zinny's quest—to clear and claim the Bybanks-Chocton Trail—seem realistic. She was inspired by some of the place names to create her own for the book, names like "Baby Toe Ridge," "Spook Hollow," and "Donut Hole."

Bloomability (1998). The tidbits give readers a rare personal look at Creech's life: the photograph on the front of the book shows Creech's daughter Karin on a mountain in Switzerland, Creech's youngest brother, and the house that Creech and Lyle Rigg lived in while he was headmaster of the American School of Switzerland in Lugano, Switzerland.

The Wanderer (2000). This is perhaps Creech's most personal story, at least to 2000. Two of the Bompie stories are her own father's tales, and the name Bompie is the name Creech's sister-in-law uses for her grandfather. Bompie lives in Thorpe, where Creech and Lyle Rigg lived and worked for many years. The sailboat journey across the ocean, which includes a harrowing experience with a storm at sea, is modeled on one that Creech's daughter Karin actually took after graduating from college.

Love that Dog (2001). Her first novel in verse, this little book includes characters that entered the story without invitation. Creech says she wanted to include Walter Dean Myers' poem, "Love that Boy," as a major feature in the novel in verse, but was "surprised when Walter Dean Myers himself entered the story." Myers' presence made her a bit nervous, since she had only met the imposing author once before, but once he found his way into the book, she could not usher him out of it.

Ruby Holler (2002). This novel is set in the place that Creech envisions when she imagines the place where her father grew up. Although she was given a photograph of the actual shack in which her father lived, after writing the book, and found that her setting is a highly romanticized, charming version of what was in reality a dirty, dilapidated shack, Creech is happy to include the holler as a tribute to her father and his home. The novel also includes some unusual touches, such as the "understone fund." Creech explains that the idea for burying money in the yard, under stones, came from a Russian friend who referred to a chipmunk who had a habit of hiding food under rocks as her "understone friend." She twisted the phrase slightly to produce "understone fund."

Heartbeat (2004). The tidbit associated with this second novel in verse provides solid information about Sharon Creech the human. First, she writes that the art assignment that is at the center of the plot is one that her daughter, Karin, was actually given to complete. Next, she says that like the protagonist, Annie, she used to love to run, and that running made her feel free and that it calmed her. Today, she takes long walks instead of going on runs, and notes that often it is during those walks that a story idea begins to emerge for her.

Replay (2005). In the tidbits that accompany this novel, Creech chooses not to reveal what her Newbery Acceptance Speech does: that the line that protagonist Leo finds in his father's autobiography: "When I am happy, I tap dance" (*Replay*, p. 56) is one that Creech has posted on the bulletin board in her home office. It is a line from her own mother's autobiography, written at age fifteen, and it inspires Creech as a reminder of her mother's zest for life.

Our reasons for wanting to know about the person who writes books that we enjoy are curious. Yet by spending some time reflecting on the life of Creech, and then examining her literary art and the influences of her teacherly tendencies in her books, we are enriched. Sharon Creech is an upbeat and uplifting person. She was raised that way, and she creates characters who learn that life is more satisfying when we seek the good things rather than expect the bad ones. In an uncommon moment of self-disclosure, the author describes herself:

> Naturally, there is drama and sadness in any family, but always I felt reassured by an overriding positive, hopeful aura. The person and writer I am today is keenly attuned to the sorrows of our world (I am a worrier), but also instructively positive and hopeful.

It is a pleasure to spend time with Sharon Creech and the families that she has created, springing from her own experiences, memories, and associations with people and places. She is an author whose work reflects light, giving her teen readers the warmth of hope.

CHAPTER TWO

SHARON CREECH: FINGERPRINTS OF A TEACHER AND AN ARTIST

R EADERS WILL DETECT the fingerprints of a former teacher of high school English as well as those of an accomplished artist throughout the novels of Sharon Creech. Sometimes the fingerprints are obvious, left by a teacher who is proudly staking claim to her territory and joyously playful with her adolescent readers. At other times, the marks are subtle, left by an artist who is gentle and compassionately respectful of her teen audience. Creech demonstrates *teacherly* allegiance to each of the areas of the traditional tripod of the discipline of English: composition, language, and literature study, by giving direct *artistic* attention to each in her novels.

OBVIOUS FINGERPRINTS

School Writing Assignments

An adolescent reader will quickly notice that Creech has left the fingerprints of a former teacher of English who enjoys helping students explore their own talents as creative writers. In the first lines of her first novel, *Absolutely Normal Chaos*, Mary Lou Finney writes, "Dear Mr. Birkway, Here it is: my summer journal…. The problem is this, though. I don't want you to read it" (2). On the next page, she actually backs up to the beginning of her story, to the first day of summer, when she pouts, "I wish someone would tell me exactly what a journal *is*. When I asked my mother, she said, 'Well, it's like a diary only different.' *That* helps" (3). With these early lines, Creech wins over not only every teacher of English who has practiced since the 1980s, but every student who has struggled to distinguish between what is too personal to include (too diary-esque), and what the teacher has asked for (a legitimate journal entry) in the amorphous "free writing journal" assignments that were as popular in the last fifteen years of the twentieth century as elaborate sentence diagramming ones had been in the 1950s.

Creech uses the journal as a narrative vehicle again in her Newbery Honor novel, *The Wanderer* (2000), this time taking advantage, perhaps, of attention in the field of composition instruction to the notion of dialogic journals. In alternating chapters, cousins Sophie and Cody present their perspectives of an amazing adventure as they sail across the Atlantic in a small vessel with only Cody's dad, two uncles, and brother. Sophie writes willingly, using words to try to sort through her feelings and confusing half-memories, nightmares, and hopes. Cody writes under duress, referring to his journal as a "dog-log." He explains to Sophie, "It was either that or read five books.... I figure it'll be a lot easier keeping a dog-log than reading all those words somebody else wrote" (24).

Vocabulary Lessons

Readers who are seeking clean sets of a veteran English teacher's and artist's fingerprints can also detect them in the vocabulary lessons that Creech includes in her novels, including the four used as representative samples here. In *Absolutely Normal Chaos*, Creech stakes a specific claim to the territory of vocabulary instruction. Mary Lou irritates her mother one time too many by saying "God!" when exasperated, and by relying on the vague "stuff" when more specific nouns would supply better information, so her mother forbids these words. Soon, Mary Lou's expression of frustration becomes, "Oh Alpha and Omega!" (152), and she begins to add diary entries that include lines such as "not much elixir happened today" (139).

In *Walk Two Moons*, Salamanca (who usually goes by the nickname "Sal") explains her unusual first name as a historic and linguistic accident: her parents thought that they were naming her after the Seneca Indian tribe to which Sal's great great grandmother had belonged. Before they realized that they were using the wrong word, they had grown used to the name Salamanca, and chose to keep it for their daughter (7).

Monikers pepper her novels, particularly the earlier ones. Creech is not shy about having family members call each other by their pet names. For example, in *Walk Two Moons*, Gramps calls Sal (and sometimes his wife) "Gooseberry," and Gram calls her granddaughter "Chickabiddy."

These terms of endearment are likely to ring true for readers familiar with northeastern Kentucky, and to intrigue those who have not heard speakers from the region or generation that Sal's grandparents represent. "Sairy," the name of "that old woman" from deep in the mountains who teaches Florida and Dallas what love means in *Ruby Holler* (2002) is a derivation of the more formal "Sara." In *The Wanderer*, Sophie is sailing across the ocean to see her English grandfather, whom she calls "Bompie," a family name that Creech admits she borrowed from her sister-in-law.

Many of Creech's protagonists have names that carry stories. Dinnie, the granddaughter of an Italian grandmother, who narrates *Bloomability*, explains hers: "Mom named her first girl ... Stella Maria. Then I came along, and she must have been saving up for me, because she named me Domenica Santolina Donne. My names mean Sunday-Southern-Wood-River. I was born on a Sunday (which makes me blessed, Mom said), and at the time we lived in the South beside woods and a river. My name is pronounced in the Italian way: Doe-MEN-I-kuh. ...so most people call me Dinnie" (5). Ironically, Dinnie's father, who is from Kentucky, once explained to Dinnie that he "was named Crick after a clear little crick that ran beside the house they'd lived ..." (*B*, 4). She goes on to note that a teacher corrected her use of "crick" and told her that it is not a real English word; Dinnie, given her rich linguistic heritage, was not convinced (*B*, 4-5). In this novel, the vocabulary lessons also include an introduction to beginner's Italian, with words such as *ciao* (hello and goodbye), *andiamo* (Let's go!), and *Dov é?* (Where is?) Creech has used *Bloomability* to set the table that she will return to when she entertains younger readers with the pinch of Italian phrases that they will sample while making pasta with Rosie, Bailey, and Granny in the delicious *Granny Torrelli Makes Soup* (2003). In *Ruby Holler*, the twin protagonists, Florida and Dallas Carter, were left at the Boxton Creek Home for Children and named by its proprietors, who noticed two pamphlets in the box in which the twins lay. Florida tells a surprised Tiller, who has asked how she got her "mighty nice name" (209), that the babies were left, abandoned, in boxes on the doorstep of the Home for Children, and each was lying atop a travel brochure—one that advertised, "Fly to Florida" and the other that read, "*Destination: Dallas!*" and that the owners of the Home then assigned each baby one of the names (210).

In *Heartbeat* (2004), the second of two novels that Creech has written in free verse, Annie relies on a thesaurus, that English teacher's lifeline, to assist her when she decides her own list of words to express herself is too shallow. Annie uses poetry as she describes her first attempts with using the resource that her English teacher insists is a "treasure of words." She spins phrases that ring with rich synonyms— "Mr. Welling says/to soar ahead and write the first draft/fast," and "later go back and/plumb/the thesaurus/for more thrilling/sensational/exhilarating/ words" (*H*, 121). She uses the thesaurus as a tool for her anger, too, when she runs into the girls' track coach, who makes her "aggravated/ ...antagonized/...displeased/.../raging" (*H*, 122).

Literary References

Finally, readers who are determined to find clear sets of an English teacher's and artist's fingerprints throughout Sharon Creech's novels will certainly want to trace her use of literary references, allusions, and quotations. She weaves Homer's *The Odyssey* into *Absolutely Normal Chaos*, as the book that Mary Lou is plodding through all summer, and the one that Carl Ray, who is ordinarily withdrawn and uncommunicative, lights up to discuss and help her understand. Creech interprets the classic work through Mary Lou's perspective, using words that are sure to appeal to adolescent readers and send them to the bookshelf, unafraid to wrestle the Cyclops or the great warrior for themselves. A poem by e.e.cummings, "the little horse is newly," is mentioned in *Walk Two Moons*. Sal's interpretation of cummings' distinctive use of capitalization in the poem, "To me that Y looked like the newly born horse standing up on his thin legs" (123) provides adolescent readers with a nonthreatening vehicle for approaching cummings' odd and brilliant words and images— and those of other poets, too. The novel draws on classic mythology: Ben's school report on mythology discusses how Prometheus stole fire from the sun and angered Zeus (155); Gramps tells Sal that people created the myth of Pandora's box out of the need to explain the existence of evil in the world (276). Then it moves closer to home, when Sal repeats a Navaho story told her by her mother about a woman, Estsanatlehi, who never dies, but who moves through the life cycle from baby to child to woman to old woman and back to baby again, living thousands of lives.

The title also draws on the aphorism, "Don't judge a man until you've walked two miles in his moccasins," a lesson that Sal, her fictitious companions, and adolescent readers, learn as they complete the journey of the story.

Aphorisms are important in *Chasing Redbird* (1997), as well. The novel opens with narrator Zinnia (Zinny) at her Aunt Jessie's kitchen table, where she spots a cross-stitched wall decoration that reads: "Life is a bowl of spaghetti ... every now and then you get a meatball" (1). Zinny challenged herself to get past the mounds of spaghetti in her life so that she could uncover the big meatball at the center. For her, the meatball became an abandoned trail behind the family property—a trail that she alone would clear. Yet she was unsettled by another wall hanging that Aunt Jessie had cross-stitched and hung in her house. This one read, "Even a monkey falls from a tree" (192). Despite her ease with being outside, alone, on the trail, would she "fall from the tree" and fail? What kinds of barriers would she encounter, and would she be able to face each of them?

In *Bloomability*, protagonist Dinnie's friend Guthrie uses Frost's "The Road not Taken" as the text on which he constructs a stirring eighth grade graduation speech. He asks his classmates to consider how they have been affected by the choice of coming to school in Switzerland, and where they are going next, then concludes to applause, "It has made—and will make—all the difference, because we will continue to affect each other's lives. ...there is something in the air of *these* yellow woods—these here in Switzerland, which we have run through and hiked through and skied through—that tells me we will take pieces of each other and of Switzerland with us wherever we go. We will! Fantastico!" (254).

Creech's most obvious and most direct employment of literary references, allusions, and quotes is (with the exception of her use of *The Odyssey* as a parallel story in *Absolutely Normal Chaos*) in the first of her novels written in free verse, the *New York Times* bestseller *Love that Dog* (2001). Young Jack narrates this story, and by page three, he is writing his own poem to his teacher in reference to William Carlos Williams' famous Imagist poem, "The Red Wheelbarrow." Jack concludes his poetic response to Williams' poem by writing, "If that is a poem ... Then any words/Can be a poem./You've just got to/make/short/lines" (*LTD*, 3).

On page four, Jack's imitation of Williams' poem appears, along with a plea to his teacher, "Do you promise/not to read it/out loud?/Do you promise/not to put it/on the board?" (4).

So much depends
Upon
A blue car
Splattered with mud
Speeding down the road. (4)

The teacher is not convinced that Jack's poem says much, but Jack reminds her that the wheelbarrow guy doesn't explain why so much depends on the red wheelbarrow, either. The teacher, whose presence the reader perceives only through Jack's side of an ongoing conversation with her, then moves the class on to study Robert Frost's "Stopping by Woods on a Snowy Evening" (6), Blake's "Tiger" (8), Valerie Worth's "dog" (16), Frost's "The Pasture" (21), Arnold Adoff's "Street Music" (31), and Sharon (Creech) Rigg's "The Apple" (35).

In the second part of the book, Jack composes a trio of poems about his yellow dog, Sky. One is an entertaining shape poem. The second, "My Sky," is a poignant poem about how his beloved Sky was killed when the "blue car blue car/splattered with mud/hit Sky" (70). The reader and Jack's teacher understand, with these lines, the significance of the blue car that Jack wrote about when imitating William Carlos Williams, and readers detect again the fingerprint of a teacher-author who cares about the hearts of young people. The third of Jack's poems, "Love that Dog," imitates the style and lifts words from "Love that Boy," a poem by popular contemporary young adult author Walter Dean Myers.

With his teacher's encouragement, the fictitious Jack invites the very real Myers to come to the school as a guest speaker. In a delightful climax and denouement, Myers agrees to appear at Jack's school (and, with a parallel in a collaboration between the two actual writers, the actual author agrees to be the central feature in Creech's story).

Today's teachers will particularly appreciate the distinct fingerprints that Creech and her editor at Joanna Cotler Books of HarperCollins left on the final pages of this book, when they chose to include full texts of each of the poems mentioned by Jack and his teacher in its eighty-six pages.

SUBTLER FINGERPRINTS

Creech's use of journals, vocabulary lessons, and literary references seems to be drawn not only from her talent as an artist, but also directly either from her own experiences as a teacher of English or years working in school environments. Her subtle uses of figurative language, natural imagery, dialect, and rhythmic syntax contribute to her artistry in ways that leave fingerprints that are less obvious on the surface, but that nevertheless distinctly identify the work of former teacher and artist Sharon Creech.

Natural Imagery

In describing the Black Hills, South Dakota, Sal says that they are not really black, just covered with pine trees that must look black at dusk. She wonders how the mountains could have been taken by whites, when, since they are sacred to the Sioux, they should so clearly still be theirs. When she says: "A cool wind blew down through the pines, and the trees swished secrets among them" (*Walk Two Moons*, 179), the juxtaposition of the questions about the sacred Black Hills and the encroachment and claim to ownership with the sense of the trees' secrets is powerful in its subtlety. It provides Sal with an opportunity to describe her mother's connection with nature in an unusual and memorable way, by telling the story of picking blackberries with her mother, in Kentucky, and having her mother patiently explain that they could reach neither for the blackberries on the ground, since those are for the rabbits, nor the blackberries in the top of the bushes, since those are for the birds, but the ones in the middle, at people-height, were for people. She sums up the memory by stating proudly, "My mother always loved anything that normally grows or lives out of doors—*anything*—lizards, trees … toads, ants, pigs" (*Walk Two Moons*, 33–34). Later, Creech picks up the blackberries as a symbol and uses them again as a way to connect the daughter to her mother through memory; Sal recalls watching her mother kiss a tree after eating blackberries, leaving a small dark stain on the tree, and now she writes in her school journal about kissing trees, too, tasting the unique flavor of each.

The title of *Ruby Holler* refers to a valley tucked deep in the mountains, a place that is as rich and glimmering as precious gems in its natural beauty. Dallas passes on what Sairy tells him about the red maple leaves for which the area is named, explaining to Florida that the leaves look like a "million bazillion rubies dangling on the trees" in the fall, a "bazillion shimmery emeralds" after summer showers wet and refresh them, and a "bazillion gazillion sparkly diamonds" when winter ice encapsulates them (78). This artistic effect is particularly useful, since it is echoed in the subplot, which involves the nasty proprietor of the Boxton Creek Home for Children, Mr. Trepid, being caught in a scheme to rob Sairy and Tiller, the couple who temporarily take in the twins. This subplot ends when Trepid mistakes a bag of inexpensive rocks that the kids had planted for him to uncover for priceless jewels, and takes the bag to a jeweler for appraisal.

Energizing Similes and Extended Metaphors

It is difficult to read *Chasing Redbird* without noticing Zinny's energy; she is committed to clearing her trail, for becoming independent, for helping her Uncle Nate deal with his "redbird's sudden death." One of the most effective ways that Creech conveys her energy is through the earthy similes that Zinny uses to describe her world. Often she uses similes to compare herself with animals or plants with which she is familiar. Examples include these:

> "This plan zipped through my brain like a dog tearing up the pea patch." (52)
> "I plunged through the nettles ... pawing at the ground like a crazed badger." (89)
> "... my thoughts were jumping around like peas on a hot shovel." (132)

Each demonstrates Zinny's earthy zest and restlessness.

Dinnie, whose list of hometowns reads like the table of contents of a United States atlas even before she goes to school in Switzerland, describes living abroad as having "double vision" in *Bloomability* (91). She goes on to explain, "I'd look at what Guthrie was pointing at and I'd see something else laid thinly over it, like a transparent photo. The grapevines on a Swiss hillside were overlaid with grapevines I'd seen in Ohio.... The castle slid behind an image of a stone tower I'd seen in Virginia...." (*Bloomability*, p. 91). This extended metaphor is an example of Creech's ability to artistically and eloquently speak through and for an adolescent's perspective. Dinnie's sense of anomie is common to those who have traveled far from home for extended periods; the frustration of seeing almost-familiar sights that leads to disappointment and often to a temporary case of the blues, coupled with the more common complications of growing into adolescence, are portrayed gently and gracefully here.

The sense of a graceful, powerful bird flying above the mountains and valleys near Boxton Creek sets *Ruby Holler* in motion, and delicately mysteriously wings it forward. The "magical silver bird" (1) that Dallas is dreaming of as *Ruby Holler* opens reappears throughout *Ruby Holler*, offering readers invitations to follow Dallas in its path and try to discover its message for him. Early in the novel, it lures him, but leaves him standing on the border of a place that he cannot yet imagine, since he has not yet experienced real love and care (80); at the close of the novel, Dallas again dreams of the magic sliver bird, but no longer needs it to tell him where he will find the magic place, since he has arrived there, with Florida, in Ruby Holler and Sairy and Tiller's loving home (308).

This sense of a graceful presence watching over the scenes of *Ruby Holler* is balanced by the dread produced by another image that Florida recalls in a poignant scene in which she is holding a tiny bird egg protectively, and accidentally cracks it. The incident provokes a memory of when she was sitting in some foster parent's kitchen as a three-year-old, smashing eggs on the floor, playing in the yellow yolks, and playing, too, in a jar of peanut butter. She had enjoyed watching the yolks seep into the floor cracks, and sealing them in with a layer of smooth peanut butter, until someone began slapping her arm and face. She recoils from the present moment when the memory overtakes her and becomes too visceral: "In the cabin loft, she stared at the broken egg in her hand, and with one mighty toss, she hurled it against the wall" (*Ruby Holler*, 46).

Rhythmic Syntax

One of Creech's most powerful, unique artistic contributions to young adult literature is the use of rhythmic syntax. For example, readers will hear the lyrical rhythms in the rising and falling of lines that seem to last the entire story, as well as the use of repetition, exaggeration, and of humor, of an Appalachian story teller when Tiller, who has lived his entire life in a tiny mountain valley, describes the time that he accidentally covered the barnyard with splotches of red paint, an accident that started when he threw some paint at an "old mangy cat" that "went bonkers" and scratched him, causing him to fling paint on a chicken, which pecked him until he tried to sling paint at it, only to hit the pig and set it into motion (*RH*, 59–60).

Creech effectively uses repetition in each of her novels as a rhetorical device, as she does here in *Ruby Holler*:

> Tiller and Sairy had lived so long in Ruby Holler that they knew every twist and turn in it, every path, every foxhole and beehive. They knew where the stream was wide and where it was narrow, where shallow and where deep. (101)

The clearest examples of Creech's use of rhythmic syntax, however, occur in her Newbery Honor book, *The Wanderer* (2000). Instead of the similes of the natural world that efflorescent Zinny creates to describe her feelings, contemplative, hopeful Sophie listens to nature with a more attentive ear. She pays attention and tries to record what the world tells her, and records lines including these as the book's opening lines: "The sea, the sea, the sea. It rolled and rolled and called to me" (1). Later, when she and her uncles and cousins are at sea during a terrible storm, she writes, "The sea, the sea. It thunders and rolls and unsettles me; it unsettles all of us" (217).

Creech experimented with this kind of rhythmic syntax in her Newbery Award novel, *Walk Two Moons*. Sal describes the sound of the wind before the cross-country trip as a sound that suggests the words "*hurry, hurry, hurry*" and "*rush, rush, rush*" (6). During the trip, the winds changed their messages to Sal, whispering repeatedly the warning, "*slow down*" (*WTM*, 101). Then, as Sal moved closer to finding an answer to her question about her mother, again the winds' whispers repeatedly urged, "... *rush* ..." (172). Readers feel Sal's urgency, and the wind itself, through Creech's poetic language.

In *Absolutely Normal Chaos*, *Bloomability*, *The Wanderer*, *Love That Dog*, or *Heartbeat*, Creech creates teachers, schools, and school assignments, and gives herself the artistic freedom to present readers with direct reader's lessons from a former teacher of English on the value of journals, on building vocabulary, and on literary allusions. In these novels, and in the three without school settings per se, novels that can be referred to as "mountain folk novels," in honor of the adult characters whose wisdom carry the adolescent protagonists through them: *Walk Two Moons*, *Chasing Redbird*, and *Ruby Holler*, Creech also introduces subtle literary elements that distinguish her as an artist. She uses natural, earthy similes and imagery to paint word pictures in ways that transform words into vivid pictures for adolescent readers to envision. She quietly tucks extended metaphors into passages so that readers can unwind them and think about them over time, allowing the metaphors to increase in meaning as the stories unfold. Her language is, at times, charged with the energy of the adolescent characters and the circumstances they find themselves in, and is, at times, muted with the comfort of the older people who help them find answers to their internal and external dilemmas. Readers can continue to turn to Sharon Creech, former teacher of English and always-artist, for lessons about what makes literature for young people work, and for the pleasure of reading books that are artistic, delicate, poetic, funny, poignant, and real.

CHAPTER THREE

ABSOLUTELY NORMAL CHAOS: SETTING THE STAGE FOR A LIFE OF WRITING FOR CHILDREN AND TEENS

S
HARON CREECH'S FIRST novel for teens introduces readers to the characteristics that have become the author's literary signature: feisty female protagonists, lovable eccentric relatives, and challenging competing cultures.

PLOT SUMMARY OF *ABSOLUTELY NORMAL CHAOS* (PUBLISHED IN 1990 IN ENGLAND, AND IN 1993 IN THE UNITED STATES, HARPERCOLLINS TROPHY)

Thirteen-year-old Mary Lou Finney starts the summer wondering how she will fill the journal that her teacher has assigned as vacation homework. Sure that her life is too dull to offer any fodder for a writer or any interest for a reader, Mary Lou begrudgingly begins her project. Two weeks later, she has already filled the first of six journals in which she chronicles a wide array of events.

One of the accounts that Mary Lou enthusiastically records involves a hastily arranged and extended visit to the Finney home from Mary Lou's odd, aggravating, and mysterious cousin, Carl Ray. Carl Ray, who comes to Ohio from West Virginia, is evasive and reticent; his habit of refusing to elaborate with any more than a "yeah" or "nope" in answer to questions makes Mary Lou suspicious of him. Readers learn, as we move through the summer with Mary Lou, that her curiosities are justified: Carl Ray has come to Easton because he has learned that he is the son of an Easton man, not the son of the man who raised him, Mary Lou's Uncle Carl. He tells no one that he has come on a quest to locate his biological father, but in a delightfully improbable plot twist, the man whom he is seeking happens to be Mary Lou's neighbor, Mr. Furtz. Carl Ray visits Mr. Furtz at Mr. Furtz' hardware store, and Mr. Furtz immediately recognizes and confirms Cal Ray's connection; the two protect their secret. Mr. Furtz hires Carl Ray to work in his hardware store; he gives Carl Ray a ring that has a significance that is slowly revealed, anonymously leaves his biological son with a sizable cash inheritance, then dies suddenly of a heart attack. After buying lavish gifts for his cousins and immediate family, Carl Ray reluctantly explains to all what he has learned. His family's shock is cushioned by their relief at finally better understanding Carl Ray's odd and secretive behavior.

An automobile accident near the end of the novel presents more suspense in this main plot: Carl Ray is left unconscious for several days, and readers are left wondering, along with his extended family and friends, whether or not he will survive. When he does, and is again the slow speaking, quietly funny, generous Carl Ray that Mary Lou has come to appreciate, everyone in the Finney family has had an opportunity to realize how much they like him, and enjoy having him in their presence.

Mary Lou also writes in her journal about minor yet significant changes in her life. In addition to recording the funny daily antics of her immediate family, where one brother is likely to be throwing eggs at a new neighbor's windows while another is in the hospital having a sliced knee repaired, or recounting the snide remarks she gets from country cousins who accuse her of being too citified when she visits them in West Virginia, Mary Lou details two of her most significant relationships: those with her long-time best friend Beth Ann, and with the boy who is becoming her boyfriend, Alex Cheevey.

During the summer, Mary Lou and Beth Ann squabble a lot, since Beth Ann's sudden interest in boys has replaced allegiance to Mary Lou. After a boyfriend breaks up with her, Beth Ann manipulates Carl Ray into asking her to a movie; Mary Lou can hardly believe what she is hearing when Beth Ann calls to tell her about the date: "... she thinks he's ... cute (pretty far-fetched, if you ask me) ... and sooooo interesting (absolutely a bald-faced lie) (ANC, 128). Her frustration over Beth Ann is mollified, however, with thoughts of Alex Cheevey, for whom she is beginning to have romantic feelings. Her innocence is revealed in Mary Lou's preoccupation with their first kiss; Mary Lou marks every step toward that kiss, and the ones that follow, with a journal entry.

Far from realistic for readers, who expect today's 13-year-olds to be sexually knowledgeable, the idea that Mary Lou would have the kinds of *questions she has about kissing, and that she would be shy about kissing a boy that she has know for years, is refreshing and endearing, even if a bit dated in its presentation in* Absolutely Normal Chaos. *By the end of the summer, Beth Ann has dated, broken up with, and started dating again the now-recovering Carl Ray; Mary Lou and Alex have moved slowly together as a pair; they have kissed, and Mary Lou declares that she loves him.*

SHARON CREECH: FINDING HER PLACE AS A WRITER IN ABSOLUTELY NORMAL CHAOS

As a first novel, *Absolutely Normal Chaos* firmly established Sharon Creech as a talented voice among contemporary writers for young people. In it, she demonstrates compellingly the ability to capture young teens' perspectives. She also provides indications of characteristics that will be more fully developed in later novels, including these: a tendency to place her novels in settings that appeal to and are familiar, even when exotic, for teens; the sensitivity to develop adult characters who contribute to teens' development without distracting from teens' opportunities to grow and find their places in the world; and the responsibility to present hope instead of darkness for her teen readers. A major theme in this novel is common in teen literature: finding one's place in the world and at home. Creech takes Mary Lou and her older cousin, the enigmatic Carl Ray, on a lovely winding road toward the theme, allowing the reader to enjoy a variety of favorite Finney family sights and unusual country scenes along the way. The greatest strength of this first of her young adult novels is revealed in Creech's ability to portray the world through the perspective of a young teen female, a perspective that she employs successfully in each of the young adult novels that follow *Absolutely Normal Chaos.*

THE MAIN CHARACTER IN *ABSOLUTELY NORMAL CHAOS*
Mary Lou: The Family's Good Girl

Mary Lou, the 13-year-old protagonist, is a lively girl who, like Creech herself, is the second-oldest of five siblings in a large, loud family. Although the novel revolves around events that affect her entire family, Mary Lou doesn't comment too often on individuals in the family, except to establish that her 17-year-old sister spends time focused on cosmetics and clothes, and she feels protective of her two youngest brothers, Doug and Tommy. She also notes that she and Dennis, who is one year her junior, are often the good and bad children in the middle, with Mary Lou doing the right things and Dennis getting in trouble for disturbing the neighbors by breaking windows and distressing his parents by careless actions that lead to injuries. With various family members rolling in and out of positions that receive prominent attention, Creech is able to suggest that the Finney family moves through the summer—and the novel— as a single unit. In scenes like this dinnertime one, the family itself assumes the role of a main character:

> We had spaghetti, and Dougie doesn't like spaghetti and was pushing it around his plate and slopping sauce all over, and so Dennis punched him and Dougie started crying and Mom told him to be quiet and eat … In the middle of all that Dad said, "Had a letter from Radene today." Radene is married to Dad's brother, Uncle Carl Joe, and they live in West Virginia.
>
> "Did you see it?" Dad said. (He meant the letter.)
>
> "No, I didn't see it. Dougie, if you don't stop that hollering right this minute—" (Just to give you an idea of how hard it is to follow the conversation.) (*ANC*, 11)

The family scene that Mary Lou is a part of is often tumultuous yet always wholesome; as a teen, she has two parents and several siblings to turn to, and a host of neighbors and relatives who are also a part of her life. Some young readers find the depiction a little too simple, too idealistic. However, many find it encouraging and uplifting, either as an escape from the family circumstances that they are used to, or as a reinforcement that it is acceptable for a young teen to appreciate his or her parents, sisters, and brothers—regardless of how irritating and annoying they are, at times.

Mary Lou: A Student Who Puts her Own Twist on Assignments

Mary Lou wants to do well on her summer journal-writing assignment, but when she begins, she isn't quite sure what a "journal" is. She asks her mom, who has time only to give her the confusing answer that a journal is like a diary, but is not exactly a diary (*ANC*, 3) before dashing off to stop brother Dennis from throwing eggs at the new neighbor's house. Young readers may empathize with her confusion temporarily, and are likely to be impressed that Mary Lou dives into the muddy waters of the unclear assignment and writes seven pages about her family for the initial journal entry.

Creech provides teen readers with plenty of clues to show them that Mary Lou is a good student. Mary Lou has chosen, from the school list, a collection of poetry by Frost and *The Odyssey* for her summer reading assignment. She admits that *The Odyssey* is a difficult tale to enter, as a reader, initially, but her difficulty propels her to identify her problems: Homer's style, and the convoluted conceit that the hero's actions are guided by a host of gods. She addresses her problem with Homer's style by putting his words and syntax into a familiar context: She compares the inverted syntax and power of the opening lines of *The Odyssey* to the oratory style of "the preacher at Aunt Radene's church in West Virginia," a man who "would make his voice really soft and then boom, he would be shouting and then soft again" (*ANC*, 61). She conquers her problem with the conceit of the god-directed hero by embracing and incorporating Homer's narrative frame as a vehicle for telling her own story of the chain of events that she experiences with cousin Carl Ray and with Alex during the summer. Eventually, Mary Lou begins to use "Zeus" to supplant her bad habit of using "Lord" and "God" as exclamations. She also borrows from Homer when selecting pet names that she and Alex use privately as terms of endearment for each other: "Athene" and "Poseidon."

What may surprise readers, though, is Carl Ray's intelligence. Creech deftly sets up by her portrayal of Carl Ray as an unusual teen with few interests and fewer words, allowing other characters to react to him by drawing on stereotypes about the low levels of intelligence that many assume run rampant among people from the mountains in West Virginia. Yet it is Carl Ray who helps Mary Lou begin to make sense of *The Odyssey*. Without prompting, he explains to her that Book Ten, in which Circe turns men into pigs, is a metaphor for the human condition, one that is as true today as it was for Homer:

"Women turn men into pigs all the time" (*ANC*, 131).

Further evidence of Mary Lou's academic prowess is seen in her tendency to connect life experiences with literary texts that she has previously read. For example, when Carl Ray was told that someone was going to give him some money, Mary Lou's interpretation of the situation is literary; she compares Carl Ray's situation to the story of Dickens's *Great Expectations*, in which, according to Mary Lou's synopsis, a boy "inherits some money and he thinks it's from this weird rich lady who sits around in this cobwebby room all day," but learns that it is really from a "spooky convict" that the boy helped years earlier (*ANC*, 91–92). As readers, we wonder if Mary Lou thinks that Carl Ray might be mixed up in some illegal activity, too. As *Absolutely Normal Chaos* unfolds, and the truth of the source of Carl Ray's inheritance is revealed, Mary Lou learns that she was closer to the truth than she could have suspected when she made her initial literary allusion.

FRIENDSHIP AMONG CHARACTERS IN *ABSOLUTELY NORMAL CHAOS*
Best Friends and Tensions

Perhaps Creech's most effective demonstration of her understanding of young teens' social development is through scenes that depict the evolving relationships between Mary Lou and Beth Ann, and those that depict the relationship that grows between Mary Lou and Alex. Mary Lou is perplexed when her place in the life of her best friend, Beth Ann, is supplanted by a series of boys in whom Beth Ann is suddenly interested (including, inexplicably to Mary Lou, even Carl Ray). This abandonment occurs at the worst time possible for Mary Lou: She needs Beth Ann's help to fortify herself against the sting of being rejected by the popular girls of the GGP Club. The double-whammy of losing her best friend to an all-consuming interest in dating and of feeling like an outcast is typical of many girls Mary Lou's age: they experience the loss of a good friend due to the friend's attraction to another—often an older boy, since the males their own age are usually physically and emotionally less mature than the girls are during early adolescence. At the same time, the social dynamics of groups necessarily shift and tilt when pairings of best friends are shaken up, and one part of the pair finds herself "single." Although she is bothered by Beth Ann's flightiness, especially when Beth Ann decides to indicate her allegiance to the popular girls of the GGP club by accepting an invitation to their pajama party—a party to which

Mary Lou is not invited—Mary Lou chooses to keep up her end of the friendship.

Close Friends and Romance

The slap that Mary Lou feels from the group of popular girls who continue to shun her is softened considerably by changes in her relationship with one particular boy in her sphere, her longtime schoolmate, Alex Cheevey. Alex is the perfect companion for serious yet funny, loyal yet independent Mary Lou. With a last name that requires stretching one's lips into a smile to pronounce, Alex first shows up on the street where Mary Lou lives, pretending to be looking for someone else. The innocence of their friendship and eventual romance will be refreshing to young teens who read other teen fiction and wonder whether they are abnormal for moving slowly, deliberately into their own relationships.

On the other hand, the fact that Mary Lou and Alex spend days and evenings together playing tennis, walking, having dinners, and going to movies without any physical contact is likely to seem silly for teens who develop physical relationships prior to social and emotional ones. Nevertheless, all young readers can appreciate the fear that Mary Lou associated with her first kiss: "I hope, when the time comes, I have a chance to brush my teeth first. I also hope that it doesn't taste like chicken" (128). Triumphantly, she is able to report, late in the novel: "He just leaned over and kissed me. It was simple as anything.... And you know what? It didn't taste a *bit* like chicken" (*ANC*, 208).

By the end of the summer, Mary Lou's social maturity is beginning to parallel her academic maturity. She realizes that the popular girls of the GGP Club have little to offer her. When Christy finally does call to invite her to one of their pajama parties, one given only for members and for those being considered for membership, Mary Lou is proud of herself when she tells them she is busy and even more adamantly refuses the "last chance" invitation a few days later. Readers also watch as Mary Lou begins to understand her changing feelings for Alex Cheevey. In chapter one, she describes Alex Cheevey as a boy whom she thought was cute and athletic, with a face that is always pink, "like he is running a race"; however, when he tells her to stop asking the teacher so many questions about the journal assignment, she determines that he is, in fact, a "jerk"

(*ANC*, 6). By the end of the novel, she has spent more time with Alex and has changed her mind about him. Both are nervous in roles that are new to them as girlfriend and boyfriend, but their mutual discomfort becomes a bond. Instead of sitting on the couch in his living room, alone, the two decide that they will go to the Tast-ee Freeze; Mary Lou reports, with delight, that Alex put his arm on her shoulder just as they walked past Artie's Automotive (*ANC*, 147–148).

She and Alex develop a deeply rooted relationship that started as friendship, and she relies on him to work with her through questions that matter. The stability of their relationship is contrasted with Beth Ann's frequent claims of "true love" when it is Alex to whom Mary Lou confides her fears, and with whom she works to make sense of the troubling aspects of her bright, protected world. When she tells him that she worries about liking people, since anyone who establishes a relationship risks feeling helpless if something bad happens to the person for whom a person cares, Alex responds to her gently but directly by asking a meaningful question: "So does that mean you shouldn't like people?" Mary Lou realizes the failure of her logic, and replies to his question, "Well, of course not! That's just the way it is. If you didn't let yourself *like* people, you'd shrivel up." He ends the conversation with a reassuring, "Exactly" (*ANC*, 225–226).

Through the depiction of Mary Lou's friendships with Beth Ann, Alex, and the other teens in *Absolutely Normal Chaos*, Creech shows readers a young teen who draws on her family's closeness for stability, then steadily, independently builds relationships based on what matters to her, not on what the popular crowd dictates. She develops an interest in Alex as a boy and learns to look forward to his infrequent but welcome kisses, she comes to terms with the vacillations of friendship with Beth Ann, forgiving her for being fickle and accepting her as she is. And most significantly, she learns to appreciate Carl Ray's unique personality and habits, instead of being aggravated by his differences.

THEMES IN *ABSOLUTELY NORMAL CHAOS*
Finding A Place in the World, Finding A Place at Home

In *Absolutely Normal Chaos* and in most of Sharon Creech's novels for children and teens, the theme of finding one's place in the world and at home, through significant connections with people who are significant, is central. Instead of adopting the trend toward using caustic street language and painting dark and gritty pictures with the realistic details of today's world, a world in which too many young people are left to fend for themselves, Creech most often presents her teen protagonists as wholesome characters who are members of large, loving families. As she moves beyond this first novel, readers are able to see Creech create more sophisticated teen characters, those whose inner struggles are represented through their physical journeys: Sal's trip with her grandparents in *Walk Two Moons* (1994), Zinny's trail building in *Chasing Redbird* (1997), and Sophie's and Cody's sea voyage in *The Wanderer* (2000) are examples.

In this first of Creech's published novels, readers grow up with Mary Lou as they see the events of her thirteenth summer through the journal: Mary Lou uses her experiences with her cousin Carl Ray and his West Virginia family, and her tribulations as the sometimes-best friend of Beth Ann, who is more interested in spending time with boys and the popular girls than in demonstrating loyalty to Mary Lou, and her solid relationship with her first boyfriend to develop a sense of who she is and where she fits in the world.

Confident and intelligent from the beginning, Mary Lou develops social relationships and an expanded understanding of family as she narrates her summer adventures. Most important to her growth in terms of finding her place in the world and in her family is Mary Lou's gradual acceptance of and appreciation for her cousin Carl Ray. It is Carl Ray's story that nudges Mary Lou to examine her understanding of family love. Near the end of the novel, after Mary Lou and Carl Ray have traveled together to West Virginia and back, the trip during which he has confessed to her that he had felt homesick and out of place when he arrived in Ohio, and after which he explained to the family that Mr. Furtz, Mary Lou's neighbor, was actually his biological father, and therefore the mysterious benefactor who left him an inheritance, Carl Ray is involved in a serious automobile accident and is hospitalized, teetering between life and death. A few days after the accident, when Carl Ray is still unconscious, Mary Lou rereads her journal entries again and again, and despairs that she wrote such insensitive, ugly things about Carl Ray and his odd habits. In her journal notes, readers see that she has developed respect for her cousin, a young man who is able to comfort his cousin at a neighbor's funeral, a young man who never has a negative word to say about other people. Mary Lou recognizes that she has been looking at Carl Ray but not seeing the person he is, and that realization causes her to wonder about her own development:

> ... I didn't notice diddly-squat. I didn't even notice anything about Carl Ray being homesick or ... how he felt after Mr. Furtz died. How could a person like me go along and go along, feeling just the same from day to day, and then all of a sudden look back and see that I didn't see much of anything? And that I've been changing all along? I don't even recognize myself when I read back over these pages. (*ANC*, 223–225)

Her growth as a person is apparent in this tender scene of self-evaluation. Mary Lou knows she has been changed, through her interactions with Carl Ray and through the other experiences of the summer, but is not cognizant of just how much she has learned or grown.

Familiar Settings

Small Towns and Big Families

Creech's talent as a writer for young adults is affirmed in her ability to imbue each setting with qualities that allow her teen protagonists to explore their perspectives and their perception in order to mature. Her skill is also apparent in the ways she uses settings, the ways she portrays adults, and the hope that she provides young readers as they move through her books, inhabiting the lives of her characters.

Through her choice of settings, Creech also shows that she has the potential to have a lasting impact as a writer for teens in this first novel. In *Absolutely Normal Chaos*, she establishes a habit of using small towns as the places in which a modern teen navigates her way toward maturity. Other examples are found in *Ruby Holler* (1994), *Chasing Redbird* (1997), and even the foreign yet intimate setting of Lugano, Switzerland, in *Bloomability* (1998). Although the settings of this first novel for young adults, Easton, Ohio, and a tiny mountain community in West Virginia, are not specifically recognizable by a majority of teen readers, they are places that are meaningful for Creech, since they reflect the places where she grew up. With these settings, she is introducing to her readers a world that she cherishes—subtly continuing her work as a teacher. Instead of relying on the more readily familiar images of television and movies that have introduced teens to the skylines and streets of large cities like New York, Chicago, and Atlanta, Creech sets *Absolutely Normal Chaos* in small, quiet communities, where it gently sways back and forth from the Ohio town to the hollers and mountains of West Virginia and back again. The small town settings invite young readers to slow down and pay attention to the details that distinguish the small Ohio town and West Virginia mountain community from less-personal cities. In Easton, readers are able to bump into the secondary characters that play roles in the lives of the main characters—people like Mr. and Mrs. Furtz, Beth Ann's sister Judy and her boyfriend Derek, Alex's parents; in the mountains, readers meet Carl Ray's siblings, all of whom have double first names; in both locales, Mary Lou and her readers experience the connections between people who really know each other, the ways that neighbors rely on each other for help. The modern day temporal setting helps offset any reading challenges that might be caused by the unfamiliar places in which the action of the story occurs.

The actual action of the novel occurs primarily in large, noisy family homes, around the school, and in a local store—places that teen readers can readily visualize. For example, the single bedroom that Mary Lou and her older sister share in the large family home becomes the perfect scene for the explosion Maggie erupts into after she is punished by their father for coming home at 2 a.m. from a date with Ken. Mary Lou records the incident in her journal, capturing Maggie's long-winded oratory as only a sister who has lived through many crises with a dramatic older sibling could.

The seemingly primitive conditions of the family home in West Virginia come to life when Mary Lou describes them, making them recognizable for today's teen readers, too. She writes about having to write by moonlight, since there is no electricity, and thus feeling "like Abraham Lincoln" (*ANC*, 152). The West Virginia experience is not all bad for Mary Lou, though. After surviving her first trip to the outhouse, she goes swimming with her cousins and discovers that the swimming hole is a magic place, hidden deep in the woods and surrounded by trees. The surprise she experiences when she finds beauty in the rural surroundings provides readers with a subtle nudge to consider our own assumptions about what life in the mountains and woods of West Virginia might be like.

Internal Setting

Some young readers may need assistance to understand that Creech has chosen to use an "internal" or psychological setting, as well, by incorporating the first-person narrative voice. Mary Lou is telling the story from her limited perspective as narrator and protagonist. She appears to be a reliable narrator, even reporting on her own failures, in scenes like the one in which she admitted to Beth Ann, "Well, maybe I was a little jealous" (*ANC*, 90) about Beth Ann's new friendships with the GPP girls. Yet in other scenes, readers have the opportunity to question her veracity—or at least her tendency to exaggerate, as when she first meets the dad of Alex Cheevey and describes him as "about seven feet" with long legs that finally ended in enormous feet that were tucked into "gigantic leather sandals" (*ANC*, 145–146). The exaggeration is not a surprise, given what we know about Mary Lou's imagination by the time she meets Mr. Cheevey. Through her depiction of Mary Lou as an enthusiastic teen who is adaptable to life in a rowdy large family home and also in a small house with unfriendly cousins, no electricity or running water, and moonlight as a reading lamp, Creech develops a spunky character that teen readers are eager to know, one they are likely to want to befriend.

Positive Adults in Teens' Lives: Going Against the Grain in Teen Literature

Creech does break away from one of the common features of popular contemporary teen fiction in this first teen novel: she creates a story in which adults—particularly Mary Lou's parents—provide support for the teen protagonist and other teen characters. In addition to a positive relationship with her parents, Mary Lou's Aunt Radene and the uncles she gets to know while in West Virginia continue to challenge what she thinks she knows about how people think, act, and live, thus helping her grow up, too. Even storeowner Mr. Furtz is portrayed as a supportive, if mysterious, friend, especially to Carl Ray. When Carl Ray moves from West Virginia and arrives in Easton, it is Mr. Furtz who gives him a job; when Mr. Furtz dies suddenly, it is Carl Ray to whom he leaves a hefty inheritance. Yet adults are not portrayed as faultless; for example, readers are left with some questions about his ways of relating to Carl Ray when they realize, shortly after Carl Ray does, that Mr. Furtz is Carl Ray's biological father.

The common patterns in teen fiction dictate that parents are left out of the storyline altogether, placed in insignificant roles, or relegated to roles in which they have a negative influence on the story and its teen characters. Creech violates the norm for contemporary teen fiction in most of her books by including strong, supportive, likable even though imperfect, adults. Examples include the following:

Gramps and Gram, who help Sal begin to understand herself and her heritage in *Walk Two Moons* (1994);

Zinny's mother, who gives the young explorer the freedom to find her own identity and strength in *Chasing Redbird* (1997);

Aunt Sandy and Uncle Max, who introduce Dinnie to a new world and new possibilities when they take her from her home in New Mexico to live with them in Switzerland in *Bloomability* (1998);

Sophie's and Cody's uncles, who teach the cousins how to survive on the sea, introduce them to Bompie, and teach them about strong family connections in *The Wanderer* (2000);

Tiller and Sairy, who provide love and stability for Dallas and Florida, the two oldest foster children living in the Boxton Creek Home for Children in *Ruby Holler* (2002);

Grandpa and Mom, who provide Annie with gentle life lessons that reach across a generation in *Heartbeat* (2004);

Miss Stretchberry, the teacher, who encourages introverted, emotionally injured Jack to write about his dog in the novel in verse, *Love that Dog* (2005).

Creech uses her skill as a storyteller—one who develops teen and adult characters that readers care about and recognize—to present to teens, through her literary work, hope.

Pointing Toward Hope

Absolutely Normal Chaos is ultimately a book about how one young teen makes sense of her world. Mary Lou's problems—finding ways to assert her voice and claim her place in a large family, to be herself when the social hierarchy at school is ever-changing, to accept differences among people without interpreting them as deficiencies—are all challenges that a clever young teenager who has a strong sense of self, and who has support from her family, can solve. She is appealing because she is an average teen whose experiences mirror those of many teens who feel like they are merely marking time during adolescence, waiting on life in the "real world"; she is too old to be a child, and too young to be an adult; she is too protected by shields of family love and care to make bad mistakes, yet too vulnerable to others' opinions and attitudes to be kept completely safe from occasional growing pains. Mary Lou's ability to record her thoughts, reflect on her life, and to develop understanding and appreciation for her family and her life during her thirteenth summer provides hope to young readers who feel like Mary Lou did when she wrote her initial journal entry, at the start of her summer of growth: "I don't know what I am. I am waiting to find out" (ANC, 5). By the end of the summer, Mary Lou has begun to understand better who she is, and has begun asking deep questions that will help her continue to find answers about herself and her place in the world:

> Aunt Radene says that you just have to do your best to make the world a better place. I said I wasn't so sure I could make the world a better place, and she said, "Oh, you already have, Mary Lou, you already have."
> How does a person ever know that for sure? (ANC, 226)

Carl Ray, an awkward older teen whose qualities are revealed very slowly, also provides hope for teenagers who feel like their differences doom them. Carl Ray is depicted as a mess throughout most of *Absolutely Normal Chaos*. He does not know even how to converse with family members when he arrives at the home of his uncle, aunt, and cousins. To every inquiry, he responds with a trademark, "Don't rightly know" or a monosyllabic "nope" or "sure" or "yeah." He is vulnerable to the manipulations of Beth Ann, who apparently enjoys dating an older guy, one who can drive her to movies, and who thrives on pointing out how "divine" her boyfriends are, as a way of elevating herself. Yet it is Carl Ray who demonstrates patience and persistence as he solves the mystery of finding his biological father. Finally, after being pestered by impatient Mary Lou, he is able to calmly state, "I came here because my mother said that my father—the real one—lived here in Easton" (ANC, 196), and then, in his own time, after he has talked with the widowed Mrs. Furtz and also after he receives a letter from his mother that gives him permission, he goes public with the "whole, long, sad, complicated story" (ANC, 208) that Mr. Furtz was his biological father. Teen readers are likely to reason that if someone like Carl Ray can find answers and live with his new self-knowledge, if Mary Lou can endure the vicissitudes of her best friend's attentions at the same time that she develops a solid relationship with a friend who becomes a romantic interest, and if the parents of Mary Lou and Carl Ray are supportive and helpful yet not controlling, then they can find reasons to have hope in their own lives and in their own sets of experiences.

Creech, the former teacher of high school English, works quietly in the background of *Absolutely Normal Chaos*, providing lessons about language structure, the universal themes of literary classics, and the rewards of working through tough texts even as she weaves this engaging story. Young readers are implicitly encouraged to move from completing one of Creech's novels into one of the classic literary works that are embedded there, as a means of sharing a favorite characters' reading path.

Creech effectively uses Mary Lou's ebullient personality, balanced against Carl Ray's stolid manner, Beth Ann's flakiness, and Alex's dogged determination, to lift readers toward hope throughout the novel. In the closing lines of the novel, Mary Lou summons up the command that Athene makes at the conclusion of the *Odyssey*, for all to "make peace," (ANC, 230). These lines resonant with teen readers when they understand that peace can occur within oneself, within and among families, and across seemingly disparate communities—even for young teens.

CREECH THE WRITER, CREECH THE PERSON, AND *ABSOLUTELY NORMAL CHAOS*

This novel is a great introduction to Creech's literature for teens because Creech infuses many of her own life experiences into the story. Readers can make inferences about the ideas and relationships that matter greatly to Sharon Creech, as an author and as a person, through attending carefully to the ways that Mary Lou grows to a deeper understanding of herself as a result of the events that she experiences and records as the story's protagonist and narrator. The author's exuberance for life, as projected through the protagonist, is infectious in this entertaining book. Readers are treated to a deeper appreciation of the novel and the author when we explore what the text suggests about Creech as an artist and as a human being.

The Importance of Family

Readers who are familiar with Creech's background will not be surprised to see that the Finney family is a large and happy one; like Mary Lou, Sharon Creech grew up as the next oldest of five siblings. Although the novel is not directly autobiographical, careful readers should be able to develop, as they move through *Absolutely Normal Chaos*, a list of family attributes that Creech considers important. The list is likely to include these traits:

Parents who listen to their children, as Mr. and Mrs. Finney do, in contrast to Mr. Winterbottom, who is distant from his daughter, Phoebe;

A sense of routine, as demonstrated in the dinner scenes in which the Finneys gather around the dinner table, spilling milk and food yet talking above the hectic din, and when the siblings all pitch in to help clean the house in anticipation of Carl Ray's visit;

The need some children have to know their biological parents, as presented quietly yet powerfully in the quest that brings Carl Ray to Easton, Ohio, from his home and large family in West Virginia;

The importance of protecting family members' privacy, and of letting them decide when they want to reveal their thoughts, as evidenced in Mrs. Finney's delicate treatment of Carl Ray's decision to wait before telling his mother and father about the money he is given, and his plans to pursue a college education with it;

The crucial role that family connections can play in our lives, as indicated by the way that Mary Lou and Carl Ray become close friends as cousins, despite their very different world experiences.

Clues about Other Ideas that Creech Prizes

Creech leaves clues about other aspects of her values system throughout the book, aspects that are apparent to careful readers of *Absolutely Normal Chaos*, such as these:

The joys of story-telling as a vehicle for sharing information and confirming connections, as revealed in Carl Ray's slow, deliberate telling of the story of how he found out about his biological father, and the roles that Mr. Furtz and the ring now play in his life;

The significance of literature, especially classic texts, for our understanding of universal human truths, as understood when readers follow Mary Lou's interpretation of *The Odyssey*, drawing on Carl Ray's useful insights to help her make sense of some of the symbolic passages, and her final realization that Carl Ray is like Telemachus—seeking his own father and thus his own identity.

The value of writing ideas down as a way to capture and then reflect on our thoughts, as demonstrated through the entire book, since Creech uses Mary Lou's summer journal-writing assignment as the narrative framework for the novel.

The importance of loyalty to friends and family, as portrayed through Mary Lou's lasting friendship with fickle Beth Ann, the promises to Carl Ray that she makes and keeps, and the growing importance of Alex, with whom she shares fears about her own inadequacies.

It is perfectly appropriate and acceptable for readers of this easy-to-read novel—to read it to merely enjoy the literary experience, and perhaps to develop some vicarious connections with Mary Lou, her family, friends, and situations. Teen readers can develop rich responses to the book without seeking connections to the author's life and without looking for clues about what the novel indicates about the author's values. However, reading it with our eyes focused on what the text suggests about Sharon Creech—writer, mother, human—can deepen and thus enhance our literary experience as we make meaning from what Creech offers us: *Absolutely Normal Chaos*.

CHAPTER FOUR

WALK TWO MOONS IN ANOTHER'S MOCCASINS WITH SHARON CREECH

S HARON CREECH CONTINUES to provide readers with a feisty female protagonist, lovable eccentric relatives, and challenging situations in *Walk Two Moons* (1994). Creech's fingerprints, ones that readers discover as evidence of her presence in *Absolutely Normal Chaos*, reappear and are more complete on the pages of *Walk Two Moons*: (1) the fingerprints of an author who gives teens' perspectives priority by allowing them to tell their own stories, using first-person voice and teenage rationalizations; (2) the fingerprints of an artist who develops settings that assume the power of minor characters; (3) the fingerprints of a former teacher who gives teens the space they need to learn and grow; and (4) the fingerprints of an adult who offers young readers a warm serving of hope instead of a cold plate of bleakness. She also makes connections among characters who appear in her first novel for teen readers, *Absolutely Normal Chaos*, and those who are featured in *Walk Two Moons*. These connections are ones that fans of her first book will be eager to locate in the second one.

HIGH HONORS FOR *WALK TWO MOONS*

Creech lifts *Walk Two Moons* beyond her first young adult novel, *Absolutely Normal Chaos*, however, in terms of literary quality and appeal for its readers. In fact, she lifts this novel above all but the finest books ever published for teen readers. In this book, which is the recipient of the 1995 Newbery Medal, Creech adds sets of clearly defined fingerprints that help readers recognize her as an author who is able to tap into the rich imaginative powers that teens possess, and an author who subtly yet unashamedly incorporates moral lessons, often through characters' renderings of classic myths, a vehicle introduced with Mary Lou's reading of *The Odyssey* in *Absolutely Normal Chaos*.

It is the addition of these new fingerprints, paired with the ones that readers found in Sharon Creech's literature for young teens through reading of her first novel, that sets *Walk Two Moons* above other young adult and teen fiction that features a teenager grappling with tough life issues. The artistic achievement of *Walk Two Moons* gives Sharon Creech a place of high honor among other recipients of The John Newbery Award, including these recent Newbery Medal recipients:

Lynne Rae Perkins for *Criss Cross* (Greenwillow, 2006)
Cynthia Kadohata for *Kira-Kira* (Atheneum Books of Simon and Schuster, 2005)
Kate DiCamillo for *The Tale of Despereaux: Being the Story of a Mouse, a Princess, Some Soup, and a Spool of Thread* (Candlewick, 2004)
Avi for *Crispin: The Cross of Lead* (Hyperion Books for Children, 2003)
Linda Sue Park for *A Single Shard* (Clarion/Houghton Mifflin, 2002)
Richard Peck for *A Year Down Yonder* (Dial, 2001)
Christopher Paul Curtis for *Bud, Not Buddy* (Delacorte, 2000)

Creech describes her disbelief the day that she learned that *Walk Two Moons* had won the Newbery Medal:

I have often told the story of how I was living in England in 1995, and one cold, gray February day (about eight months after *Walk Two Moons* was published), I was struggling with the end of the next book, *Chasing Redbird*. As I stepped our into our tiny backyard to scream, the phone rang. On the other end was Kathleen Horning, calling from the American Library Association convention in Philadelphia. She informed me that *Walk Two Moons* had received the Newbery Medal.

To say I was shocked is a vast understatement. I had no idea my book was even being considered, nor how the awards were made. I think I kept asking Kathleen Horning, "Are you kidding?" At the end of the call, the entire committee shouted (from the background), "Huzza, huzza!" [Gram's upbeat expression].

When someone from my publisher called shortly afterwards, I asked, "How many of these medals are given out each year?" She replied, "One, Sharon. One." You might think I would be deliriously excited—and I was—but I was also terrified, because I didn't know what to expect next. I was not prepared for the deluge of calls, faxes, and deliveries, for the requests for interviews and for information. It took me a long time to get over the surprise that people were interested in my book and in how it came to be written.

[The Newbery Medal] gave me a feeling of immense freedom—freedom to write, and freedom from the worries that many writers have (like "Will a publisher want to print my book?" and "Will anyone find my book?") It forced me to learn how to give a speech in public (something I dreaded in the beginning but now enjoy). It also gave me the chance to travel to conferences and schools all over the world, meeting readers and teachers and librarians. It is an enormous gift, the Newbery Medal, and I am grateful for it. (www.sharoncreech.com, 2006)

Walk Two Moons is also identified by young adult literature specialists as one of the "Best YA Books of the 1990s," taking its place among *Holes*, by Louis Sachar (Frances Foster, 1999) and *Out of the Dust*, by Karen Hesse (Scholastic, 1998), two other Newbery Medal Award books on the list of "Best YA Books of the 1990s" (Hipple and Claiborne, 2005). International awards for *Walk Two Moons* include the United Kingdom Reading Association Award, 1995, and the Children's Books Award, United Kingdom, 1995; Literaturhaus Award, Austria, 1997.

Another kind of international honor that *Walk Two Moons* has earned is that it has been published in at least five languages in addition to English, and released in translation in five countries in which English is not a native language, according to the Association for Library Service to Children, which in 2002 tasked its International Relations Committee to search the OCLC WorldCat data base to identify Newbery Medal winners that have been translated into languages other than English (http://www.ala.org/ala/alsc/alscnews/news.htm). In Denmark, Creech's novel is published in Danish and titled *Mält med evigheden*. In Israel, it is published in Hebrew and titled *Shene yerehim*. In Italy, the Italian translation is called *Due Lune*; in Spanish-speaking countries it can be purchased in translation as *Caminar dos lunas* and as *Entre dos lunas* (www.alsc.ala.org).

PLOT SUMMARY OF *WALK TWO MOONS* (HARPERCOLLINS TROPHY, 1994)

Thirteen-year-old Salamanca Tree Hiddle (Sal) reluctantly agrees to go with her father's parents, Gramps and Gram, on a summer road trip from Ohio to Idaho. The trio traces the route that Sal's mother took a year earlier, prior to totally disappearing from Sal's life for reasons that Sal only begins to unravel and understand during the trip. Sal does not understand, at the start of the journey, why her mother has not come home, and blames herself, assuming that her mother didn't love her enough to return. The true reason for her failure to return—that she was killed in a bus crash when traveling to visit sites that were of spiritual significance to her, including the Black Hills, the Badlands, and Mount Rushmore—is not revealed fully until the penultimate chapter.

While they drive across country, Sal entertains her spunky and story-loving grandparents with tales of her new friend Phoebe, "a quiet girl who stayed mostly by herself," and who "had a pleasant round face and huge, enormous sky-blue eyes" with hair "as yellow as a crow's feet—curled in ringlets" (13). Phoebe's mother has also disappeared, and Phoebe is sure that a "lunatic" is responsible for the disappearance. Sal finishes the story just before she, Gram, and Gramps arrive at the end of the route: Phoebe's mother returns home and announces that she has been located by the son whom she had given up for adoption. This son turns out to be the same person whom Phoebe had misidentified first as a stalking lunatic, then as a mystery lover with whom her mother had secretly been spending time. For Sal, the story is an especially sad one, since it reminds her that her mother is not coming home. Ever.

When Sal's grandmother suffers a stroke and spends her last night in a hospital in Idaho, Sal takes Gramps' truck and drives over a mountain to the spot where her mother spent her final moments—-the spot where the bus in which she was riding went over the side of the road, killing Sal's mother and every other passenger except one: Mrs. Cadaver.

Until taking the trip with Gram and Gramps, Sal had not accepted her father's friendship with their new neighbor, Mrs. Cadaver, a friendship that gets closer when Mr. Hiddle moves the family from the home place on a farm in

Bybanks, Kentucky, where Sal recalls seeing her mother pick wildflowers and raise her arms wide to welcome the wind, to Euclid, Ohio, where the houses of their neighborhood looked "like a row of birdhouses" (WTM, 2) and where there are no physical landmarks that can remind her father or her of her mother.

Finally Sal learns that it was Mrs. Cadaver who was sitting beside Mrs. Hiddle when the bus crashed, and that Mrs. Hiddle had been talking about her daughter, husband, and their home in Bybanks, Kentucky, to Mrs. Cadaver for six hours prior to the bus crash. The fact that Mrs. Cadaver was the final person to speak with and comfort Sal's mom becomes apparent only near the end of the novel, in a poignant soliloquy in which Sal acknowledges her jealousy that Phoebe's mother returns home while hers will not, but in which she also confirms Sal's strength and her ability to continue to live as her mother and Gram, who dies before the trio leaves Idaho, would want her to live.

FAVORITE CHARACTERS IN *ABSOLUTELY NORMAL CHAOS* RETURN TO *WALK TWO MOONS*

A feature of *Walk Two Moons* that attracts young fans of Sharon Creech to this novel is its many connections to the first novel, *Absolutely Normal Chaos*. Teen readers will enjoy meeting, again, several of the characters who became their friends in the earlier novel.

Salamanca Tree Hiddle, called Sal, is a 13-year-old girl who is new to Euclid, Ohio. She is befriended by Ben Finney, cousin of Mary Lou Finney, who is the protagonist in *Absolutely Normal Chaos*. Because they have the same last name, Sal assumes that Ben and Mary Lou are siblings, but Sal's first friend, Phoebe, explains that the Finneys are cousins. Phoebe tutors Sal in the gossip of the neighborhood: "Apparently there was always at least one stray relative living at the Finney's temporarily" (ANC, 46). This observation is an allusion to cousin Carl Ray's memorable if temporary stay at the Finney home in *Absolutely Normal Chaos*.

Also familiar and potent when told through a teen's perspective is the "chaos" that permeates the happy Finney home, where Sal remembers seeing Mary Lou's brothers "sliding down the banister and leaping tables," while Mr. Finney escaped the pandemonium by lying in the bathtub—fully clothed—and Mrs. Finney rested, lying on the roof of the garage (WTM, 46–47).

In *Walk Two Moons*, Sal comments on her new friend Mary Lou's use of unusual expressions; savvy readers of Creech's first novel will recognize that Mary Lou is merely using terms that she picked up from her study of *The Odyssey*: "King of kings" (*WTM*, 47), "Omnipotent," (*WTM*, 12), and "'Alpha and Omega'" (*WTM*, 14) are examples.

Further familiarity is accomplished by the reappearance of a minor but important role in *Absolutely Normal Chaos*: Mr. Birkway. Although this English teacher is never physically present in the first novel, it is his assignment—one that requires the rising seventh graders whom he will teach in the fall to keep a journal of events during the summer—that causes Mary Lou to pen the pages that provide the commentary for *Absolutely Normal Chaos*. Since Salamanca is new to town and to the English class, she arrives without a journal; Mr. Birkway, who dramatically and flamboyantly refers to her as a "deprived child" (*WTM*, 82), because she was unable to enjoy writing a summer journal, asks her to compose a "mini-journal" so that she, like the other students, will have entries to share with classmates. Sal makes references to Mr. Birkway's strange habits, such as a fondness for having his students engage in exercises like a 15-second free-drawing session in response to the monosyllabic prompt, "soul," and which leads the class to discover that Sal and Ben have, unknowingly, drawn exactly the same symbol, a sugar maple leaf, to represent their souls, and ends when Mr. Birkway proclaims, "We now have everyone's soul captured" (130). She describes him as "one of those energetic teachers who loved his subject half to death and leaped about the room dramatically, waving his arms and clutching his chest and whomping people on the back" (*WTM*, 80) and someone with "enormous deep brown cowlike eyes that sparkled all over the place, and when he turned these eyes on you, you felt as if his whole purpose in life was to stand there and listen to you, and you alone" (*WTM*, 80).

Mr. Birkway's presence also lends depth to the novel through his attention to poetry, including Henry Wadsworth Longfellow's "The Tide Rises, The Tide Falls," which in its closing lines reflects Sal's forlorn searching:

> The day returns, but nevermore
> Returns the traveler to the shore.
> And the tide rises, the tide falls

and his assignment of e.e. cummings' "the little horse is newly." Curious readers of Creech's novel are likely to find and read cummings' poem, and those who do will have to work to make sense of enigmatic lines that include phrases and original compound words like "smoothbeautifully" (*WTM*, 123). As readers, we are invited to try to connect these lines, phrases, and words to Sal and her world, and to our own world as well. The references to Longfellow and cummings also enhance the sense that this is a novel with depths to be explored by young teen readers who are willing to peek beneath the surface.

Readers who hope to see Mary Lou's relationship with Alex Cheevey, which flourishes into a romance that includes kissing in *Absolutely Normal Chaos*, may be slightly disappointed in the references to Alex and his relationship to Mary Lou in *Walk Two Moons*. In *Walk Two Moons*, Alex is first referred to as "pink-cheeked Alex" (12), a reference to his always-blushing complexion. This description reminds readers of the one in the early portion of *Absolutely Normal Chaos*, in which Mary Lou described Alex as looking "like he's just been running a race" (*ANC*, 6). Instead of progressing, their relationship seems to take a few steps backward, a reversal that is aided by the fact that Mr. Birkway reads the first few pages of Mary Lou's journal aloud, including a section in which she refers to Alex in unflattering terms. Later, Mr. Birkway starts to read from early entries in the summer journals aloud, and in doing so, he unintentionally causes trouble among the classmates: "Alex avoided Mary Lou because of what she had said about his being a pink jerk, and Mary Lou avoided Beth Ann because of what Beth Ann had written about the chicken kisses" (228).

CREECH'S STYLE: PUTTING HER FINGERPRINTS ON *WALK TWO MOONS*

The Teen's Perspective

Creech convincingly depicts teens' perspectives by allowing 13-year-old Salamanca Tree Hiddle to tell the story of her cross-country trip with her Gram and Gramps. The trip is a quest that takes the trio to every locale from which Sal had received a postcard from her mother, who disappeared a year earlier, and whose failure to return Sal cannot understand.

The teen perspective is provided through Salamanca's narration of her own summer, including the trip with her grandparents to retrace her mother's final trip. Sal also provides readers with commentary on

Phoebe's struggle to find her mother (and avoid a lunatic) through a clever structural effect: Creech has Sal telling Phoebe's story to her grandparents, as a vehicle for entertaining them while the trio travels across the country. Gramps and Gram know that it is time that Sal learns the truth, that her mother has been killed and thus is never going to return home—and that her mother's leaving was not Sal's fault. Lewiston, Idaho, is the final destination. Along the way, they visit the Black Hills, Mount Rushmore, the Badlands, and Coeur d'Arlene, all of which were places from where Sal's mother mailed her a postcard a year earlier. The postcards express the loneliness and love that Sal's mother felt regarding her daughter, but when her mother doesn't return, Sal is left to question the sincerity of cards on which her mother recorded sentiments from each stop on her final journey, like the one she sent from North Dakota that tried to assure her daughter, "This is Mount Rushmore, but I don't see any Presidents' faces, I only see yours" (*WTM*, 56).

In a subplot that has strong thematic ties to the main plot, Sal tells the story of the disappearance—and eventual return—of her friend Phoebe's mother, Mrs. Winterbottom. The parallel story focuses on her friend Phoebe's struggles with her mother's disappearance. In telling it, Sal reveals many of her own concerns and fears, especially about whether or not she was the cause of her own mother's disappearance, and whether or not her mother loved her enough to come home.

During her disappearance, Phoebe's mother comes face-to-face with Mike Bickle, the sheriff's (adopted) son. Mike has contacted Mrs. Winterbottom and announced that he is her biological son. Readers see the two together for the first time at the moment that Phoebe and Sal do; Mrs. Winterbottom is sitting on a bench with Mike, and she kisses his cheek. Because neither Phoebe nor Sal knows that Mike is Mrs. Winterbottom's son at the time they observe the kiss, they mistakenly assume that Phoebe's mother is having an affair with the young man who turns out to be her son. Finally she returns home to set the record straight: Mrs. Winterbottom admits to her husband and daughters that he is her son, one whom she had given up for adoption in an earlier phase of her life, and questions emerge.

Phoebe, along with the young readers who are engaged in her story, are left to wonder whether or not Mr. Winterbottom will be able to forgive his wife for remaining silent about her son, and about how Phoebe and her sister will adjust to having an older brother in the group. These questions hang like ominous storm clouds over the Winterbottom family and the story; they do not pass across the horizon quickly to leave sunshine in their place, but are broken to emit rays of light by Mr. Winterbottom's act of acceptance, which Sal describes this way:

> I was sad for Phoebe and her parents and Prudence and Mike … sad for myself, for something I had lost.
>
> Then [Mr. Winterbottom] did what I think was a noble thing. He went over to Mike and shook his hand and said, "I did always think a son would be a nice addition to this family." Mrs. Winterbottom looked relieved. Prudence smiled at Mike. Phoebe stood motionless off to the side. (*WTM*, 249–250)

Sal's perspective, one that suggests that she is still counting on the adults to make things right, is not one that Phoebe can champion. Phoebe's father does not initiate a search for her mother; when Mrs. Winterbottom does return home, he is at first unable to even look at her, because he suspects that the young man who she brings home with her is her new lover, instead of asking for her explanation first. Phoebe is not ready to trust either parent.

Here, as in *Absolutely Normal Chaos,* adults have an important role in teens' lives, but it is the generation of Sal's grandparents that adds stability throughout much of this award winning novel. Sal's father could not tell her about her mother's death, and thus hides it from her, allowing her to hope for the miracle of her mother's return, for over a year. Eventually, the relationships between parents and teens are worked out, but it takes growth for all involved in order to open the communication between them.

An exception to the difficulties faced by families is the Finney family, a group that is still filled with energy and playfulness. Sal describes the contrast of the kind of participation that Mary Lou's parents and Phoebe's parents demonstrated at a school sports day when she reports that her parents "don't usually participate," whereas the Finneys are fully engaged in running, jumping, falling, and having fun during the day. Phoebe comments about the embarrassment that Mary Lou must feel because of her parents' silly behavior, but readers hear, in Sal's reply, a wistfulness that she had a family with whom she could play freely; she believes that Phoebe wishes that for herself, as well.

Familiar But Unusual Settings in Walk Two Moons

Creech also stays true to her literary signature, first established in *Absolutely Normal Chaos*, of using familiar yet unusual story settings—the small town of Euclid, Ohio, is the starting point of this novel, and a family farm in Bybanks, Kentucky, provides the setting of its final scene. (Bybanks is the fictitious name of Quincy, Ohio, the small rural town in which Creech spent many summers as a child, playing with her cousins and siblings.) Sal is unhappy to have moved with her father to Euclid; she misses the sugar maple and other trees and the multitude of birds that dotted the landscape of her home on a farm in Bybanks, Kentucky. She associates the move to Euclid with her father's need to be near his new friend, Mrs. Cadaver, who lives with her blind mother near Sal and her father. This association with a new woman in her father's life—only a year after her mother's disappearance—contributes heavily to Sal's bad feelings about Euclid. Her only real happiness while in Euclid seems to occur when she is in school interacting with other middle school students.

Between the two map points of Euclid and Bybanks, and the temporal points during which she did not know about her mother's death and the time that she knows the truth, Sal travels with her grandparents to the Black Hills, Mount Rushmore, the Badlands, Coeur d'Arlene, and Lewiston, Idaho, tracing the steps of her mother's final adventure.

Relationships between Adults and Teens in Walk Two Moons

Creech continues her effectiveness in presenting adult characters who contribute to teens' development without interfering with the teens' need to learn some lessons for themselves. In this novel, though, not all adults are admirable. For example, Sal's father is unable to free himself from his grief in order to share the truth about her mother's death with her; surely readers would prefer to see him be direct and honest with her, so that she is not left to wonder, for a year, whether or not her mother is coming home, whether or not it is her fault if her mother chooses to stay away. Similarly, the disappearance of Phoebe's mother, and the irresponsibility a mother shows by failing to phone her children or their father during her absence, raises questions about her dedication to their happiness. While young readers are likely to be familiar with the notion that even their parents sometimes have to protect their own feelings, the failure of Phoebe's mother to make contact during her investigation into the claims that Mike is her biological son reminds readers that parents are not immune to emotional, spiritual, and social confusion.

Here, unlike in *Absolutely Normal Chaos*, the older members of the family are featured, through Creech's depiction of Gram and Gramps. They use pet names for each other (Gooseberry) and for Sal (Chickabiddy) that today's readers might become bored with or find to be too precious … yet they give us information as readers about the personalities and strong relationship of Gramps and Gram. Gramps and Gram use expressions colorfully, too, as Gram demonstrates in this passage:

> "Being a mother is like trying to hold a wolf by the ears," Gram said. "If you have three or four—or more—chickabiddies, you're dancing on a hot griddle all the time." (53–54)

The wisdom of this older pair is revealed slowly; at first, they seem comical in their language and enthusiasm for a road trip; Gramps anticipates seeing "the whole ding-dong country!" while Gram is eager to spend time with her "favorite chickabiddy," Sal, who was unable to predict what to expect from this peculiar pair of grandparents (*WTM*, 5–6).

This introduction of family members who help create a bridge between a teenager and her parents becomes a trademark of many of Creech's books that follow *Walk Two Moons*, including these: Zinny's deep need to create a place of her own in the world is mirrored by Uncle Nate's need to keep a place in the world in memory of Aunt Jessie, whom he loses suddenly to illness in *Chasing Redbird* (1997). Aunt Sandy and Uncle Max remove Dinnie from her normal surroundings to introduce her to the world while providing her with the stability that her restless parents cannot in *Bloomability* (1998).

Three uncles and a cousin doubt Sophie's relationship with the grandfather, Bompie, but Sophie is led to him across the sea by the power of their connection in *The Wanderer* (2000). Odd but lovable old Tiller and Sairy teach orphaned and previously abused twins Dallas and Florida positive life lessons in *Ruby Holler* (2002). In *Heartbeat* (2004), her grandfather's heartbreaking, gradual loss of mental acuity provides a balance in Annie's world view, since she is expecting the arrival of an infant sibling at the same time that she watches her grandfather slip into forgetfulness.

The Warmth of Hope in Walk Two Moons

Creech's desire to present hope, ultimately, instead of darkness, is a feature that makes this novel a welcome choice for today's young readers. Although Sal learns that her mother will never return from Idaho, since she was killed in a bus crash there, she is finally able to accept the idea that her mother had loved her. Sal learns, too, that her mother's leaving Kentucky to go on a long road trip was the result of her need for the freedom of travel, but that it was not driven by a need to be separated from her daughter.

When Gramps, Gram, and Sal finally arrive in Idaho for the last leg of their trip, to retrace the stops that Sal's mother made during her final adventure, Gram has a stroke and dies, in a hospital far from home, but with Gramps beside her. The stroke is possibly related to a snakebite that Gram suffers when the trio makes an impromptu stop to wade in a river. The situation forces Sal to think about her mother's life, and the accidents and incidents that marked it, too. Sal wonders, for example, if her mother would still be home and happy if she had not miscarried after running, with Sal cradled in her arms, from the tree that Sal had climbed and fallen out of when her mother was almost ready to deliver a baby. The juxtaposition of Gram's critical condition and Sal's questions about her mother's life and disappearance are powerful. Sal concludes that

> a person couldn't stay locked up in the house.... A person had to go out and do things and see things, and I wondered, for the first time, if this had something to do with Gram and Gramps taking me on this trip. (*WTM*, 257)

The final scene, in which Sal admits that she harbors three jealousies, resonates with the realistic voice of a teenager who is trying to put together the pieces of her world that help her make sense of it. After admitting a petty jealousy about whomever Ben Finney wrote about in his journal, she then moves to more substantial confessions, ones about the jealousy she has felt in knowing that her mother had longed to have a second child, as though Sal was not a grand enough prize for her mother, and about the lasting jealousy that "Phoebe's mother came back and mine did not" (*WTM*, 278–279).

There are indications that the adults around Sal have grown through some of their grief at the loss of Sal's mother, too. Her father is able to move with his daughter back to Bybanks, Kentucky, without the fear of being haunted by too many painful reminders of his wife's absence. Gramps, comforted by a beagle and a lifetime of memories, is continuing, without Gram, in his role as Sal's confidante and traveling friend. Mrs. Cadaver, the nurse who had been seated beside Mrs. Hiddle and who comforted her as she lay dying after the bus crash, is becoming a close friend of Mr. Hiddle; she and her mother, Mrs. Partridge, are set to visit Sal and Mr. Hiddle in their Kentucky home when the book closes, thus drawing more caring adults close to Sal and her father.

The teenagers have learned to have hope for their futures, too. Sal's friendship with Phoebe has continued to grow, despite Sal's move to Kentucky. Sal's romance with Ben flourishes; Ben entertains her using long distance mail with his truly bad attempts at writing love poems, including this one, sent to Sal in October after she has returned to Kentucky:

> Roses are red,
> Dirt is brown,
> Please be my valentine,
> Or else I'll frown. (*WTM*, 279)

Some adults read *Walk Two Moons* as a novel that is too bleak for young teens to read. They are bothered by the deaths of Sal's mother and grandmother, and by the disappearance and eventual return of Phoebe's mother, as well as by the fact that Mrs. Winterbottom had hidden the truth about her son from her family for almost two decades. However, those critics are in the minority; more readers, teens and adults alike, find a transcending sense of hope in the novel, through its gentle treatment of death and life issues.

EXTRAORDINARY ART IN *WALK TWO MOONS*

Aspects of this novel that set it apart from others young adult books that Kenneth L. Donelson and Aileen Pace Nilsen, in the all-time best-selling book on young adult literature, *Literature for Today's Young Adults,* seventh edition (Boston: Allyn & Bacon, 2004), call "the new realism," include Creech's masterful ability to capture teen girls' imaginations, her ability to write convincingly, as if she were an extremely articulate 13-year-old female herself. This novel also showcases her talent for weaving American poetry and American Indian mythology into the narrative in which her characters live.

Sal and Phoebe: Teens with Larger-than-Life Imaginations

The parallel story that offers a subplot to Sal's journal to find out about her mother's disappearance and death is peppered by humor, adding balance to the novel. Sal describes Phoebe as "a quiet girl who stayed mostly by herself … huge, enormous sky-blue eyes … hair—as yellow as crow's foot—curled in short ringlets" (*WTM,* 13). Given her demure manner, readers are surprised to learn that Phoebe's imagination runs rampant and sometimes amok. Phoebe gathers a collection of unusual—and thus disconcerting—notes that are left by a secretive messenger on her family's doorstep, and eventually takes them to her father, urging him to go to the police. When he refuses to take action, Phoebe takes the notes to the police herself. The unlikely circumstances become more and more plausible to Sal when Phoebe's belief in them intensifies. The message collection grows to include these:

> "Don't judge a man until you've walked two moons in his moccasins." (51)
> "Everyone has his own agenda." (60)
> "In the course of a lifetime, what does it matter?" (105)
> "You can't keep the birds of sadness from flying over your head, but you can keep them from nesting in your hair." (154)
> "You never know the worth of water until the well is dry." (198)

Phoebe is sure that a roaming "lunatic" is leaving the notes, and even spots "him" once or twice at her doorstep. However, her attention is turned toward her family when she discovers her mother, who has not yet returned home, sitting beside the mysterious stranger on a bench, kissing his cheek. When her mother returns home, Phoebe is shocked to find that she brings along the mysterious stranger, and that he is the "lunatic" whom she has spotted at her front door. She is further shocked when she learns that the "lunatic" is actually her own half brother, and accepts the truth only after she discards the entire series of explanations regarding the lunatic, the stranger, and her mother—explanations that she had invented and had begun to believe.

Sal has an active imagination, too, and it is revealed when she describes her relationship with trees. Instead of sounding traditional spiritual notes, Sal prays to trees. She explains that, praying to trees is "easier than praying directly to God" since "There was nearly always a tree nearby" (*WTM*, 7). This praying foreshadows the scenes in which Sal remembers a special tree from her childhood in Kentucky, a scene that, when recalled, tells readers something about Sal's ability to pay close attention to nature, to turn to nature as a friend. In it, Sal tells how she once heard beautiful birdsong emanating from the top of her sugar maple tree, a "true birdsong, with trills and warbles," but that when she looked for the singing bird she saw only leaves stirred by the wind (*WTM*, 99–100). Her conclusion was that the tree itself, not birds in it, was singing for her. This memory also serves to keep Sal close to her mother, in her mind, since her mother loved trees, too.

Early in the novel, readers learn that Sal's mother's real name is "Chanhassen," a Seneca Indian word for "tree sweet juice" or "maple sugar" (*WTM*, 16), and that she prefers her Seneca name to "Sugar," the Americanized version that she is called by everyone except her own mother. Sal finally acknowledges to herself that her mother is not returning when she finds her mother's tombstone in Lewiston, Idaho, near the site of the bus crash. She arrives on her mother's birthday, and sees that the tombstone has an engraving of a tree. While Sal is sitting before it, in reverie, she hears a bird singing sweetly in a nearby willow tree. She is comforted by the birdsong and the continuity of the singing tree: "'Happy birthday,' I said.... 'She isn't actually gone at all. She's singing in the trees'" (*WTM*, 268).

Subtle Moral Lessons

Creech skillfully laces moral lessons like the one associated with the unkind use of the word "lunatic" and the relationship of people and nature throughout the novel. In addition to humor and action, a subtle message about how we talk about people whom we don't understand, including those with mental illnesses, is introduced in the subplot. Sal follows Ben one morning and finds that he has gone to the psychiatric ward of a hospital. He tells her later that he was there visiting his mother. That visit to his hospitalized mother explains why Ben has been living at his cousin Mary Lou's home, Ben's discomfort when he hears Phoebe use the term "lunatic," (64–65), and causes readers to wince at Phoebe's use of the term, too.

The strength of the marriage between Gram and Gramps is reflected in the motif of the "marriage bed" that Creech weaves throughout the journey. Sal understands the significance of a stable bed as a metaphor for a life filled with the love of a spouse and an extended family. The marriage bed became significant on the night that Gram and Gramps were married, since, as Gramps tells Sal, when he carried his bride over the threshold of their hand-built wooden home, they found that his family had moved his parents' own bed, the bed that he and each of his brothers had been born in, into the middle of the single bedroom of the little house. The day that Gram dies, Sal and her Gramps share a poignant moment of resolve. While lying down, staring at the ceiling, he confides in Sal, "Chickabiddy ... I miss my Gooseberry ... this ain't ..." Sal is able to finish the sentence for him, since she has heard him on each night of their journey pat the bed for Gram to join him, before saying "This ain't a marriage bed" and after five minutes, he rises and completes the familiar sentence, "but it will have to do" (*WTM*, 273).

Another moral lesson is quietly introduced in the scene in which Phoebe's mother, Mrs. Winterbottom, confesses that she would have been considered "unrespectable" if anyone had known that she had given birth to a son many years prior to her marriage to Mr. Winterbottom. Creech deftly foreshadows the secret by portraying the coldness that separates Mr. and Mrs. Winterbottom, and prevents Mrs. Winterbottom from hugging even her daughter Phoebe. Finally, Mrs. Winterbottom acts on her own, disregarding what "respectable" people will say, and meets her now-grown son:

> She had tried very, very hard all these years to be perfect, but she had to admit she was quite imperfect. She said there was

something that she had never told her husband, and she feared
he would not forgive her for it…. "Mike is my son." (*WTM*,
246, 248)

This scene reinforces the theme that a mother's love is strong and ultimately dependable. It also reminds readers that even mothers can buckle
under pressures to be perfect people. Sal's mother left on a journey across
the country when her baby died, feeling that she had been an inadequate
mother. However, Sal learns from Mrs. Cadaver that it was Sal and Mr.
Hiddle who were the topic of conversation just before Mrs. Hiddle died
(270); this revelation demonstrates to Sal that her mother was thinking of
her family even when she needed time away to collect herself while she
grieved the loss of the baby (110). Sal succinctly sums up the lesson that
she is just beginning to accept in these words: "We couldn't own our
mothers" (*WTM*, 176).

Myths and American Indian Stories

Walk Two Moons is laced not only with moral lessons, but also with inte-
grated references to classic myths. At school, Ben and Phoebe present
oral reports on Prometheus (155) and Pandora (171) that resonate with
the struggles that Phoebe is having, and lead Phoebe to argue that Ben's
interpretation—that Zeus sent Pandora to Prometheus as punishment in
the form of a woman—preferring, instead, her take on the story—that
Zeus gave man a "present" in the form of "a sweet and beautiful woman"
(172). The idea of Pandora's box mirrors the caution that Mr. Winterbottom provides as he refuses to explore possibilities related to his wife's disappearance, as well as Sal's insistence on finding her mother and trying
to bring her back to Euclid or to Bybanks.

The myths that Creech laces into the novel are not only Greek ones.
Sal tells Gramps Navaho stories that her mom had told her, and he especially likes the one about the woman who never dies, but continues to
rotate through life cycles as baby, woman, old woman, baby … (*WTM*,
278). Readers who enjoy the novel—due to its main plot, or the sentiments attached to the two girls' longing for their missing mothers, or the
fun of the mystery surrounding the messages left on the Winterbottom
family's doorstep, or even the relationships that are continued from

Absolutely Normal Chaos—are likely to close its final page with an increased awareness of the wisdom of the Native American axiom: "Don't judge a man [or person] until you've walked two moons in his [or her] moccasins."

A Challenge for Readers Who are Up for a Challenge: Reading *Walk Two Moons* with an Eye Toward the Portrayal of Females in the Novel and In Society

Readers who enjoy the trip that they take through *Walk Two Moons* will amplify the depth and quality of their literary experience by reflecting on the text with feminist lenses—a perspective that can help them zoom in on how the characters bend, break, or reinforce society's stereotypes about females. Creech has provided at least five intriguing female characters, Sal, Gram, Sal's mother (Chanassen Sugar Hiddle), Phoebe, and Mrs. Winterbottom, each of whom readers can examine successfully with these feminist lenses. She has also created male characters who help readers consider expectations that society holds for males, including Gramps, Sal's father—Mr. Hiddle, Ben Finney, and Phoebe's father— Mr. Winterbottom. The sixteen question sets that follow are ones that a feminist reading of *Walk Two Moons* can raise:

1. What lessons about how females are expected to act does Sal learn from these female characters: her mother (whose presence in the novel is implied), Gram, Mrs. Winterbottom, Mrs. Cadaver, Mrs. Partridge?

2. Does Creech portray Gram as more emotional and intuitive, but less intelligent, than Gramps? Is this portrayal one that builds on stereotypes of women? Senior citizens?

3. Does Creech lead readers to conclude that Sal's mother, Chanhassen (Sugar) Hiddle, is a "bad mother" because she lost one baby to a stillbirth and left on an adventure without her only child?

4. How accurate is Mrs. Hiddle's self-evaluation, that she is "rotten in comparison" (*WTM*, 109) to her husband, and that her life proves that she is "not brave … not good" (*WTM*, 110)?

5. What does the response of Mr. Hiddle to his wife's death say about his (in)ability to express himself? To face reality? To be honest with his daughter? Is this response one that is expected of a male character? How would a female character respond to the death of a spouse? Are stereotypes perpetuated in the answers?

6. Gram is portrayed as strong but also hapless; her zest for life is eventually responsible for her death. What stereotypes does Creech bend, break, or reinforce through the character of Gram?

7. What expectations for Gramp's response to Gram's death are realized, and how does his response defy expectations? Would readers accept a similar response from Gram, if Gramps had died?

8. How do readers feel about Mrs. Winterbottom's disappearance? Does her goal of meeting her once-abandoned son excuse her failure to contact her family regarding her safety?

9. Is Mrs. Winterbottom an attractive, strong character, since she pushes through her shame to meet her son, or is she a weak, unattractive character since she feels that she has had to hide from her husband and family the existence of her son, who was born after she had an affair with a man whom she did not marry?

10. Consider the ways that Creech uses physical contact, or lack of contact—between spouses, parents and children, friends, and romantic pairs—in this novel. Is the willingness to demonstrate affection through physical contact associated with females? Males? Does Creech bend, break, or reinforce stereotypes through the scenes in which physical contact is important?

11. What about Phoebe is typical, according to readers' expectations for a young female who is confused about her mother's behavior? What is exceptional in her actions and attitudes?

12. What kinds of stereotypes about women does Mrs. Cadaver reinforce? Which stereotypes does she break?

13. What expectations does our society have for the attitudes and actions of an older, blind, woman? Did Creech rely on stereotypes when she drew the character of Mrs. Partridge?

14. How does Creech's portrayal of Mr. Birkway work to dismiss or perpetuate stereotypes about male English teachers?
15. In what ways does Creech bend and break stereotypes about teen male behavior through the character of Ben?
16. When the adult male characters (Gramps, Mr. Hiddle, Mr. Winterbottom) are compared and contrasted, in terms of their treatment of their wives, their children, and their own identities, which ones defy social expectations for male behavior? Which ones reinforce expectations? In what ways? Which of these males is the most admirable character?

A final set of questions that readers might address when reflecting on *Walk Two Moons* from a feminist perspective is this:

How does being male or female influence the ways that you respond to this novel?

If you changed your reading to read from the other gender perspective, which aspects of your response to the novel would change? Why?

This final question set moves from a consideration of the text to an explicit focus on the reader, and therefore might help teen readers account for their own "gendered" reading of the novel. A discussion of these readings is likely to be thought provoking and rich in terms of personal responses and readers' connections of the text to broader contemporary social definitions, expectations, attitudes, and actions.

CHAPTER FIVE

CHASING REDBIRD WITH SHARON CREECH

O
N THE BACK cover of *Chasing Redbird*, an excerpt from a *Publisher's Weekly* starred review proclaims that this novel is "Creech's best yet." This evaluation is high praise for a book that follows *Walk Two Moons*, for which Creech won the most significant American prize for literature for children, the Newbery Medal (1995). And that high praise is deserved. In *Chasing Redbird*, readers will find Sharon Creech's characteristic fingerprints: a feisty female protagonist, lovable eccentric relatives, and challenging competing cultures. In this novel, the female is protagonist Zinny Taylor, a quiet 13-year-old stuck in the midst of seven siblings. The eccentric characters are her Aunt Jessie and Uncle Nate, with whom Zinny spends a lot of time, since they are better able to pay attention to her than are her own, too busy, parents. The cultural clash is rooted in the moral differences between two people who live in the same town, Zinny and Jake, instead of in the geographic differences that readers have found in the previous two novels: the physical and cultural distance that separates Mary Lou from her country kin in *Absolutely Normal Chaos*, and the distance from Bybanks, Kentucky, to a new home in Euclid, Ohio, that Sal longs to abolish in *Walk Two Moons*.

Chasing Redbird is also filled with Creech's specialties. In it, Creech portrays life from an adolescent's fresh, lively perspective, with connections across novels to characters that Creech's readers have met. She uses a setting that breeds adventure, one that is similar to one that her readers explored with Mary Lou in *Absolutely Normal Chaos* and that becomes vaguely familiar, since it is the place that Sal longs to return home to in *Walk Two Moons*. Creech includes realistic adult characters who, even when they are exaggerated, demonstrate true concern for adolescents, and who assist them instead of thwart them as they reach for their goals.

And Creech builds into the novel a sense of hopefulness emerging from the protagonist's self-discovery, her appreciation for the qualities and uniqueness of those around her, and her emotional and social growth.

In addition to the presence of these characteristic features of Creech's literary art, Creech challenges readers more than she has previously, in *Chasing Redbird*. In this novel, she draws readers more completely into the world of the protagonist by weaving threads of two important subplots into the fabric of the main plot line. She also fascinates and unsettles readers by bringing them face-to-face with sensitive, delicate, painful, and confusing issues related to the ways that people react to the death of family members. In *Chasing Redbird*, Creech's presentation of death is visual and visceral. In her previous novels, the deaths of family members, even the central issue of the death of Sal's mother in *Walk Two Moons*, are described from a temporal and geographic distance. In *Chasing Redbird*, the deaths are depicted with disturbing proximity and clarity.

Creech also showcases, in *Chasing Redbird*, her talent for using natural imagery and strong, colorful dialogue in ways that have been only hinted at in the previous novels. It is the attention to intricately woven subplots that complement the main storylines; attention to death from Zinny's personal, close, perspective, and the ways that Zinny's ideas about death occupy her throughout the novel; and with Creech's use of natural imagery in the fabulously fresh language of characters' speech and recorded thoughts, that set this book apart from other works of fiction for adolescents, including the author's previous books. Perhaps it is this deep and wide blend of elements found in *Chasing Redbird* that is responsible for the novel being named a "Best Books for Young Adults" by the American Library Association (1997), and an enduring staple of contemporary young adult literature.

Creech explains that, following the success of *Walk Two Moons*, she determined that she would write a story about someone who could have been Sal Hiddle's friend. Creech notes, in a section called "Inspiration" on her personal Web page that is devoted to *Chasing Redbird*, that she "imagined Zinny living in a large family and being lost in that family" then goes on to note that Zinny's town, Bybanks, is based on Quincy, Kentucky, where her cousins lived on a farm:

I remembered my cousins' farm and the woods nearby, and all the trails we used to follow. And so, the idea of Zinny finding a trail came to mind. As I was writing, I was vaguely aware that the trail was working on many levels. Not only was it a real, literal trail in the woods, but it also seemed to mirror the trails we all follow in our lives (Which way should we go? What should we do?) and also to mirror the writing process (Which way will this story turn? Why can't I see where it's going?). (www.sharon-creech.com/novels/04.asp. Retrieved December 1, 2006)

Synopsis of *Chasing Redbird* (HarperCollins Trophy, 1997)

Thirteen-year-old Zinny is tired of being just another one of the seven Taylor kids. Her mother, who is permanently distracted by doing chores or investigating calamities caused by one of the rowdier children, seems to forget her name. Even her beloved Uncle Nate and Aunt Jessie think of Zinny as someone else. They see her, Zinny believes, as a living replacement for their own daughter, Rose, who died of whooping cough when Rose and Zinny were four. Zinny, who also had whooping cough, suffers deep guilt, assuming that it was she who infected her cousin, and thus that it was she who was responsible for Rose's death.

This summer, though, she finds a way to make her mark on her family and her town, Bybanks, Kentucky. She plans to uncover the long-forgotten Bybanks-Chocton Trail, and to plant zinnias all along it as a floral homage to herself. The trail, which begins in Zinny's back yard, covers twenty miles that cross mountain ridges, creeks, hollows, and holes on the outskirts of Bybanks. Convincing her parents to let her live on the trail while she works on it, dealing with her loneliness and grief over the sudden death of Aunt Jessie, working in locations that have names such as "Bear Alley," "Shady Death Ridge," and "Spook Hollow," and trying to understand Uncle Nate's odd behaviors, are challenges she faces while she works on the trail.

Zinny is also troubled by the erratic behavior of attractive 16-year-old Jake Boone, who has returned to Bybanks this summer. Jake is eager to show Zinny that she is the Taylor girl who has caught his eye. Although Zinny's older sister, May, incorrectly assumes that his intention is to win her heart, Zinny is the recipient of a series of gifts from Jake. Zinny becomes ashamed of the gifts when she realizes what no one else knows: the gifts, including a gold and ruby ring and a puppy, are things he has stolen in his attempt to win her attention and affection. Jake's stealing crosses the line, in Zinny's mind. He also crosses the line with his insistence that she needs him to keep an eye on her, from a distance, while she camps and works on the trail. She resists his help, and yet it is Jake who helps Zinny when she most needs help. Jake assists as Zinny struggles to take Uncle Nate, on a borrowed horse, to the cabin in the woods. The cabin that they take Nate to is a memorial site, one that Uncle Nate has built as a place in which he imagines that his baby Rose and his "redbird," Jessie, are still alive and with him.

Zinny's goal for the summer is reached by the conclusion of Chasing Redbird. *She has single handedly uncovered and rebuilt the trail, and named it in honor of her Aunt Jessie, "The Redbird Trial." She has accomplished more than the physical labor, though, by establishing her own identity as someone who is stronger and smarter than the oddly quiet little sister whom her family and the people of Bybanks recognize. En route to uncovering the trail, she has pieced together bits of memory about herself and her cousin Rose and the times that they spent as babies and children together, has grown into to a greater appreciation for Uncle Nate's need to imagine Jessie alive and flourishing in the mountains that she loved, and has begun to recognize that she likes Jake, despite his objectionable behaviors, and that their relationship has the potential to grow into more than friendship.*

CONNECTIONS TO *ABSOLUTELY NORMAL CHAOS* AND *WALK TWO MOONS*

The setting of *Chasing Redbird* is familiar to readers of *Absolutely Normal Chaos*, because it is reminiscent of the "holler" in West Virginia where Carl Ray, his parents, and his host of brothers and sisters live, the home that he and Mary Lou visit during the summer of her story. It is also familiar to readers of *Walk Two Moons*, since the town in which Zinny lives, Bybanks, Kentucky, is the town that Zinny's best friend, Sal Hiddle, leaves after Sal's mother permanently disappears.

Zinny refers several times to her best friend, Sal Hiddle, whom readers have met in *Walk Two Moons*. Zinny had learned to ride Sal's horse, Willow, before Sal had to move to Ohio. In an ironic twist, it is Willow that Zinny borrows from its current owners, without asking, to take Uncle

Nate to his hidden cabin, and to return with help when he has a heart attack there.

Jake, upon his return to Bybanks, recalls the friendship that Zinny and Sal shared, and asks Zinny about it. When she replies, she notes that Sal's move has left "another big empty hole" in her life. In this scene, Zinny also connects Sal's leaving with her own mother's abandonment, and tells Jake that Sal promised to return, but that Sal's mother, who died while on a trip, had made and broken the same promise (*CR*, 12).

Other reminders of the girls' friendship appear throughout the novel. For example, Zinny knows her way to the farm where Sal used to live even with her eyes closed. And although she had been doubtful that Sal would ever return, late in the novel she gushes with a report that she has received a postcard from Sal, with four longed-for words: "*Coming home to Bybanks!*" (254). The connection that binds the two girls, in this example, is not only that Sal and Zinny are friends. Astute readers of both novels will recall that Sal is communicating with Zinny like Sal's mother had communicated with her—in short but potent bursts of words on a postcard. The difference is that Sal, unlike her mother, is able to keep to her promise and, as readers know from *Walk Two Moons*, she does return to live again in Bybanks.

LITERARY ELEMENTS THAT PRESENT STRONG CHARACTERS AND CULTURAL CLASHES

Zinny: Who AM I?

Zinny is a bright, quiet girl and an active listener. She knows that some people assume she is a bit dull, since she rarely talks, but explains that she finds little reason to add her voice to others', when there is not much new to be said. She becomes even more interesting as a listener than a talker when she serves as the perceptive, observant narrator. She is also aware that she had been a physically fragile baby and young child, one who was frequently sick, but she is a determined, independent, focused young teenager who vows to become known for something grander than being the "strangest and stingiest dirt-daubing doodlebug" or "a little mashed up fritter at the bottom of the pot" (*CR*, 52) of the Taylor family, or for being an "agent of death" and doom within the family.

She decided that the act by which she would earn a positive name and reputation would be to clear the 20-mile Bybanks-Chocton trail that

winds over the mountain ridge. She determined that she would name the
trail after herself, and plant zinnias all along the way as a note on her
name, and that hikers would have to get her permission before she would
allow them to use it (*CR*, 52). A symbol of her emotional growth is that
at the end of the summer, after she has tamed the trail, she names it
"Redbird Trail," after her aunt who dies during the summer, instead of
after herself.

The job of clearing the path would require constant work for an
entire summer, and since she would move further and further from home
as she made progress, it would eventually require that she camp out,
alone, in the wooded hills, in order to get an early start from a distant
point on the trail, the next day. After she talks herself into the plan, Zinny
becomes impatient with her parents, who are not immediately convinced
that it is the right thing for her to do. She explodes, uncharacteristically,
one day, when trying to talk them into giving her their permission to
camp out on the trail as she continues working on it, complaining about
the crowded conditions, the lack of personal space and things: "Bonnie
wears my shoes, Sam took the pillow off my bed"; she concludes her ti-
rade by telling herself, "I didn't think I ought to mention about feeling
that if I didn't finish the trail, I was going to be struck down by the hand
of God" (*CR*, 137).

Finally, Zinny's mother begins to listen between the lines of her
unhappy daughter's words. She surprises Zinny and Mr. Taylor when she
announces that she thinks Zinny "needs" time away from the house (*CR*,
139), and Zinny's parents astonish her when they tell her that she can go,
so long as she agrees to abide by some conditions related to her safety,
including coming back home every ten days to restock her food, shower,
and sleep in a bed.

The wisdom of Zinny's mother, and her often-hidden awareness of
her daughter's special qualities, is highlighted when Zinny and her three
sisters decide to wear clothes that will help their mother associate them
with their names: May chooses **m**ulti-colored ribbons for her hair;
Gretchen wears only **g**reen; Bonnie wears **b**lue. Zinny decides to paint a
zinnia on each of her shirts, but the colorful label proves unnecessary. In
a gentle scene, Mrs. Taylor assures Zinny: "I know who Zinny is. I know
what she sounds like, smells like … what she—radiates. I know who she is"

(*CR,* 20–21). Although Zinny needs to learn about herself, to find her own place in the family, the community, the world, she has already established a unique place in her mother's heart.

Uncle Nate: Chasing Memories

Creech enjoys peopling her books with eccentric characters; in this novel, that character is Uncle Nate. Zinny knows him as a "restless" and "frisky" man (*CR,* 16). He is also a kind-hearted man, a livestock farmer who is unable to raise chicken and pigs because he would be expected to slaughter them for food after he raised them, and he cannot bear to kill a living creature (*CR,* 16), and a dairy farmer who must give up on his plans to raise dairy cows after most of the "sweet creatures" in his herd catch a disease and die (*CR,* 17).

The only exception to his self-enforced prohibition against killing animals that Uncle Nate tolerates is killing snakes, since snakes have always frightened Aunt Jessie. The symbol of a snake becomes an important one to track through the novel. One day in the barn, Zinny shows Aunt Jessie two of the treasures that she has uncovered while digging on the trail: one is a snake, which Zinny had kept trapped in a box, and the other is a medallion that Zinny has found under a rock. Aunt Jessie reacts powerfully to Zinny's show and tell, and it is that night that Aunt Jessie pulls out her drawer, curls up in it, and dies. Zinny believes that the sight of the snake caused her to have a heart attack. Later, though, readers learn along with Zinny that it was the medallion that arrested Jessie's heart, and increased her resolve to get to heaven to be with her Rose. The medallion that Zinny uncovered was one that had belonged to Rose. Zinny had taken it when it slipped from her dead young cousin's hand, then she had run into the woods and buried it there while her little cousin Rose still lay dead in the drawer-coffin at home. It is not until she rediscovers the medallion and asks Uncle Nate about it that she recalls the night that she took it, buried it, then hid on the ridge, a frightened 4-year-old who was sure she was responsible for the death of her cousin—her best friend. Uncle Nate's resistance to the death of any creature is heightened after the sudden death of Aunt Jessie; he seems unable to reconcile the sad reality with his lively visions of her, and imagines that he sees Aunt Jessie, whom he calls his "Redbird," fluttering in nature all around him.

Uncle Nate is likely to remind readers of Gramps, in *Walk Two Moons*. His language is spiced with the sounds of the mountains and hollers. For example, one day, when on the mountain ridge with Aunt Jessie and all of the Taylor children, he proclaims, "I never heard such a noisy bunch of tadpoles and pumpkins in all my born days," and when he kicks at some rocks and uncovers a portion of the Bybanks-Chocton trail, he declares that he has kicked at the "dag-blasted trail," in words reminiscent of Gramps' language in *Walk Two Moons* (CR, 26).

Like Gram in *Walk Two Moons*, who developed "Huzza, Huzza" into a personal expression, Uncle Nate and Aunt Jessie have their own trademark: a segment of the Andrews Sisters hit, "Boogie Woogie Bugle Boy of Company B," a song that was released in 1941 and became one of the most popular World War II songs in the United States. When Uncle Nate sings the refrain, "Tottle-ee-ah-dah," Jessie responds with the line, "Make the company jump." This shared song dates Nate and Jessie, establishing them as a couple who had gone through the World War II era together. Zinny reflects on the ways that her aunt and uncle used the musical phrases between themselves when, unexpectedly, Uncle Nate bellows out a *Tottle-ee-ah-dah* to her when they are hiking on the trail, and she automatically responds, as Jessie, would have, with a happy burst of *"Make the company jump!"* in a tone that suggests, *"... Live! Live it up!"* (CR, p. 125).

What Zinny and her parents don't realize is that, while Uncle Nate chases Aunt Jessie's spirit, and slowly begins to lose some of his connections with the reality of the present world, he ambles further and further down the mountain ridge and into the woods. There, he has built a cabin in which he creates a secret altar to memorialize his dead baby, Rose, and his beloved Redbird. When Zinny discovers the cabin and peeks through the shuttered windows to view its contents, she glimpses some pots on a shelf, and then zeroes in on Jessie's coat, and finds herself unsure of what to make of the scene: "—oh, it was wonderful, oh, it was terrible, terrible. It was Aunt Jessie's coat.... *The sight of that coat! ... That instant joy, that instant horror!*" (CR, p. 223).

In this last line of repetitions and exclamations, Creech evokes other authors of powerful psychological mastery, such as Edgar Allan Poe and Joseph Conrad.

Uncle Nate's gentle nature is revealed further in his sense of deep loss when Aunt Jessie dies. Zinny struggles to describe the changes that she observes in him, and in doing so, eloquently says as much about her confusion regarding how she expects others to act in the face of the death of a loved one, as she does about Uncle Nate's grief. She notes that, although he sometimes acted the same—gentle to the kids—there were other times when, according to Zinny, he would aimlessly go off chasing his Redbird, or would look at her and mistakenly call her Rose, then stop and stare at her in a way that made her feel like he imagined that Rose or Jessie were standing beside her (*CR*, 48–49).

Jake Boone: Charming Teen Thief

Zinny is surprised when she walks into Mrs. Flint's store in Bybanks, the summer of her trail-building adventure, and is greeted by a tall, handsome teenager who is working behind the counter. It turns out that the stranger is Jake Boone, whom she knew when she was a child. After they make (re)introductions, Jake admits that he remembers her as "a scrawny little pipsqueak"; she remembers him as the "dirt dauber" from church, long ago, a boy who cried when her sister May shoved him into a bush after he tried to give her a flower (*CR*, 10–11). Jake's presence sets into motion two sources of tension around which subplots of the story unfold. One centers on Zinny's assumption that Jake is interested in her older sister, May. Jake does everything possible, however, to show her that he wants Zinny to notice and like him.

At first he is a delightful country suitor; he gives her a handful of pebbles and then a cricket, which he is proud to teach her to use as a thermometer. He instructs Zinny to count the number of chirps she hears each minute, then to divide that number by four and add thirty-seven in order to determine the temperature (*CR*, 55). This kind of nature-based courting is exactly the kind that we have grown to expect Zinny to respond to with favor.

When Zinny resists Jake's homespun charms, though, assuming that he has eyes for her pretty and prissy sister May, Jake begins to take more desperate actions. He steals a puppy and gives it to Zinny as a gift; she insists on knowing why he wants to give her the pup, sure that he intends it for someone else, probably her sister. In good-natured frustration, Jake admits to Zinny that she is a difficult friend to win over (*CR*, 72), but he proves to be game for the challenge of breaking through her resistant shell. When she begins to suspect that Jake has stolen the dog, Zinny realizes that she doesn't want to tell anyone, and she acknowledges that she does not know whether her aim is to protect Jake or to protect herself from embarrassment. Jake is contrite when Zinny catches him up on the trail that she considers her own, and blushes a confession, saying he is sorry about the dog. Zinny holds him responsible, despite his contrition, and scolds him about "Stealing an old lady's innocent puppy ..." to which Jake can only respond, with head hung, ..."—I don't know—I just wanted you to have it" (*CR*, 99).

Jake's moral code is much more conditional than Zinny's is. He steals a puppy, a ruby ring, and a car in hopes of attracting Zinny's attention and affection. For Jake, some ends—like pleasing Zinny—justify questionable means—even stealing. For Zinny, who has lived with the horrible misconception that her actions led to the death of her cousin Rose when she and Rose were four, and the death of her Aunt Jessie, every action is either right or wrong. When Zinny chooses to take Uncle Nate onto the trail, so that she can show him that she has discovered his secret cabin, the one filled with memories of Rose and Jessie, Zinny realizes that there is only one way she can get him across the mountain ridge, and that is on horseback. Since she doesn't own a horse, she cuts the fence of a neighbor and sneaks out Willow, the horse that her friend Sal Hiddle had taught her to ride summers earlier, the horse that Sal owned until she moved to Ohio. Suddenly, due to her urgent need, Zinny reconciles stealing with her own moral code.

On one hand, she chides herself with pointed thoughts: "Selfish Zinny. Thief!" (*CR*, p. 201). She almost bursts with guilt (*CR*, 202) when she thinks of stealing Willow, even temporarily. Yet she is able to justify her actions for Uncle Nate's sake, and out of her love for her uncle (*CRI*, 202). In this poignant scene, Zinny determines that by helping Nate see his Redbird one more time, she will be freed of some of the guilt that she has carried for what she falsely clings to, in her mind, as her role in Rose's and Jessie's deaths. Upon realizing that her reasons for stealing the horse are propelled by love and care for Uncle Nate, Zinny is forced to reconsider her harsh evaluation of Jake's behavior. She becomes more forgiving of him when she learns, through her own experience, that people's actions do not always reflect the purity of their motives. It is Jake Boone, Zinny's long-time friend and a good-looking 16-year-old, whom she credits as the person who "tried to get me out of that swamp" (*CR*, 9), the swamp of despair in which she was floundering after Aunt Jessie's death.

SPECIAL STYLISTIC FEATURES OF *CHASING REDBIRD*
Subplots that Add Texture

In this novel, the third of her novels for adolescents, Creech demonstrates an increasingly sophisticated use of subplots to support and add texture to the main plots. Perhaps this development is due to the fact that the author better understands, or pays more attention to, the capabilities of her readers at this point, seven years following the publication of her first novel for adolescents. In her first novel for adolescents, *Absolutely Normal Chaos* (1990), Creech adds interest to the main plot, which revolves around the impact of cousin Carl Ray's long stay with Mary Lou and her large family. Gradually, information about Carl Ray's biological and familial identities are revealed in entertaining but minor subplots in which Beth Ann's actions as a suddenly boy-crazed teen and sometimes disloyal friend are examined. In her second novel, the Newbery Medal-winning *Walk Two Moons* (1994), the main plot follows Sal's journey to retrace her mother's last steps and the growth that results. This plot is coupled with a subplot that has powerful parallels to the main plot, since it involves the search that Sal's friend Phoebe conducts to find her mother, who has, like Sal's, disappeared.

In *Chasing Redbird*, the main plot, which focuses on Zinny's efforts to uncover the trail, corresponds with her efforts to establish her own identity. This plot is supported by two significant subplots. One focuses on Jake Boone, who breaks the law, disrupts her family, and demands that Zinny make some decisions for herself about what she considers right, and wrong, at the tenuous time that she is seeking to become more independent of her large and close family. The other subplot entwines Uncle Nate's increasingly bizarre behavior, weakening health, and unquenchable desire to get in the woods, with the development of Zinny's own self-understanding. Since both subplots correspond with Zinny's self-realization, the thematic emphasis on coming of age during a journey is intensified through the subplots.

Creech reconciles the elements of this subplot by having Zinny learn more about herself by virtue of learning more about her family; ironically, in order to establish her identity as someone other than just one of the Taylor girls, Zinny has to be pulled back toward her family, where her identity is formed and strengthened. The story demands that Zinny consider, from the more mature stance that she gains during the summer of her trail-building, the significant role that her entire family has in defining who she is and what she values. This subplot is laced with the delicate images of Zinny's literal discoveries of the cabin in the woods in which Nate has created a memorial for Rose and Jessie, her discovery of Rose's medallion, which she had hidden in the woods upon Rose's death, and her recovery of memories about the dolls that she and Rose shared, and the time they spent together—more as sisters than as cousins.

Disturbing Images of Death

Death is a difficult topic to address in books for adolescents. It is not, however, a topic that Creech avoids. Through her first three novels, she moves increasingly closer to the subject; Mary Lou narrates the death and funeral of a neighbor in *Absolutely Normal Chaos*, and Sal comments on the deaths of her mother and her grandmother in *Walk Two Moons*. In those novels, the deaths occur outside of the view of the reader or narrator. In *Chasing Redbird*, Creech poignantly depicts Zinny's memories of her cousin Rose, as she lay in a drawer that Aunt Jessie insists should serve as the child's coffin, and Zinny watches as Aunt Jessie follows her daughter, curling up into a drawer and calling out for death.

In *Absolutely Normal Chaos*, Mary Lou describes the sudden, unexpected massive heart attack and death of her neighbor Mr. Furtz, who "Looks like one of those really healthy types ... always running around in his gym shorts and tennis shoes" (*ANC*, 53). Mary Lou reacts as many young teenagers would: she asks questions, most of which occur only in her mind, about the death, how it will affect Mr. Furtz's family and friends, who were "just going along, doing the dishes and stuff and then all of a sudden the telephone rings and ... wham, it's the most awful news" (*ANC*, 57). It causes her to think with apprehension about her family's vulnerability, too: "... my mom and dad ... seem so healthy too. Please, please, please don't let anything happen to them" (*ANC*, 57–58).

She also tries to imagine how Mrs. Furtz will select a coffin, and whether she will choose one "because it is pretty or because it is sturdy and won't, sort of, *leak*?" (*ANC*, p. 58). She writes nervously in her journal about the viewing of the body and the funeral, wondering for a while if, in the coffin, he would be propped up as though he were reading a newspaper, with elevator music playing in the background.

Readers are given the opportunity to think through questions about life and death as they affect the immediate family, and how an innocent comment can pierce a teen who has suffered the incomprehensible loss of a parent, when reading *Walk Two Moons*. References to the accident in which Sal's mom is killed are made, and readers follow Sal as she struggles to see through the trees covering the embankment where the bus carrying her mother crashed, the crash that only Mrs. Cadaver survived. Where a path of severed treetops ends, she glimpses something "shiny and metallic" and recognizes it as the wrecked bus, the "one thing [she] had been looking for" (*WTM*, 262). A stranger who is also looking down the cliff tells Sal that he had arrived on the scene after the crash, and witnessed the rescue workers hacking through the brush, trying to get to the bus. He tells Sal, with the self-satisfied pride of an eyewitness, "Only one person survived, ya know?" to which she responds to herself, simply, "I knew" (*WTM*, 263).

Creech uses words that evoke physical pain and emotional longing when Sal crawls down the embankment and gets a closer look at the bus, inside and out, describing for instance the rubber tires as "punctured and grotesquely twisted" and the side of the bus as having "enormous gashes torn into the side" (*WTM*, 264–265). Readers also are told, along with Sal, that Gram has died, during the trip, while in a hospital far from home. Yet these scenes are narrated without any direct images of a dead person.

In *Chasing Redbird*, however, there is a direct picture of a dead body, and the image is especially disturbing since the body is that of a 4-year-old child. The picture occurs early in the novel, creating a kind of discomfort for readers just as they are trying to get to know the narrator and protagonist, 13-year-old Zinnia—Zinny—Taylor, who talks directly about the death of her cousin Rose, whom Uncle Nate and Aunt Jessie were raising as if the girls, who were the same age, were sisters. She describes Aunt Jessie's curious ritual of pulling out a dresser drawer in which she placed Rose, with her baby quilt, which became the child's coffin, and her own curiosity about what being dead meant for Rose—and for herself. Zinny peeks at Rose as the little cousin lay in the drawer-coffin, and for a while, almost expects that Rose will wake up and step out of death. That does not happen, of course, and Zinny finds herself drawn to her cousin and friend, even in death:

> People said, "Don't touch her!" but I did, once. I tapped her hand, and it scared the beans out of me. It wasn't her hand. It was like a doll's hand, stiff, neither warm nor cold. I studied my own hand, wondering if it was going to turn into a doll's hand like Rose's …
>
>   … In my four-year-old mind, I knew I was responsible for Rose being in that drawer, and I waited for someone to punish me…. (CR, 3–5)

Phrases like "scared the beans out of me" offer readers some relief as they move through this disturbing picture of a small child displayed, in death, in a dresser drawer. The passage also allows readers to see that although Zinny still feels the horror of the days surrounding Rose's death and the days of grieving that followed, she is able now, as a 13-year-old, to reflect on the events with some degree of detachment. Nevertheless, Zinny and readers are left to wonder whether or not Zinny's own mother, who had seven babies of her own, felt guilt over having so many children while her in-laws had lost their only daughter. On page 158, readers get a stronger sense of how close Rose and Zinny were—now that we know more about Zinny: Zinny reflects on what a teacher has told her: that infants do not have memories because they don't have the words with which memories are filed, yet. Zinny is skeptical of that teacher's assertion, because she frequently remembers Rose's infant face from a time that preceded their ability to use a spoken language (CR, 158).

Creech goes even further to reinforce the fact that Zinny has distinct memories of Rose and her death by recasting it in a flashback in which Zinny recalls a pair of life-sized dolls that she and Rose had shared and treasured, dolls that had been dressed in the girls' clothes and that had hair the color of the girls. As soon as the memory surfaces, she longs to see the two dolls (CR, 192–193). She later finds them in Uncle Nate's cabin, and is haunted by the fact that they have been lying side-by-side in the bottom dresser drawer, as if dead, there (CR, 242). Zinny, like Creech's readers, are left to wonder what kind of message Uncle Nate, who is responsible for slowly taking items that remind him of Rose and Jessie and hiding them away in his secret cabin, was intending to make by placing both dolls together in the bottom drawer.

Just two pages after she provides the memory of Rose as she lay dead in the drawer-coffin, Zinny reports another significant death, that of her Aunt Jessie. It takes a long time for Zinny to come to terms with Aunt Jessie's absence. She is not able to objectify Jessie's death in any way. Therefore, instead of providing the kinds of details that fill in the picture of baby Rose's death, such as the baby doll hands, she describes her own, and her uncle's, sense of helplessness and loss following the middle of the early spring night that Aunt Jessie was "snatched away" suddenly:

> Her death ... left us all dazed and jittery, as we stumbled around
> trying to get our bearings. It was as if we'd all been slapped, hard,
> by a giant hand swooping down from the sky. (CR, 8)

The actual scene of Jessie's death is too intense and disconcerting for Zinny to talk about directly, right away. Zinny circles back to the day Aunt Jessie died. She describes seeing Jessie pull out a dresser drawer, line it with a quilt, and try to curl up inside it. While Nate and Zinny were begging her to stand up, to fight to live, Jessie seemed to have already started on her journey to be reunited with her baby Rose.

Zinny's description of the death scene includes her use of the quaint phrase, "plonked [the drawer] in the middle of the room" and the understated one, "She was a bit big for the drawer," but these touches of Zinny's colorful language are not weighty enough to provide balance for the heft of the unnerving scene.

After Aunt Jessie's death, Uncle Nate started wandering around, apparently aimlessly, snapping photographs and talking to himself and to invisible people. He spoke often, out loud, to his Redbird, Aunt Jessie, and, in his grief and confusion, spent much of his time chasing after her. Readers are left to wonder whether he thought he saw her, or whether he was chasing her spirit, her lasting essence (CR, 8). Creech adds the poignant detail that as he chased after his invisible partner, he always carried a stick, so that he could beat snakes, which she feared greatly, away from her.

Zinny is shaken not only by grief, but also by unreasonable yet powerful guilt when Jessie dies. She convinces herself that she is largely responsible for it, since she had shown Jessie two things that caused her to react with immediate pain, and that she believes eventually stopped Jessie's heart: a snake, and a medallion that Zinny had found on the trail—a medallion that Zinny later understands is the one the had belonged to baby Rose years earlier. The impact of grief and guilt is strong: "… I felt as if someone had tied me up and dropped me in the middle of a swamp, where I was in danger of sinking.… I was like a walking mummy, all sealed up against the world, sinking, sinking, sinking" (CR, 9).

Later, Zinny notices that Jessie's death has affected others in her family in addition to Uncle Nate; her mother has become easily distracted, and her father seems, "as helpless as a turtle on its back" (CR, 49). No one is left untouched by Jessie's unexpected death. Careful readers will find subtle hints that Jessie died because she did not take her insulin, a shot that was required to manage her diabetes; without the insulin, she fell into a diabetic coma and death.

Zinny's most alarming and repugnant contact with death, however, is self-initiated. One night, when sitting with Nate while the others have left the farm for an evening in town, Zinny listens to him as he sleeps, and notices that he is struggling with his dreams of flying into his Redbird's arms. Zinny, watching over him, tries to comfort him by smoothing his pillow and wiping the sweat from his forehead, but when she moves his pillow, she finds beneath it a silken, embroidered cloth that she recognizes as the one she had placed in the casket with her aunt when Jessie was buried. The discovery, juxtaposed with Uncle Nate's fitful sleep, so "spooked" Zinny that she moves, without thinking, to place the pillow over her uncle's face in order to end his misery and set him free to be reunited with Jessie and Rose. She admits to herself, "I don't know what came over me. I was somebody else. I was God," and releases the pillow before she is able to suffocate Nate (CR, 196). Nevertheless, the scene is heart-stopping; it is difficult to reconcile the images that are presented of Zinny, the loving, dutiful, respectful daughter and niece, and Zinny, fulfilling her self-imposed nick-name as "Agent of Doom," or "Zinny Taylor: Killer."

This kind of moral complexity, like the issues relates to stealing, challenges and honors teen readers, because it acknowledges what teens know: that many of our daily actions carry life and death consequences. The moral complexity of what looks, at first, as if it will become a scene of euthanasia, is resolved ultimately by Zinny's backing away from the choice of killing Nate to end his pain; she opts for life. Later, Nate kids her good-naturedly about her action with the pillow, subtly telling her that he was aware of what she had almost done, aware that she chose life.

Creech's books do not glamorize death; the death scenes are not gory or extraneous. Instead, Creech uses the voices of teenaged protagonists to narrate their encounters with death. Through them, she is able to address issues from the perspective of adolescents who are uncomfortable with death and with the rituals that surround it in their own, and others', modern American families. The images of death in the novel are potent and difficult to shake—for Zinny and for Creech's readers.

Fabulously Fresh Language

In this novel, Creech uses language in more advanced ways than in her previous novels, as well. The language that Creech uses in *Absolutely Normal Chaos* is enriched with hints of dialect used by the Finney family's West Virginia kin, such as this passage when Aunt Radene asks for Mary Lou's help: "I'm gonna ask you something strange, and if'n you'd rather not do what I'm gonna ask you, you just tell me straight on out and I'll abide by that" (*ANC*, p. 163). The narrative is also dotted with Mary Lou's youthful experimentation with an Americanized version of Homer's language. She addresses her blank journal page with "Ready, O Muse?" (*ANC*, 82), and when her mother insists that she stop using the expression, "O God!" she draws on Homer again, using "Oh, diety!" or "Oh, Omnipotent!" or "Oh, Alpha and Omega!" (*ANC*, p. 138). Thus, in her first book, Creech demonstrates that she is an author who can successfully stray from the language of much of the literature that is written for adolescents, the sometimes pedestrian language that reflects the speech of contemporary teens.

In *Walk Two Moons*, Creech continues to demonstrate her ear for language, and to offer her readers entertaining hints of unusual usage, such as the expressions of endearment that Gram and Gramps use with each other and with Sal: "chickabiddy" and "gooseberry" (*WTM*, 3), as well as their continual mispronunciation of Phoebe as "Peeby" (*WTM*, 176) and Gram's trademark expression for enthusiasm, "Huzza huzza!" (*WTM*, p. 37).

It is in *Chasing Redbird*, though, that Creech seems to release the power of her language potential. This novel becomes a treasure of figurative language. The language itself, which is rich with similes and metaphors that incorporate elements of the natural world, reinforces the setting and supports the theme of the importance of finding one's place in the world. Most notable in the extraordinary use of figurative language in *Chasing Redbird* is Creech's rich use of animal and plant imagery—imagery that complements and amplifies Zinny's focus on the natural world as she explores the trail and her own identity. A handful of examples best demonstrate Creech's accomplishment in the language of this novel:

1. Zinny describes the woman who lives in the former home of Zinny's friend Sal Hiddle: "Her hair ran all the way down her back like thin gray rat tails" (*CR*, 78–79).
2. Confused and frustrated with the certainty that Jake had stolen in an effort to please her, Zinny heads to the woods and works frantically on the trail: "... pawing at the ground like a crazed badger" (*CR*, 89).
3. The effect of spending time alone is that it sometimes releases, in Zinny's mind, unexpected memories, which "fly out ... like little birds rising suddenly from the branches of a tree" (*CR*, 150).
4. When Zinny experiences the contentment of finishing the trail and naming it for her beloved Aunt Jessie, and finding, at the same time, her own identity in the process, a sense of deep happiness washes over Zinny and causes her to exclaim joyfully:

> For several glorious minutes there, I was about the happiest person on the face of this planet.... I heard, in my head, the soft refrain of a song Aunt Jessie used to sing: *Lay your burden down, girl, lay your burden down.*
> And then I had the oddest feeling, warm and comforting, as if a gentle hand had reached down from the heavens and stroked my hair." (*CR*, 250)

CONCLUDING WITH THE MANY CHASES IN *CHASING REDBIRD*

This novel leads its readers on a wonderful adventure with Zinny as she uncovers the abandoned trail across mountain ridges and valleys, and as she discovers the depths of her own identity. The notion of a "chase" has, in fact, many dimensions, each of which rewards readers' careful attention. For example, the title refers, at least on the surface, to Uncle Nate's habit of chasing his wife, his "Redbird," whose elusive presence permeates the home place and woods where they lived together for so many years. It also takes on a literal meaning when Zinny takes Nate to the cabin on the trail, and discovers the truth about the memorial to Jessie and Rose that he has created there.

The novel includes figurative chases, too. Zinny is caught up in chasing meanings that Aunt Jessie took with her in death: Zinny tries to find clues that will allow her memory to be reconciled with reality, in order to shed her self-assigned moniker, "Zinny Taylor, Agent of Doom," and "Zinny Taylor: Killer." During her chase for answers, Zinny's progress is often stalled by a confusing overlay of memories on the present. She dimly recalls two life-sized dolls that represented Rose and herself; she flashes back to a scene in which she is holding a medallion that she took from Rose's hand before Rose's casket was closed in burial. Zinny is desperate to better understand why she, one of seven siblings, got whooping cough and lived, while her best young friend and cousin Rose, the only child of her Aunt Jessie and Uncle Nate, died. She finds herself face-to-face with a decision about how to help the grieving Uncle Nate, and almost chooses to suffocate him with a pillow so that his agony will end and he will be reunited with Jessie and Rose in death.

And Zinny is also chasing questions about who she will become. Among her questions are these: Is it possible that someone who is older, experienced, and sometimes misguided, like Jake, can be interested in a quiet, odd, girl like her? Will the work on the trail bring her an identity that others will respect, one that will establish her as more than one of the seven Taylor kids? Reflecting on the days before she earns her parents' permission to work on the trail, Zinny acknowledges, "It didn't occur to me that I might be escaping something or even chasing something" (*CR*, 52). Zinny, always a realist, acknowledges that she has not caught everything she has been chasing when she finishes her labor on the trail. She tells readers, "Sometimes I wonder about other trails. Maybe I'll check at the museum for more maps. I can see myself running across the whole country, chasing—what? Who?" (*CR*, p. 258).

In an interview conducted in the United Kingdom, where she lived when *Chasing Redbird* was first published, Sharon Creech noted:

> When I was writing *Chasing Redbird*, my life was very busy and chaotic, and I longed for the quiet of the woods, and so I followed Zinny into the woods every day. It was inevitable that the characters and I would also have interior journeys on these treks, and for me that is much of the excitement of writing: discovering what the interior journey is, how it changes the traveler. (www.achuka.co.uk/interviews/creech.php. Retrieved December 2, 2006)

This novel is an accomplishment. Readers will find many examples of Creech's concern for family, for rural landscapes, and for strong female characters throughout *Chasing Redbird*, and attending to these features will enhance readers' enjoyment of the book. Creech has left her fingerprints on the adolescent characters, the familiar scenes, the positive adults. She has added new marks, too, through the rich use of subplots to advance the major storylines, her treatment of disturbing images of death, and the fresh figurative language that leaves the taste of the novel on readers' tongues. Readers finish the book with an image of Zinny, energetic explorer and compassionate person, who will be forever listening attentively for a crisp staccato of a redbird's call, one that is close enough to hear, but that is just out of sight, over the ridge.

CHAPTER SIX

WHAT'S BLOOMING IN SWITZERLAND? SHARON CREECH'S *BLOOMABILITY*

"It seemed as if anything could happen, anything at all.
The *bloomabilities* were endless."

(Creech, 1998, 263)

What is *"bloomability,"* anyway? In Sharon Creech's fourth novel for teen readers, the word is a derivation of "bloomable," which is synonymous with "possible." Is it an actual English word? Perhaps only to Dinnie Doone, 13-year-old narrator of *Bloomability* (1998), and her international group of friends who attend an American School that is located in Switzerland. Dinnie explains that it was Keisuke, a Japanese student, who unintentionally coined "bloomable" by choosing the term over the less interesting word, "possible" (B, 100–101).

Bloomability is, first, a novel about possibilities. It is an often funny and sometimes serious examination of the possibilities that Dinnie recognizes and responds to during her thirteenth year. Some of the possibilities are obvious, such as those that spring up for her as she travels to Switzerland, where she makes friends with an international group of teens. Other possibilities are more subtle and include what may happen when Dinnie gives herself permission to define "home" as the places and people she carries with her in her heart, mind, and memory. Throughout the novel, Creech, herself a teacher at an American school in Switzerland where her husband was headmaster when she wrote *Bloomability*, draws attention to the kinds of possibilities for creating happiness and making global contributions that are propelled by teenagers' positive energy.

Bloomability is also a novel about the ways that teens learn to reconcile conflicting feelings about identity, home, and personal values. Dinnie's struggle to come to terms with her past and present, her sense of where "home" is and where she is a visitor, is a problem that she refers to as her "double vision." Sometimes, she feels alienated even from her family; she is a wanderer who retreats into a personal bubble in order to isolate herself from contact with an unpredictable world. Yet during the year in Switzerland, she begins to find her bubble too crowded and begins to risk stepping outside of it. One day, after a hike with her good friend Guthrie, she reflects on her conflicts of past and present, of a sense of dislocation and connection. She struggles to explain her sense of "double vision," in which the images she encounters in Switzerland are "overlaid" with similar scenes from the life she had known in the United States—the grapevines on a Swiss hillside seem to be painted atop her memory of grapevines in Ohio; the walls of an ancient castle draw up memories of the stones of a house in Virginia. Her intelligent comparisons conclude with a blend of the two voices—one mature and confident, the other playful and uncertain—that we, as readers, learn to associate with Dinnie: "Even the gelato was submerged beneath an ice cream cone I'd eaten in Wisconsin.... It was if I were carrying around all the places I'd ever lived ... all smooshed together" (B, 91).

Bloomability is, finally, a book about journeys. Journeys are a frequent conceit in Creech's novels; they serve as physical manifestations of emotional, psychological, and social movement for main characters. In *Bloomability*, as in her earlier novels, Creech encourages readers to consider our own physical and inward journeys. Creech readers will recall that Mary Lou, in *Absolutely Normal Chaos*, learns to look beneath the surface before judging people when she travels to West Virginia to visit cousin Carl Ray's unsophisticated rural home. We remember that Sal, in *Walk Two Moons*, uncovers portions of her own identity, including some that are related to her role as daughter, when she travels across the country with her grandparents in order to learn more about her mother. We reflect on how Zinny, in *Chasing Redbird*, begins to understand herself and her family better as she moves across the twenty miles of abandoned trail that she clears the summer after Aunt Jessie suddenly dies. In a similar vein, Dinnie, in *Bloomability*, reluctantly leaves her parents who are living in New Mexico to go to school in Switzerland. There, she learns much more than academic lessons. She discerns how important her family is to her and begins to treasure her father's restless energy, which is mirrored in her new friend Guthrie's contagious enthusiasm for life. She realizes that the definition of "home" does not always refer to a specific place, but always refers to a specific set of connections to the people we keep with us in our minds and hearts. The journey is a particularly important vehicle for characters' growth in two of Creech's novels that follow *Bloomability*, *The Wanderer* (2000), and *Ruby Holler* (2002), too.

In her earlier novels, Creech focused on differences and similarities among neighbors, friends, and relatives who live in small, close-knit towns in the eastern United States. *Bloomability* is a novel that moves with Creech and her narrator, Dinnie, to an international setting to consider the significance of family, identity, and values within and across varied cultures. It beckons to readers who are eager to explore, vicariously, what it would be like to feel constantly like a visitor in our own lives, unsure of the customs and attitudes, the likes and dislikes, the language and expressions used by those around us. As readers, we get to decide whether we would respond by seeking shelter in our own personal bubbles, as Dinnie sometimes does, or whether we would respond with enthusiasm to the myriad of possibilities, the *bloomabilities*, presented to us there as Dinnie does as she gains confidence and achieves contentment.

SYNOPSIS OF *BLOOMABILITY* (HARPERCOLLINS, 1998)

Domenica (Dinnie) Doone and her older brother and sister are living with her mother and, when he is not traveling to pursue other opportunities, her father. Their latest residence is a small town in New Mexico, but that location is only one in a string of spots where the Doones have lived the last few years. Dinnie's mother and her Italian Grandma Fiorelli recognize that the frequent moving has contributed to the restlessness of Dinnie's sister, Stella, who is now an unwed mother. They are also frustrated with the effects that the lifestyle is having on Dinnie's brother, Crick, who is continually in trouble with the law. The summer of her thirteenth year, Dinnie's mother and Grandma Fiorelli determine that Dinnie needs a better life. When Dinnie's Aunt Sandy and Uncle Max offer to take Dinnie to Switzerland, where Max will serve as headmaster of an American school for international students and Sandy will teach, the women decide that Dinnie must go. Dinnie's father is disturbed by the decision, in part because he doesn't want Dinnie to leave the country for a year, but also because he does not like his wife's family and resents their interference.

When Aunt Sandy and Uncle Max take Dinnie to Switzerland, she travels as she has traveled from town to town in the United States: with one small box that holds all of her belongings, her treasures. Initially, she resists the move, but gradually she begins to appreciate the beauty of the Ticino portion of Switzerland, where she learns to speak the Italian of the region, and where her world is expanded through her friendships with Guthrie, whose American father lives somewhere in Canada; Lila, whose demanding parents live at present in Saudi Arabia; and other students at the school.

Dinnie's physical journey to Switzerland parallels her emotional and psychological journey to understand herself and the world. She realizes that she is a scholarship student, one who could not attend the pricey school except for her uncle's role as headmaster. The realization helps her become more sensitive to those who are treated as deficient merely because they are different. As she participates in "Global Awareness Month," her awareness of global poverty increases and helps her put her own situation in perspective. After watching a movie about genocide in Rwanda, then hearing a Rwandan classmate describe the day he watched his mother being killed, Dinnie and her best friend Guthrie want to take some kind of action to help, but find that, as 13-year-olds, their possibilities are limited. They have to be satisfied, at least for the present, with Uncle Max's admonition that teenagers like them, who have privileges, need to "know about art and beauty and music and laughter" in order to be prepared, one day, to "change the world" (B, 155–156).

While in Switzerland, Dinnie also experiences adventures that would appeal to many active teenagers, including hikes and ski trips in the Swiss Alps. Of course, life is not perfectly idyllic for Dinnie while she lives in Switzerland. She is terrified when an avalanche, set off by the boom of military testing, almost takes the life of her friends Guthrie and Lila. She feels abandoned by her own parents, and as if seeing her life played out in front of her, she sits helplessly as Lila leaves school, and wonders what the odd, candid, unhappy girl's home life is really like. However, the trying times are overshadowed by awe-inspiring ones; she observes the kind of beauty that

Uncle Max suggests can change the world when she listens to clear church bells, watches the white-on-white of winter snowfalls, and attends to the lyrical Italian voices of children around her. She remains connected to family, too, though not her parents, through a stream of postcards that her father's sisters, her Aunt Grace and Aunt Tillie, send. Their sincere cards remind her of their simple yet satisfying life in Kentucky.

When Dinnie's year abroad is finished, she prepares to return to the United States at the same time that her father has decided to move the family yet again. This time, the move itself holds possibilities and offers more hope than the previous moves, with their vague and ambiguous directions, since Dinnie's dad will relocate the family to his hometown, rural Bybanks, Kentucky. Dinnie is confident that she will be able to take lessons about the real value of friends, family, and the world with her as she reunites with her family.

Bloomability continues Sharon Creech's trend as the author of high-quality literature for children, adolescents, and young adults. It has been recognized by a *Parenting Magazine* Reading Magic Award (1998) and an International Reading Association Children's Choice Award (1999).

CONNECTIONS TO PREVIOUS NOVELS: FAMILIARITY IN PLACES, PEOPLE, AND POSTCARDS

Settings Far and Near

In this novel, Creech takes her readers far away from the small-town Ohio, Kentucky, and West Virginia landscapes that we recognize as the author's usual settings. Domenica (Dinnie) Doone is sent away from her family's current home in New Mexico to live and attend school near Lugano, Switzerland. Dinnie hardly knows her mother's sister, Aunt Sandy, and Sandy's husband, Uncle Max, so she is unhappy when she records that her "second life began" when she is, in her words, "kidnapped by two complete strangers" (B, 9). Soon, though, she begins to feel comfortable with her aunt and uncle and with her new circumstances. Her Swiss home is, specifically, "in a casa on the Via Poporino between Lugano and Montagnola in the Ticino in Switzerland in Europe on the planet earth," (B, 26) as Uncle Max explains to her upon their arrival. Previously, Dinnie and her mother, brother, and sister had followed her father to live in small "forgotten" towns in Kentucky, Virginia, North

Carolina, Tennessee, Ohio, Indiana, Wisconsin, Oklahoma, Oregon, Texas, California, and New Mexico, in that order (*B*, 2). At age twelve, all of her personal belongings fit into a single small box. Dinnie has learned to travel light, to think of home as people instead of as a place.

Despite the dramatic changes in settings from one continent to another, however, the small Kentucky town that is featured in *Walk Two Moons* and *Chasing Redbird* becomes an important setting in *Bloomability*, too. Dinnie's father, a truck driver, mechanic, and wandering opportunist, grew up in Bybanks, Kentucky, a setting that Creech fans will recognize as one that has appeared in earlier novels. It is the same rural town where Sal Hipple lived before mother died, and where Sal and her father return at the end of *Walk Two Moons*; it is also the home base from which Zinny wanders as she uncovers the twenty miles of an abandoned trail in *Chasing Redbird*. Upon Dinnie's return from the year abroad, she rejoins her parents by returning to a town she had no real memory of, and to a house where she had never lived (*B*, 269).

Even before she learns that her parents have decided to return to Bybanks to live, the town has a significance for Dinnie: her father's sisters, Aunt Grace and Aunt Tillie, still live in Bybanks. These paternal aunts frequently send humorous postcards to Dinnie while she is living in Switzerland, thus helping her feel connected across the continent to her own family and home. Creech's regular readers will recall the significance of postcards in *Walk Two Moons*: Sal's mother sent cards as a way to identify the places she stopped along her final journey, thus providing Gram, Gramps, and Sal a set of points on the map that they were able to retrace. Creech fans will also recall Zinny's joy, in *Chasing Redbird*, when she receives a postcard from her friend Sal, exclaiming that Sal is returning to Bybanks to live once again.

In *Bloomability*, Aunt Grace and Aunt Tillie recount for Dinnie the minutiae of their daily lives on postcards. Grace makes fun of the cheesecake gelatin dish that Tillie proudly brings to family gatherings, and Tillie complains about Grace's dry pot roasts. In their handwritten messages, they also unintentionally reveal a lack of acquaintance with much of the world beyond Bybanks. For example, in the first postcard that Dinnie receives, Aunt Grace asks, "How is it there? Do you need to speak Switz or what?" (*B*, 33). In her first card, Aunt Tillie asks Dinnie whether or not she has to wear "those leather shorts and kneesocks ..., " or if that practice is reserved for boys, only (B, 34). A few weeks later, she announces to Dinnie in another card, that she is getting her teeth "fixed," and that she will soon look like Marilyn Monroe (B, 63). She admits, in a follow-up card, that her teeth didn't turn out quite like the movie star's, then advises her niece to take good care of her teeth (B, 95). Despite their lack of sophistication, the Kentucky aunts use their homespun conversation to communicate their constant concern and love for Dinnie. In contrast to their regular interest and attention, the young teen gets little communication and no confirmation of either concern or love from her parents.

People: Family Relationships as a Familiar Theme

Although Dinnie's situation takes her away from her parents, the relationship that develops between parents and their children is an important theme in this novel. Creech's readers know that family is a high priority for the author and for the characters she creates. In *Bloomability*, Creech focuses on family relationship—not only through the protagonist, Dinnie, but also through the circumstances of Dinnie's schoolmates. For example, as readers we are led to think about our own relationships with our parents and our place in our families when observing Lila's strict and cold father, who refuses to leave behind his "Important Business" (B, 225) to come see her even after she is hospitalized after being caught in an avalanche, and Guthrie's attempts to please his father, who is traveling across Canada and can't be located when Guthrie is hospitalized after the avalanche.

Though Dinnie longs to have a close, dependable relationship with her parents, she does not. They disappoint her by sending no cards, by conducting telephone calls that are regulated with an egg timer, and by sending a Christmas package that doesn't arrive until February. Still, they are her family, and she misses them while she is in Switzerland. Her place as a member of the family is important to Dinnie; her loyalty to her family is, perhaps surprisingly, not snuffed out by her parents' apparent ambivalence toward her. Readers finish the novel with reason to hope that the lessons Dinnie learns about family, while she spends the year abroad, will give her strength and wisdom in building better connections with her own parents.

People: The Roles of Extended Family as Caring Adults

In *Bloomability*, Creech employs one of her favorite patterns: placing aunts, uncles, and cousins in featured positions in a novel. In *Absolutely Normal Chaos*, cousin Carl Ray and his West Virginia family provide balance and a new perspective for Mary Lou and her siblings in small-town Euclid, Ohio. In *Walk Two Moons*, it is grandparents instead of aunts and uncles who assume a paternal role for Sal Hiddle, a teen who needs to learn the truth about her mother's disappearance and death, and her father's new relationship with Mrs. Cadaver. In *Chasing Redbird*, Zinny's search for self-identity is shaped by her need to determine whether or not she is responsible for the death of both her baby cousin Rose and, years later, Aunt Jessie; she matures, too, as she learns to pay attention to Uncle Nate and his eccentricities.

In *Bloomability*, Aunt Sally and Uncle Max represent positive progress, success, and sound decision-making as adults who know how to care for teenagers. They are the educated family members who are able to step in to offer Dinnie encouragement to grow and learn through providing her with an education in the private school in Switzerland. Because Max is the new headmaster and Sandy is a teacher in the school, they are able to provide constant monitoring of her activities, and protection when needed, too—home luxuries that Dinnie had not previously enjoyed. The most important gift that they give Dinnie is stability, so that the roots of her identity can grow strong. Without their intervention, Dinnie is destined to run into trouble. Her father is constantly chasing a new job opportunity, none of which pans out, and each of which forces the family to continue to move from town to town. Stella, who is Dinnie's older sister, has taken advantage of an absence of parental supervision by hanging out with a variety of rowdy guys, and finds herself pregnant and unmarried. Crick, Dinnie's older brother, is constantly in trouble, not only with his parents, but also with the law, and eventually is ordered to either go to jail or into military service. He chooses to join the Air Force. As the youngest child in the family, Dinnie is her mother's final ray of hope, a last indicator that can signal that she has not failed in raising her children.

Dinnie's initial anxiety about moving to Switzerland is typical of the reaction that many young teens would probably have, since normalcy, even when it is infected with problems, is preferable to major change. When Dinnie's father realizes that Dinnie has left home while he is one of his trips, and that she will soon leave to spend at least a year in Switzerland, he telephones her and cries. At that moment, Dinnie feels almost immobilized inside her bubble, as though she is watching her own life from a distance, unable to change her course. She vows that she will stay tucked inside her bubble, where she can effectively keep an eye on the world, and plan her escape (B, 13). Once she gets to know Aunt Sandy and Uncle Max, though, and has time to befriend Guthrie, Lila, Keisuke, Belen, Maria, and the others at the school—some of whom also feel abandoned by their parents—she grows determined to begin living life outside of her bubble. Nevertheless, she is aware of how tenuous her connections to her immediate family are, and worries when she begins to enjoy her life in Switzerland, since she is afraid that accepting Switzerland may require rejecting her family and the kind of life they have shared. She asks herself, "What if I adapted completely, what if I forgot about them, what if they forgot about me?" (B, 44–45).

Later, her sense that she has betrayed her family shifts, and she decides that it is her family that has forgotten her, instead of she who risks forgetting them. When Lila cries about how fortunate Dinnie is to have Uncle Max and Aunt Sandy as resident family members, so that she doesn't have to "be alone," Dinnie admits to herself that she feels like her parents have shipped her off "like a spare parcel," and that they hardly noticed her absence. She cannot tell Lila that she thinks about her family and home constantly, and that she feels as if she is "drifting, floating, lost in the air" (B, 69).

By the end of the story, after spending a year in their care, Dinnie accepts Uncle Max and Aunt Sandy as family. During the trip to the airport in Zurich where she will board a jet for home, Sandy and Max kid her about the "kidnapped" signs that she posted in her bedroom window upon arriving in Switzerland, and give her a couple of them as funny souvenirs. Dinnie knows that Aunt Sandy and Uncle Max will welcome her if she decides to return to the Swiss school after the summer break. Dinnie has left her snow skis in their closet, just in case. But she knows that she needs to take the summer to think about her life and her world before she decides whether to return to Switzerland, or to stay with her parents in Bybanks. Because she makes her decision after the end of the story, readers get to determine for themselves which choice they think she will make, and which one they want her to make. In this way, they get to accompany Dinnie on her continued journeys.

Strong Characters, Led by a Feisty Female
Domenica Dinnie Doone

Domenica Dinnie Doone's lineage as one of Creech's characters is recognizable to readers who have enjoyed Creech's other novels, and she is recognizable to all teens who struggle with finding their own place in the world. Dinnie is strong willed and creative, intelligent and sensitive, but she has trouble recognizing these traits in herself. Through much of the novel, Dinnie describes a figurative bubble that she has inflated around herself. She uses the bubble regularly as a means of sealing out the possibility of being disappointed, of getting too close to new friends, or of being vulnerable to the quirky decisions made by her mother, father, sister, or brother. When she inflates it as a barrier, Dinnie demonstrates her ability to assess her own identity in order to evaluate how she relates to the rest of her world, and to consider where she fits in it.

Unlike Mary Lou, in *Absolutely Normal Chaos*, or Zinny in *Chasing Redbird*, Dinnie's home is not teaming with so many siblings that her mother can hardly distinguish among them. Nevertheless, as a young adolescent, she feels as if she is virtually invisible to peers and adults. She refers to herself as "Miss Average," citing as evidence not only her average height and weight, but also her nondescript facial features, such as her gray or green or blue eyes and a personality that led teachers to urge her to speak up more often, to be more assertive, in classes (B, 80).

Skilled as a "new kid in school," Dinnie adds that she is more "jumbled up" about her identity when she moves to Switzerland than she has been as a result of other moves. The difference, she explains, is that in Switzerland, she cannot blame her feelings of being odd or different on being the new person, the quick descriptor that she has learned to rely on since her family has moved so often from town to town. Switzerland is different, because everyone at the school there is from a different place; everyone is a "new kid" with a different accent. She makes comments about the ways that people tend to make assumptions about others based on stereotypes of appearance, and in doing so, reinforces an important theme of the novel—that everyone has individual strengths and can make individual contributions, therefore, we should look for what is unique in others, not only what is most similar to ourselves (B, 81).

Eventually, readers see that Dinnie is able to achieve a goal that many adolescents strive for: she fits into the international group of students and into the family unit comprised of Sandy and Max; she also establishes for herself a unique individual identity, as well. In fact, she uses her own experience to silently disagree with her sister, Stella, when Stella strongly advises that she always "wait and see" how people in each new town dress, talk, and spend their time, so that Dinnie can then imitate them and be accepted as one of the crowd. Dinnie thinks over Stella's advice, and determines that although she longs to be accepted as the same, she also longs, deep inside her bubble, to be different and therefore interesting, though she admits that she is unsure about how anyone "[gets] to be interesting" (B, 78).

One day when she is fishing with the rod her father gave her when she turned eight, an item that she keeps in her single box of things that she carried from move to move, Dinnie feels a disturbing conflict regarding her family at home and her new place in Switzerland with Aunt Sandy and Uncle Max. In an eloquent blend of attention to her emotional bubble and the bubbling of a river, she describes what happens when she looks into the water:

> I would see things that … were inside me. And that day as I sat on the riverbank, what I saw was my father and my mother and Stella and Crick and the new baby and even Aunt Tillie and Aunt Grace.… They were in my mind, but they were more real here, as if they were floating out in front of me, rising up from the water. (B, 99)

The episode left Dinnie feeling happy, because the feeling brought her close to her family, in her mind, but also homesick, since it emphasized the actual distance between her and her family. Dinnie seems to be speaking for teens who have to deal with a sense of growing distant, either geographically or emotionally, from the families that they have grown to depend on, the families who accept them as they are.

Dinnie realizes, just prior to the end of the school year, that she has actually made a new home in Switzerland. She seems surprised at her realization, and proud of it, too. She looks out on the scene in front of her, noticing the stillness of Lake Lugano, the power of Mt. Bre and Mt. San Salvatore that drew Guthrie and her there on hikes. She recalls the times spent drinking cappuccino with friends in the village of Montagnola. The realization that she has established a home in Switzerland catches her by surprise; the intensity of her passion for Switzerland leads her to claim: "I felt as if this was my home, and I was no longer a stranger" (B, 261). This is one place in the novel in which the journey motif is fully realized; Dinnie has grown from being a stranger into a sense of belonging. Her growth is reflected in willingness to claim Switzerland as her own home.

This strong sense of connection with a home place, a connection that is solid enough to withstand a continental move, is an uplifting conclusion to Dinnie's search. Dinnie longed for a place in which she felt at home for her entire life. She now realizes that even if her father continues to move the family from town to town, she can take the people whom she gets to know and appreciate there in her mind and heart, wherever she goes. With that attitude and ability, she will never be without a home place again.

Early in the novel, Creech provides us with an effective metaphor for Dinnie's feelings, using Dinnie's narrative voice. The surprising comparison that Dinnie makes is one in which she equates herself with the roots and leaves of a spider plant: the leaves stretch upward, while the roots dangle in the air (B, 31). Dinnie's sense that she is suspended in air, without firm roots, is reinforced later in the novel through further self-assessment. By the end of the novel, she doesn't feel lost and weightless, but buoyed by the hope she has for her future, hope that emerges when she is offered choices. The spider plant that Sandy gave her when she arrived in Switzerland has evolved into a positive symbol of Dinnie's growth and the possibilities that have opened up for her. When she leaves Switzerland, she leaves the plant on the windowsill, where it will continue blooming and continue sprouting new, floating shoots (B, 271); the comparison with Dinnie is strong.

As readers, we are rewarded by paying special attention to the fact that Creech wrote this novel just prior to her family's return from Switzerland to the United States. She and her husband, with her children, had spent years in Switzerland; her husband was the headmaster at a school for international students, and Creech taught English there. We can imagine that Creech's thoughts regarding her departure from Switzerland laced excitement about returning to the States together with a poignant sense of loss toward the place where she had spent years as teacher, mother, and participant. And as readers, we identify the author's deep passion for Switzerland in the passages above, and are awed by her connection to the beauty of the country, its people, and the sense of home that she established there.

Peter Lombardi Guthrie the Third, or Just "Guthrie"

Creech includes significant male characters in her novels, but until *The Wanderer*, published in 2000, she does not position a male character in a primary role. Guthrie, however, is an important secondary character in *Bloomability*. His relationship with Dinnie is similar to Carl Ray's relationship with Mary Lou in *Absolutely Normal Chaos*, and Jake Boone's connection with Zinny Taylor in *Chasing Redbird*: each of the three is a male counterpart with whom the female protagonist is able to talk with honestly about her feelings, fears, and future. Each of these male characters presents a perspective that assists the female protagonist as she learns more about who she is and where she fits in her world.

Although he is officially "Peter Lombardi Guthrie the Third" (B, 51), a name that school founder Mrs. Stirling uses to hint at his aristocratic heritage, Guthrie shrugs off his full name and insists on being referred to by only his last name. He is the kind of teenage boy whom almost all of us would like to have as a friend. He is generous and adventurous, both logical and impetuous. He has unbridled enthusiasm for life, and his energy is contagious. Dinnie greatly admires Guthrie, who is the first friend she makes in Switzerland, and describes him as "an electric cloud of whirling energy" who loves the school, the people, and especially Switzerland itself: "'Svizzera!' he would boom. 'Bella, bella, Svizzera!'"(B, p. 56).

Even Uncle Max, headmaster, is charmed by Guthrie, who has spent two years at the school already, and who has picked up a lot of Italian.

Max admits, "Guthrie fractures the language sometimes, but nobody seems to mind too much because he does it with such gusto" (B, 57). As readers, we might ask, "Is the alliteration of *Guthrie* with the descriptive *gusto* intentional or accidental on Creech's part?" Regardless of the answer, we recognize that the parallel works effectively. Guthrie lives with gusto; he walks down streets and breaks into a shout of "*Sono libero!*" (I am free!) (B, 79), pronounced with an exaggerated accent so that each vowel resonates throughout the hills.

In homage to Ralph Waldo Emerson, and as a repetition of the book's epigraph, "I become a transparent eyeball," Guthrie refers to himself as "a transparent eyeball," and associates his frequent outings with Emerson, too, since the poet and philosopher frequently went into the woods, where "he could see everything and was a part of everything: one big huge transparent eyeball!" (B, 90–91).

Dinnie learns a lot about Switzerland, and also about how to take risks, from Guthrie. His perspective as a transparent eyeball, but not an invisible person, and his zest for observing the world and participating fully in it, contrasts sharply with Dinnie's initial preference for living inside a bubble and looking out into a world in which she refused to participate fully, joyfully, playfully. When pressed by Uncle Max to talk about her feelings for Guthrie, Dinnie admits that she would like to be a fly on a wall, following Guthrie through the summer that they will be apart. Upon further reflection, she realizes that one of the things that attracts her to him is similar to what makes her father irresistible: they both have a way of making a person want to travel along with them, to "see the world as they saw it" (B, 257). Perhaps one of Guthrie's greatest contributions to Dinnie is that he helps her better appreciate her father for his adventurous energy and his yen for traveling to find out more about the world.

When Guthrie gives a speech at graduation and encourages his classmates, including Dinnie, to think about how much their shared experiences as students and friends has meant to each of them, Dinnie responds with a rush of longing to make the year last a little while longer (B, 255). With the most powerful example of personification in the novel, Dinnie gives voice to her conflicting feelings by saying, "I felt as if time was pressing in on us, rumpling our clothes and our emotions" (B, 255).

It is appropriate that Guthrie is one of the main speakers when the students gather for the commencement ceremony at the school. He uses Robert Frost's "The Road Not Taken," as his text. Dinnie and the others listen as he talks about the roads that have led each of them to the school, and that will take them home—to Rome, Osaka, Barcelona, Kentucky, and other locations across the globe. He ends his speech by imploring his classmates to pause, before they travel on, to consider how their time at school has made and will make "all the difference" in their lives (B, 254). Although he is too humble to acknowledge his positive impact, Guthrie has made a huge and lasting "difference" in Dinnie's life, too.

Lila

Lila is another significant secondary character in *Bloomability*. Much of the time, she is irreverent and rowdy, disrespectful and selfish. Most of the students avoid contact with her, but she is one of the first people whom Dinnie meets in Switzerland, and Dinnie feels obliged, somehow, to stick by her side throughout the novel; despite Lila's lack of popularity, Dinnie is loyal to her, and fascinated by her: "Being with Lila was like watching a movie. You couldn't believe she was actually doing and saying some of those things, but you stuck around to see what would happen next" (B, 68). Despite Dinnie's loyalty to her, though, Lila serves as the personification of the story's "Ugly American." Her attitudes toward people who are different from her are often so outlandish, and her behavior so spoiled, that as readers we recoil against her. However, each time we reject Lila because of her prejudices, we are forced to step back and check our own attitudes against hers. Sometimes we see ugly parts of ourselves in Lila.

When she and Dinnie meet for the first time, Lila exudes confidence and enthusiasm, and exclaims her intention to "start fresh" at the Swiss school (B, 41). Dinnie immediately realizes that Lila fails to explain where she is starting from, or why, at age thirteen, she needs a fresh start at all. We begin to assume that she has had an unhappy childhood, and that she may have been bumped from setting to setting by parents who are detached from her everyday life. As we follow Lila's actions and conversations, we are able to draw some fairly solid conclusions about the kind of home and school life Lila has experienced in the past, and may even develop concern for a teenager like her, who wears such a defensive exterior. We wonder, like Dinnie does, what she is hiding beneath her tough shell, and why she is covering it.

Lila is often belligerent; when she learns that she has a Spanish roommate, she complains vociferously to Max, demanding that she should have an English-speaking roommate, especially since her parents are paying so much for her to be at the school (B, 64). Lila frequently demonstrates her disregard for others. One instance of this disregard occurs when she meets Mrs. Stirling, the regal founder of the Swiss school, as well as similar schools in France, Spain, and England. Mrs. Stirling is hosting a formal tea at her Swiss home, Casa Stirling, which is an imposing, four-hundred-year-old edifice perched on the edge of campus, complete with its own bell tower (B, 48). While the other students are either awed or intimidated by Mrs. Stirling, Lila addresses her boldly, unceremoniously, asking her whether the two can chat about Lila's room. That afternoon, Mrs. Stirling deftly deflects Lila by asking Max to help Lila with her questions about her room (B, 53). However, the scene foreshadows a truly unpleasant incident in which Lila, while at dinner with Uncle Max, Aunt Sandy, and Dinnie, spouts a long, bitter list of complaints about how the Japanese, who "never look at you," drive her crazy, and insisting that even if it is inappropriate in their country to look others in the eyes when talking, they should at the school, when around Americans like her (B, 71). Lila then moves into complaints about the Spanish students, whom she finds rude since they talk in Spanish (B, 72), the Italians, because of their flashy dress (B, 72), the Germans, whom she finds to be pushy know-it-alls (B, 72). She finally suggests that everyone should defer to Americans at the school, since it is designed as an American school. This discomfiting passage prods readers to think about our own assumptions about the vast array of people with whom we share the globe.

Before the novel ends, Lila departs—or is removed from—the school. As readers, we are left to wonder, with Dinnie, what has happened to her, and whether or not she will return. We suspect that her vitriolic attacks on people from non-American countries has erupted because she is angry and frustrated; her parents are living in Saudi Arabia for the next two years, and she is therefore without a home to return to, or a familiar school to attend (*B*, 188). As readers, we sense that her behavior is a screen for her insecurity and sense of dislocation, and for her lack of a secure relationship with her own parents. Her story is an unsettling one; she is not an attractive character, yet the protagonist, whom we feel sympathy toward, continually defends her. Too many threads are left loose around Lila for us, as readers, to know with certainty, or even with well-informed speculation, what becomes of her once the school year ends. Lila reminds us that teenagers do not always find their way to happiness.

SPECIAL FEATURES IN *BLOOMABILITY*

In each of her novels, Creech adds special stylistic or narrative features that lend artistry and interest to the text, and that invite readers to engage in the literary experience of living through the characters, plot, and settings. In *Bloomability*, one of Creech's special features is the inclusion of postcards from Dinnie's aunts, as described in the "Connections to Previous Novels: Familiarity in Places, People, and Postcards" section earlier in the chapter. The postcards help Dinnie connect with her sense of family and the world she came from. Another special stylistic narrative feature is developed through Dinnie's vivid reports of her own dreams. These dream accounts provide us with a second source of information about Dinnie's interior world, and her sense of connection, identity, and values. Dinnie merely writes down her dreams in a journal, without commenting on or attempting to interpret them, then she drops them into the narrative text of the novel. As readers, we are left with that opportunity to form our own interpretations, and our efforts help shape our interpretation of the novel as a whole. A third special stylistic narrative feature in *Bloomability* is Creech's introduction of some of the words and phrases of the Italian language, a language with rhythms and intonations that enchant Dinnie as they enchant the author. The dream motif and the introduction of Italian words and phrases, when combined with the sweetly quaint postcards from Dinnie's Kentucky aunts that are scattered throughout the novel, are artistic features of *Bloomability* that deserve special attention.

The Dream Motif

Dinnie records her dreams and intersperses them, as narrator, in many chapters, under the italicized heading, "The Dreams of Domenica Santolina Doone." The dreams weave a thread that holds together Dinnie's imaginative and actual lives, without the intrusion of Dinnie's direct narration. Readers are left with the task, if they choose to accept it, of trying to tie each dream to what is going on in Dinnie's world at the time.

Most of her early dreams are disturbing. When Dinnie is trying to get used to the idea that her mother is sending her to live in Switzerland with Aunt Sandy and Uncle Max, who are at that time virtual strangers to her, she has an unsettling dream in which her mother packs her into a cardboard box, tapes the box, and gives it to strangers, who place the box in the luggage compartment of an airplane, with Dinnie inside. She hears a dog bark from inside the box next to her, and finds a dog biscuit, which she eats when she becomes hungry, in the bottom of her box (B, 9).

Readers are left wondering why Dinnie would dream about herself as equal to a dog being hauled across the sky in the carrier of an airplane, but are likely to understand the source of her feeling that she is being crated and sent against her will. Dinnie makes the connection more explicit with the narration that immediately follows the recorded dream: "My second life began when I was kidnapped by two complete strangers.... my mother's sister and her husband: Aunt Sandy and Uncle Max" (B, 9).

In a third example, she dreams about her limited ability to use Italian, even though she has been complimented by her Italian teacher for her linguistic flexibility (B, 6); instead, in this dream, she gets a sack of letters from her brother, who has written them in what she thinks is Italian, and she is unable to read them; when she shows them to others, they tell her that the words are not Italian at all (B, 60–61). This dream seems to indicate her frustration with assimilating into a new culture, and with learning a new language, while away from her family, her sense of security.

Another dream account follows a series of class sessions in which one of Dinnie's teachers challenges his students' thinking, and asks them to consider the question, "What would you sacrifice for someone else?"

(*B*, p. 175). Dinnie records her dream, which begins with her lying on an operating table, with a doctor leaning over her, asking her, "Did you say we could take one kidney or two? Can we take your leg also? And maybe an ear? A heart?" When she asks the doctor whom the parts are for, the doctor gives her brother Crick's name. At that point, with her decision regarding how much she will sacrifice for Crick still undetermined, she awakens (*B*, 176).

Although most of the dreams are foreboding, almost nightmarish, and they stop before they come to a conclusion, a few are happy and uplifting. An example is the dream in which Dinnie realizes that her bubble, her self-protection from direct contact with the rest of the world, is finally gone. It had been eroded by the reality of the close encounter with death that Guthrie and Lila endured when they got caught beneath an avalanche, and Dinnie helped rescuers locate them. The rush of cold mountain air that she feels gives her an emotional surge: "Something was different. My bubble was gone.... I understood exactly what Guthrie mean when he shouted *Libero*! It was a celebration of being alive" (*B*, 229).

The dream motif is a particularly effective narrative technique. Dinnie records her dreams but does not interpret them. As readers, though, we do want to try to make sense of the dreams. We can track the dream accounts, moving from one to the next as they occur in the text, in order to follow the development of Dinnie's preoccupations, fears, and concerns. For example, readers might focus on what the dreams that appear early and later in the text suggest about Dinnie's growth. We can start with the dream on page 9, which is Dinnie's description of being crated in a cardboard box and loaded onto an airplane. The dream is reported just prior to Dinnie's narration of her first-ever plane trip—one she takes to Aunt Sandy and Uncle Max's home before they fly to Switzerland. A dream that follows, after she has arrived in Switzerland, is recorded on page 25. In this one, Dinnie is holding Stella's baby and waving and shouting to her father, who is standing across a mountain. He neither sees nor hears her. This is a fear she experiences when she contemplates how distant she is from her family. We notice a change in the nature of her dreams when we come to page 76, where Dinnie recounts the dream of her protective bubble. She notes that it is expanding, filling the pores with the new images, new relationships, new understandings that she is developing. She notices that the walls of the bubble are growing thinner and thinner, and fears that it will pop, but it does not (B, 76).

In the last portion of the novel, Dinnie's dreams reflect her realistic concerns but also her optimism. On page 266, she reports on a dream in which she is flying down a ski slope, without the aid of ski poles, arms stretched out to her sides. She sails across the school, and she wonders where she will land. The question of where she will land is a real concern, but within the answer she finds possibilities, not fears. Her response suggests Dinnie's new sense of hopefulness that grows from her newfound freedom to make choices about her future.

Italian Language Lessons

Readers learn that Switzerland is a country in which four languages are spoken: Italian (as is spoken in the Ticino, where Max and Sandy live), German, French, and Romansh. Slowly, readers are introduced to several Italian words and expressions, and a sense of the rhythm of the language. We also learn that Dinnie is familiar with the sounds and rhythm of Italian because she has heard it spoken by her maternal grandmother, Grandma Fiorelli, and by her mother, who uses phrases including *andiamo* ("Let's go!") and *ciao* ("hello" and "goodbye") at home. Dinnie and her classmates in Switzerland learn Italian together. The language enchants Dinnie. She enjoys hearing little Italian children "jabbering away" in Italian, and notes that, "When I heard a boy command his dog to sit: *Siediti!*... I thought, *Wow, even the dog knows Italian*" (B, 57). Her own mistakes, like the time she tells her teacher that she is three hundred and thirty years old, and the time she asks her classmate, "How much does the time cost?" amuse Dinnie. These humorous linguistic miscues are familiar to all readers who have tried to learn a foreign language or use one to conduct even mundane daily conversations.

The music teacher asks choir members to use *voci bianchi*, "white voices," when she wants them to sing with pure, soft clarity. This phrase takes on a special meaning for Dinnie, who recalls it, longing to hear her friend Guthrie's "white voice," while she watches as rescuers search for Lila and Guthrie as they lay buried beneath the deadly white weight of an avalanche. It is Guthrie's exuberance that Dinnie and others react to most eagerly. At graduation, he closes a moving speech by promising his classmates that each of them will take a part of each other and of Switzerland with them, wherever they go, and punctuates his speech with his trademark expression, *"Fantastico!"* to which his friends respond, *"Viva! Viva! Viva!"* (B, p. 254).

It is interesting to note that Creech, always a teacher, pays attention to the challenges that English-language learners have when they participate in schools in which English is the language of instruction. Dinnie notes the challenges of learning a new language: "When [the non-English-speaking students] asked me 'How to discover them gym?' or 'Do you habit America?' they were making more sense in English than I was in Italian" (B, 59).

Dinnie's attempts to make sense of the English used by her classmates from different countries, and to learn Italian as a foreign language, help her develop sensitivity and respect for the many students at her school who come from non-English-speaking backgrounds, and who therefore must be able to learn math, science, history, and all of their school subjects in a foreign language. Creech leaves her fingerprints as a teacher at an international school when she gives respectful attention, in these passages, to the challenges and opportunities offered by linguistic variety among a diverse group of adolescent students.

CONCLUSION: LIFE IS IN FULL BLOOM
FOR DINNIE DOONE

When we first meet Dinnie Doone, she is an unhappy 13-year-old. She is being compelled, by her mother and grandmother, to follow her aunt and uncle, whom she hardly knows, to spend a year at a school in Switzerland. She feels as if she has been taken without her assent and abandoned by her family. She is sure that the trip itself will end in disaster. Dinnie has lived all over the United States, always traveling with her parents by car. She has never traveled on a plane before she boards one with Uncle Max and Aunt Sandy to fly to Sandy's home in Washington, DC, two weeks prior to their long flight across the Atlantic Ocean to Switzerland. Her description of what she sees offers us insights into what Dinnie, a careful observer, thinks about herself and her life at the start of her eighth grade year. The description itself, which is representative of Creech's artistry, is as fresh as a gust of winter wind:

> In the plane, you saw it all spread out beneath you, a living map, a wide, wide living photograph, and you were suspended above it and you knew where you were. You were a dot, miles and miles above the state of Oklahoma where you had once lived on a speck of dirt ... You little dot.
>   Or rather *me*: Dinnie the dot. (B, 12)

By the end of the novel, Dinnie knows that she is not merely a dot on the landscape, and that the experiences that have comprised her life up to that point in time, including the many moves and a year-long separation from her family, have helped her grow up and grow into her own identity. At the final banquet of the school year, during which Uncle Max, as headmaster, and school founder Mrs. Stirling, along with several of her classmates give short speeches, Dinnie makes careful observations and thoughtfully reflects on what she hears and feels. Her reflections provide not only a summary but also a synthesis of the lessons she has learned about others and about herself.

Dinnie listens proudly to Uncle Max's "funny, gentle speech about Variety," and Mrs. Stirling's stirring talk about the obligations that this group of privileged students now carry with them into the world (B, 250). She attends intently to Mari's confessions about the fears she felt, initially, as a new student at the school, and imagines that Mari is speaking for her when Mari says that the fear has finally "'slipped away silently and secretly'" (B, 251). Dinnie is awed by friend Belen's beautiful voice and well-hidden talent, and is amused and touched by Keisuke's insistence that "here he had learned that anything is *bloomable*" (B, 251). Her friend Guthrie's speech, based on Frost's "The Road Not Taken," inspires Dinnie to think directly about the paths she has taken, the distances she has gone, and the family and friends who have traveled with her. Following the banquet, Dinnie applauds her own insightfulness, her realization that despite their differences in languages and cultures, "we were all more alike than not"; this observation makes her proud, and makes her "feel grown-up" (B, 256).

The experience of living among an international group of friends, and of growing into adolescence with them, has changed Dinnie. On the flight home, she sits on the plane by herself, watching as Switzerland and Europe pass from view. Instead of feeling fear or indifference about yet another move, this time to her father's and his sisters' hometown, Dinnie begins to daydream about going to Bybanks—about the smell of it, the feeling she will have when she first sees her family; she concludes her thoughts on a very positive note: "What would I find in Bybanks? It would be an opportunity, I told myself. A new life" (*B*, p. 272).

No longer seeing herself as a dot, or her future as an insignificant speck, Dinnie knows that she has a place in the world, and that there are many possibilities open to her. Dinnie finally, joyfully, experiences "bloomability."

CHAPTER SEVEN

HIDDEN TREASURES BENEATH THE SURFACE OF SHARON CREECH'S *THE WANDERER*

IMAGINE THAT YOU ARE on the Atlantic Ocean in a boat with five of your relatives—two who are about your age, and three who are older—the age of your parents or teachers. Now imagine that the only way the boat will reach its destination, England, is if all six of you work together to make sure that you are fed, safe, and entertained for the duration of the trip. The boat is 45 feet long, or about fifteen yards—the distance between one and a half hash marks on a football field. You do not have any room for yourself; you sleep in a tiny bunk bed below the deck, in a room with all five of the others. You cannot escape contact with your five relatives, and you cannot escape the constant rocking of the boat, even when you prepare food in the cramped kitchen galley. How do you respond?

Imagine that slowly you learn to accept the conditions in which you have chosen to live. You are glad, after all, that you convinced your family that you were old enough, strong enough, focused enough, to take part in this adventure across the sea. You have learned to ignore the idiosyncratic oddities of your relatives, and are happy to feel the ocean breezes, see the brightness of the stars at night.

Suddenly, though, the gentle sea starts to buck and kick like a rodeo bull. The sky, which had delighted you just a few hours earlier, becomes menacingly dark, lit only when lightning strikes on the water nearby. Waves build to frightening heights and seem to flex their muscles at you and the boat as they curl and roll around you, pushing the boat in every direction. Remember: the success of the trip is up to you and your five relatives, even when the voyage includes a mighty storm that crushes the boat under the powerful, horrible waves. How do you respond?

These scenes are similar to ones that Sharon Creech creates for cousins Sophie and Cody, two of the six-person group that sails a boat across the Atlantic, with the goal of arriving in England where they will see their grandfather. *The Wanderer* (2000) is an adventure story, but it is a much darker and more disturbing novel than the ones that she has written previously.

The Wanderer is also much more complex and challenging for readers, demanding that we attend to cues and clues, hints and innuendos in order to make sense of the intricately designed, multi-layered story. The plot follows Sophie, her two cousins, and her three uncles, on a sailing voyage across the Atlantic to see their grandfather and father. The storyline slowly reveals the truth about Sophie's past, what happened to her parents, with that revelation, Sophie's own identity.

Creech handles her craft expertly when she sails in new directions with *The Wanderer*. This novel has earned numerous awards, including designation as a Newbery Honor Book, an American Library Association (ALA) Notable Book, an ALA Best Book for Young Adults, a *School Library Journal* Best book, a *Booklist* Editor's Choice Book, and an International Reading Association Children's Choice book. Readers who set sail with Creech in *The Wanderer* experience an invigorating, confusing, challenging, and ultimately uplifting adventure.

SYNOPSIS OF *THE WANDERER* (HARPERCOLLINS TROPHY, 2000)

Thirteen-year-old Sophie has talked her parents into allowing her to join her two cousins, Brian and Cody, and her three uncles, Brian's father Stew, Cody's father Mo, and Uncle Dock, for the adventure of a lifetime: The six will travel together on Uncle Dock's 45-foot sailboat, The Wanderer, from the northeast United States, across the Atlantic Ocean, to the British Isles. Their goal: to visit Bompie, who is the three teenagers' grandfather, and the three uncles' father. Bompie is now living alone in his family's home place, in the English countryside. During the adventure, the sailing crew stops to visit some of Dock's friends, and eventually we learn that the stops are all related to his desire to gather information about a lost love, Rosalie, who miraculously appears once the crew reaches England. This unobtrusive sub-plot is overshadowed by the action of the story: as we predict when reading, the sailboat is caught in a terrible storm, and is almost lost at sea.

The experience of the storm helps the crew better appreciate the connections among them, including the father–son relationship between Stew and his young clone, Brian, and Mo and the son who irritates and disappoints him, Cody. The interrelations among all three uncles and all three cousins also improve as a result of their close call with death. Their family connections are improved even more when they arrive in England to find that Bompie is suffering declining health. They gather around him and tell stories of their shared childhood adventures; the storytelling unites them.

Even the action of the trip, the storm, and the reunion with Bompie is overshadowed, though, by the story about Sophie that unfolds as the plot moves forward. Finding answers to questions about Sophie's past, especially about what happened to her parents, her claim to be Bompie's granddaughter, and how she knows his stories, becomes her cousin Cody's focus, and our focus, too, as readers. Like Cody, Sophie presents us with images from the flashbacks of a "little kid" that we suspect is Sophie herself, because that little kid reports vague, incomplete memories of her parents, of a trip to the ocean and a big wave that swooped her up, and other details that we begin to realize might be related to Sophie's history. As early as page 2, we realize in retrospect and with rereading, Creech foreshadows what we will learn about Sophie and her tragic past. Sophie, in a mysterious narrative, tells us about her present dream, one in which the sea gently rolls in and invites her to come out, and the recurring nightmare to which she links her pleasant dream, one in which a "wall of water, towering, black," sneaks up on her and hovers above, threatening to crash upon her (TW, 2–3). The tension that joins her present dream of traveling across the sea with her cousins and uncles to see their Bompie, and the haunting nightmare that fuels her enormous fear of the power of the ocean, builds throughout this intricately woven novel.

… but …

Sophie mentions her terrible recurring nightmare several times during the voyage, and eventually she links the wave of her nightmare (and memory) with the actual giant white wave that almost overturns The Wanderer in the storm at sea (in her present experience).

Creech masterfully weaves together foreshadowing and flashbacks to prepare us to pay special attention to the "little kid" that Sophie talks about, and the recurring nightmare, but we are surprised, nevertheless, when we are finally able to stack the many layers of Sophie's story together to make sense of it. This is what we finally understand:

Sophie, when she was four years old, was on a blue dinghy in the ocean. A blue dinghy is mentioned by one of the uncles when he is recalling his adventures as a child (TW, 173–175). When Sophie hears the story, she is confused by her strong reaction: "I had to go down below because I couldn't get that image out of my head, of them floating out in the ocean in the dinghy without any paddles" (TW, 176).

She was with her first set of parents, the couple who gave birth to her and raised her for the first four years of her life, but not the pair whom she refers to as her parents in the present tense (TW, 28–29). The sea became storm-tossed, and the couple and their young girl battled against it into the night. Finally a giant black wave curled over the dinghy, and her parents were lost. This is the wave that Sophie recalls, in her subconscious, when she has nightmares of the black wave (TW, 2, 142, 165–167, 208). Eventually, the nightmare is manifested in the present, as The Wanderer *is caught in a storm. Everyone on* The Wanderer *survives this second wave. Sophie then combines, in her mind, the memory of the black wave with the giant white wave of the present. The two waves become one in her mind (TW, 235, 256, 283).*

Sophie's parents were able to keep her afloat during the night of the black wave, perched on the dinghy. She was rescued (TW, 286). She has flashbacks to the funeral services for her parents, and reacts oddly when she hears "Amazing Grace" played in the present, but is unsure why the tune bothers her (TW, 103). (As readers, we assume that "Amazing Grace" was played at the funeral for her parents, when Sophie was four years old.) She recalls adults assuring her that her parents had gone to heaven, a beautiful, perfect place, but their words do not comfort her: As a child, she constantly wonders why her parents didn't take her to that perfect place, too (TW, 231). Instead of going to heaven, she finds herself moving from one foster home to another, until she finally is adopted by the couple to whom she refers in the present as her "parents" (TW, 269–270). Her new mother has three brothers: Stew, Mo, and Dock, and their father is Bompie (TW, 5).

Sophie has never met Bompie before she introduces herself to him when he is lying in his sick bed in England. But unbeknownst to the others on the boat or to us as readers, she has been in communication with him for three years. When she was adopted, he became an active, though geographically distant, grandfather. He decided that he would regularly write letters to her, as a way of welcoming her to the family (TW, 279–285). Each letter contains one of the stories that she claims, while on the boat with her cousins and uncles, are "Bompie Stories."

The only difference between the stories that Bompie wrote to her, in his many letters, and the stories she tells as "Bompie Stories" is that in her rendition, there is always a reference to water as a threat—Bompie is driving a car and has to cross a flooded creek in it (TW, 59); he is walking across a train track that crosses a river, and must jump into the swirling water to avoid being run over by the train (TW, 83–85), he jumps into a swimming hole and bangs his head on something, again and again (TW, 156). In these stories, though, Bompie always survives and is whipped by his father and rewarded with a pie—usually an apple pie—by his mother.

This fascinating plot and its storyline roll peacefully in places, and they tumble turbulently in others. In its movement, the novel reflects and reinforces the rhythm of the sea, creating a synthesis of meaning and form that is powerful, challenging, and rewarding for us as readers of *The Wanderer*.

FAMILIAR LITERARY CHARACTERISTICS AND QUALITIES IN *THE WANDERER*

As readers, we can approach *The Wanderer* from several different perspectives, including these three: *The Wanderer* as representative of Creech's attention to a set of characteristic preoccupations and themes, the novel as a source of evidence of Creech's fingerprints as an artist and former teacher, or *The Wanderer* as a multi-layered puzzle that we have to work steadily and conscientiously to solve.

We can conduct one rewarding level of examination of *The Wanderer* by considering how the novel fits within the artistic framework that we have learned to associate with Sharon Creech. As in her other books for adolescents, Creech incorporates attention to preoccupations and themes associated with attending to adolescents' perspectives, creating significant settings, providing strong characterization, and leaving readers with hope in *The Wanderer*. These reflections of Creech's characteristics are worth exploring. We can engage in another satisfying level of examination of *The Wanderer* by searching for evidence of the fingerprints that Creech, as an artist and as a former teacher, has left on the novel. These fingerprints include her attention to the importance of writing as a mode of thinking, the introduction of vocabulary words that enhance our enjoyment of the story and give us insider status, and the use of literary references to add layers of interpretive possibility to the novel. If we choose to examine *The Wanderer* with our eyes focused on signs of Creech's fingerprints, we also will need to look carefully for more subtle marks that the artist and former teacher has left on the book: the use of figurative language, natural imagery, comfortable dialect, and rhythmic syntax.

These focal points are appropriate and useful if we read *The Wanderer* as an engaging novel that is representative of Creech's contributions to literature for young people. We will give attention to these approaches to the novel in the section that follows. However, we have to go further and work harder as readers in order to find the treasures hidden in this novel. It is the multi-layered complexity of this novel that distinguishes it as different from Creech's earlier books. This complexity requires that we move, as Creech has moved, from attention to the traits that are common across the works in her literary collection, to an examination of special narrative features that are distinctly incorporated in this novel in order to fully experience the depths of the novel. These special narrative features include Creech's complicated, careful use of interwoven examples of foreshadowing, flashbacks, and a recurring nightmare. The book bubbles to life when we look beneath the surface; it rewards us if we dive beneath the smooth water of the surface, to the place where we experience undercurrents and riptides. It is beneath the surface, in these powerful hidden currents, that the treasure of the novel can be found.

ADOLESCENTS AS STRONG CHARACTERS

We notice first that that the perspective of adolescents has priority. *The Wanderer* introduces two adolescents, Sophie and her cousin Cody, who serve as narrators and the storytellers. We move through the novel relying on Sophie's and Cody's views of the world, of the others on the boat, and of the significance of family that provides one of the main purposes for the journey. Creech develops the characters of adolescents in the novel, giving Sophie, Cody, and the other adolescent, Brian, room to grow and learn.

Sophie

The most dramatic growth toward self-awareness and an understanding of her place in the world occurs for Sophie. Apparently, Sophie is unconsciously aware of her own tragic past, or unwilling to admit it, having pushed the memories of her parents' drowning death and her own relocation from one foster home to another into a part of her brain that she has closed to entry. Instead of a plot line marked with details that identify the points in time and the people who have filled her life prior to the journey with her cousins and uncles, we begin to understand Sophie's story through synthesizing various sources of information, including stories about Bompie, the little kid, the recurring nightmare, and stories about her parents.

She tells Bompie stories that even Bompie's sons, Uncle Mo, Uncle Stew, and Uncle Dock don't know; she leaves her cousins and uncles to wonder whether or not she has invented the stories or if she has some kind of secret connection to the old man who has returned home to England, the man toward whom they are sailing. She recounts stories of "a little kid" to her cousin Cody, whom she trusts with her tales, and we suspect, with Cody, that the "little kid" is actually a younger version of Sophie. Like Cody, we aren't sure whether or not Sophie recognizes herself as the "little kid" of her stories. She experiences flashbacks in the form of nightmares about a huge black wave. During the novel, the wave of her nightmares materializes as a wave that almost kills the group of six while they are out at sea. She has to reconcile the dream wave with the real wave in order to make sense of her own history, but it is difficult for her to accomplish the task. Sophie lets us see inside her mind by her refusal to acknowledge that her adoptive parents are not her biological parents, too. Whenever she is asked about her "real parents," she starts by claiming that her mother and father in Kentucky are her real parents, although we know that she has lived with them for only three years, then she changes the subject all together. Sophie may not realize how many gaps in her self-identity she has to fill when the journey begins. By its end, though, when she meets Bompie, she has filled most of them with information. She gains assurance that she is now living with parents who love her, and that she has a grandfather who loves her enough to share his private stories with her through scores of letters that he has sent her from England for the past three years, in order to establish a relationship with her.

Cody alerts readers that Sophie is different from many young teens. Characteristically direct yet kind, he succinctly, sensitively relates part of her story and comments on her demeanor when he says, first, that Sophie has been allowed to accompany the guys on the trip only because, as Uncle Stew says, she is an "orphan" (*TW*, 28); Cody cringes when he hears Sophie referred to that way, yet admits that he is baffled when Sophie talks about his aunt and uncle as if they were her actual parents, since she moved in with them only three years ago, at age ten. Cody is inclined to find the positive in situations, though, and concludes that it is a "kind of neat" that Sophie pretends that her adoptive parents have been her parents all along, instead of "sitting around moping about being an orphan" (*TW*, 28–29).

Although we have Cody's account regarding Sophie's status as a fairly newly adopted member of the family, Sophie will not confirm his account. In fact, when he asks her directly, "What really happened to [your parents]?" Sophie refuses to give Cody any details about how she became an orphan, and almost convinces him that she does not realize that she has ever had another set of parents. Without skipping a beat in the conversation, Sophie responds to Cody's sincere question by claiming, confidently, "Nothing happened to them. They're back in Kentucky—" (*TW*, 97) then moves immediately into a new topic of discussion. Cody is aware that she is dodging the truth, but neither he nor we, as readers, know what the truth is at this point. When Brian asks her the same question, she again deflects the question. This time, the three cousins are watching birds and dolphins, and, according to Cody's journal entry, Brian was watching baby dolphins imitate their mother, and wonders, aloud, what happens when dolphins are orphans—whether or not they learn anything. Sophie responds with a double meaning: "I guess they're smart enough to figure it out on their own. They probably don't have a lot of choice" (*TW*, 155).

Brian follows up by asking whether she had figured things out on her own, too, but Sophie is finished with the comparison and shifts her attention, immediately and without turning back, to the activity of the leaping dolphins, then she disappears beneath the deck of the boat, where Cody finds her later, juggling a bag of pretzels, clearly upset (*TW*, 155).

In a dramatic follow up to this scene, Sophie tells the story about Bompie in the swimming hole, and his struggle to surface after bumping his head several times. Brian has grown impatient with her stories and is, at this point, insensitive to her background. Cody reports on Brian's efforts to push Sophie to recognize herself, and her own fears, in the Bompie stories. Notice that Cody tries to step in and help Sophie; he becomes her protector, shielding her from any sudden sickening or painful self-realizations:

> "If he always gets in trouble in the water, why does Bompie keep going in the water?" ...Sophie's lips were pressed tightly together, and suddenly she looked so fragile to me.
>
> ..."Maybe," [Cody] said, "he's afraid of the water, but he keeps going back to it because he has to—there's something he has to prove—"
>
> "Like what?" Brian said.
>
> "I don't know," [Cody] said, "But if you think about it—if you conquered the thing that scared you the most, then maybe you'd feel—I don't know—you'd feel free or something. You think?"
>
> Brian said, "Well, that's stupid." Sophie ...went over to the railing and stood there like she does, staring out over the water. (*TW*, 158–159)

Understanding Sophie, Creech's most complex character, requires the unraveling of many layers of cues, clues, and hints. As readers, we benefit from revisiting the passages in which Sophie shares flashbacks and foggy glimpses of memories, as when she vaguely recalls visiting Block Island (*TW*, 26–27), those passages in which Sophie's past foreshadows danger in the voyage, and her apparent obsession with water as a threat, including the Bompie stories and the black wave that she sees again and again in her dreams. We will look closely at these in the section

"Special Narrative Features of *The Wanderer*: Foreshadowing, Flashbacks, and a Dream of the Wave," which follows later in the chapter.

Cody

Cody's growth is related to changes in his self-image and attitudes as his relationship with his father and his relationship with Sophie deepen. At the beginning of the novel, Cody is cocky and relaxed. Sophie describes him: "loud, impulsive, and charming in a way my mother does not trust..." (*TW*, 5). Early in the novel, he doesn't take seriously the need to learn nautical jargon or to pull his weight while on the boat; he doesn't take seriously his assignment to record the trip in his journal, which he calls a "dog-log" (*TW*, 24). However, we learn that Cody actually has several dimensions, some of which he keeps hidden beneath the surface. Those hidden qualities, such as sensitivity to Sophie and to her confusion about her past, begin to emerge as the story continues. It is Cody, for example, who intercedes on Sophie's behalf whenever Brian asks her pointed questions about her parents, and when Brian claims that Sophie was invited to go on the trip only because Uncle Dock felt sorry for the "orphan" girl. Cody records, in his journal, a typical scene in which he and his cousin Brian interact. He refers to the entire day as "stupid," and notes that Brian was blabbing too much about his voyage specialty, points of sail. Brian interrupts himself to tell Cody that he realizes that Cody prefers Sophie to him, and Cody quickly admits that Brain is right. With no apparent remorse for possibly making Brian feel bad, since he had simply told the truth when asked for it, Cody shifts his thoughts to the next day, when Sophie would tell her first Bompie story. Cody records his anticipation in the journal: "Now, *that* ought to be interesting" (*TW*, 51).

We also see Cody's gentleness toward nature in his eagerness to observe birds, dolphins, and other living creatures, and to be sure they are safe. The toughest quality for Cody to reveal is care for his father. He spends the early parts of the novel feeling as if his father, Sophie's Uncle Mo, is antagonistic, an enemy who is always finding fault in him. For example, when Uncle Stew decides that each of the sailors will come up with something to teach the others during their voyage, Cody decides that the talent he will teach is juggling. At first, his father is disgusted with what seems to be a frivolous choice. After all, the others' choices are more serious: Brian plans to teach points of sail; the uncles will teach how to form knots, how to read nautical charts, and how to use a sextant. Sophie will tell Bompie stories. Eventually, however, Cody's contributions to the crew become apparent. He assumes the role of tension breaker; his positive attitude becomes as essential to the success of the voyage as the bilge pump, wind, and sails.

During the novel, even Cody's father begins to practice juggling, at first in private, as if he is embarrassed, then in front of the others. As readers, we sense the release of anxiety that comes with the physical activity and the total concentration it requires. Two other circumstances draw the father and son closer together during the time span of the story. First, Cody learns, by overhearing the end of an infrequent phone conversation between his parents, that his father and mother are not happy with each other. He watches in stunned silence when he sees his father cry, for the first time ever. Although they do not talk about the incident directly, Cody senses a vulnerability in his father that he had not recognized before. Second, when the sailors all fear that they are going to die in the major storm, Cody and his dad talk gently to each other. His dad confesses to him that Cody has "been a good son" but that he has "been a bad father" (*TW*, 196), and Cody disagrees, stating that it is he who has been the bad person in the relationship. When the danger has passed, they treat each other with more respect and kindness, and we are led to believe that the changes are ones that will continue to develop, and that will last. Cody reflects on what he is learning:

> I feel as if I've been asleep my whole life, and I wish I'd been asking questions like Sophie does, and I wish I knew more things. But … I don't know how to turn into a person who asks questions, who knows more.
>
> And my father—…he looks like a complete stranger to me. (*TW*, 240)

Brian

Brian is a younger version of his father Stew, in appearance and in attitude. Sophie describes him as "quiet, studious, serious" (*TW*, 5) in demeanor, awkward in physical appearance and movement. As Sophie notes, father and son both "walk in a clumsy, jerky sort of way, as if they are string puppets" (*TW*, 15). Like his father, Brian is determined to create order, and is disturbed by Sophie's ambiguities regarding her life, as well as by Cody's insouciance. Brian's growth occurs as he learns to occasionally relinquish his desire for control. He also learns to replace the need to acquire information with the need to demonstrate compassion. When Uncle Dock and Cody fill in the gaps of Sophie's story, Brian does not ask questions. He reacts only by putting his head in his hands and exclaiming, "Oh, oh!" (*TW*, p. 270). By the end of the novel, we do not know enough about Brian to know how the voyage, the storm, or the truth about Sophie affects him.

The Three Uncles: Mo, Stew, and Dock

The three adult brothers, Mo (Moses), Stew (Stuart), and Dock (Jonah) are typical of Creech's adult characters in one important way: They provide the teens in their care the kind of adult help that they need in order to reach their goals. Yet they also provide readers with a look at adults who have problems to overcome themselves and show us that it is not only teenagers who sometimes seek answers to questions about who they are and where they fit in the world.

Dock is the brother who seems to be the oldest; it is he who enters Bompie's house and asks about him first, and who is in charge of the trip itself and owns the boat, his "baby" (*TW*, 14). He is, according to Sophie, not easily bothered by "all the work that needs doing, or the mishaps that occur—like when Brian knocked over a can of varnish … or when Uncle Stew tangled the lines" (*TW*, 16). Dock's challenge is to find Rosalie, a long-lost love whom he lost when she married another man, but who is now single again. The two are reunited, at last, when Dock and the others reach England, but the reunion is short-lived. He decides that he will stay in Thorpe, England, with Bompie, since the old man wants to live out his days in the home of his youth. Since Dock has no family waiting for him in the United States, his brothers agree that he is the one who should stay. (Thorpe is the name of the town in which Creech first worked as a teacher of English in an American school; it was there that she met the man who would become her husband, Lyle Rigg.)

The other two adult brothers have their teenage sons on board: Stew is Brian's father, and Mo is Cody's. The nickname Stew, which takes the place of the uncle's actual name, Stuart, works well, since it is indicative of his demeanor—he is the uncle who worries about everything, who "stews" over situations as if each one is going to present a problem (*TW*, 15). Stew supports Brian to the point of exaggerating his son's strengths and accomplishments, like many proud fathers do. Stew's challenge during the voyage is to accept the fact that he has been fired from his job as an insurance adjuster, and that he does not know what kind of employment or career would make him happy.

Mo, on the other hand, is disappointed by his son, Cody, and fails to recognize his son's talents, at least during much of the voyage. Sophie describes Mo as a "chubby" man who lounges around as if his job is to sunbathe while he barks orders at everyone, an image that contrasts with his son, who is "fit and muscular, always humming or singing, and smiling that wide white smile" that draws girls' attention whenever he goes (*TW*, 16). Mo chastises Cody by shouting demeaning and unhelpful remarks like, "You knucklehead doofus" (*TW*, 16) at him. Mo's primary challenge during the voyage is to build a relationship with his son, one that is grounded in mutual respect, before he risks losing both his son and his wife. He has to release his negative attitude about Cody and look for the contributions of his son, whose light spirit and good heart are especially important for Sophie. Mo and Cody share a talent for pencil drawing, a talent that neither knew the other possessed, until each began drawing while on the voyage. When they are preparing to leave Bompie near the end of the story, Mo presents Bompie and each of the five who traveled with him a drawing. The one he created for his son is special; it shows Cody juggling all five of the relatives. This drawing indicates that Mo has paid close attention to Cody, and that he acknowledges that even his son's juggling is a worthwhile contribution to the voyage.

Sophie recognizes another challenge that Mo and Stewart need to address: both have settled in jobs that they are unhappy doing every day. Mo is a computer systems "number cruncher" (*TW*, 115), and Stew has just lost his job as an insurance adjuster. She asks each why he has a job that is not what he wants to do, and subversively challenges her uncles to consider following their dreams instead of living in a productive but unsatisfying rut. She interprets Mo's talent for drawing as an indication that he has a creative side that is being hidden in his computer job. When he talks about the dolphins, she is further convinced of his submerged creative side. He tells her, wistfully, that the dolphins remind him "of being a child, with all that curiosity and energy. They remind you that this is what you could be, not what you should grow out of…" (*TW*, p. 153). Sophie sees the fact that Stew has lost his job as a benefit, since it has the potential to free him to do whatever he wants. The problem is that Mo responds to her questions and prompting as evidence of the wistful optimism of youth (*TW*, 116), and Stew has organized others' lives so long that he no longer has any idea what he wants to do as a profession. These are adult characters who remind us, as readers, that age alone does not help us find who we are and determine where we fit in the world. Creech shows respect for her readers by including portraits of three adults who have challenges to face and struggle through, alongside the portraits of three teens who struggle with their own identity and place issues.

Bompie

Neither Sophie nor Cody is able to provide us with much direct information regarding Bompie, the grandfather and father who is the focal point of the journey to England. What we do know, though, we learn from Sophie's telling of stories of Bompie's youth, messages sent over the telephone by Sophie's adoptive mother about her father's declining physical and mental health, the uncles' stories about his home, and his own behavior when the six relatives arrive in England. The stories that Sophie tells suggest that Bompie was an adventurous and happy boy who loved to be outside. The fact that he shares the stories, in a series of long letters, to his newly adopted granddaughter describes an older man who is warm, gentle, and caring. Sophie's mother is worried about his health, though, and sends a message that she has found him "fuzzed up" (*TW*, 69) when talking with him on the telephone. This comment leads Sophie to recall a conversation during which she asked her mother to explain how Bompie remembered so many stories. Her mother explained that for Bompie, memory is "like a picture in his head" (*TW*, 74). That idea would have satisfied some teens, but not Sophie; it led her to worry about what would happen "if the picture got erased," a possibility that her mother would not indulge.

Sophie, of course, has already experienced the partial erasure of her own memories of her parents, her life with them, and their death. She knows that memories can evaporate. When the six sailors arrive to visit Bompie, his memory has apparently been diminished; he mistakes his sons for his brothers, at first, in a scene that is realistic and recognizable for any reader who has had a similarly unsettling, unnerving experience. This is not the first time that Creech has portrayed older characters with mental deterioration. Uncle Nate believes he sees his "Redbird," Aunt Jessie, in *Chasing Redbird*, and he sets up a shrine in the woods to his deceased wife and daughter. These portrayals suggest that as we change, our definitions of what matters most to us also change. The slender thread of attention to the transitive nature of memory that Creech weaves into *The Wanderer* provides subtle yet significant cohesion throughout the novel. Creech leaves us, as readers, wishing that we had known Bompie prior to his illness, and that we had more time to spend with him at this current stage of his life. Ironically, Sophie learns that Bompie's real name is Ulysses, the Latin name of the Greek king whose leadership in the Trojan War, followed by his struggle to return home, is legendary. Creech, the former teacher, spins the tale of Ulysses' battles and victories, *The Odyssey*, into the texture of *Absolutely Normal Chaos* as a more direct metaphor for the travels and travails of the secondary character, Carl Ray. In *The Wanderer*, the reference to leadership, struggle, and travel is constantly present.

THE SETTING

Sharon Creech characteristically develops settings that assume as much significance as minor characters in her novels. In *The Wanderer*, she adds an element that is unique, to date, for her fiction: the primary action takes place on sailboat while it is traveling across a constantly changing ocean. The setting becomes part of the story, since the sea and the boat it supports are benevolent and warm, then violent and frigid, in turns. The sense of change ranges from Sophie's invocations, her dreamy "The sea, the sea. It rolls and rolls and calls to me... I love the sea, I love the sea" (*TW*, 126) to her horrific premonition, "The sea, the sea, the sea. It rolls and boils. It feels as if *The Wanderer* will be swallowed up, and I'm afraid"

(*TW*, 201), to Cody's forcefully blunt, "It's all wind and walls of water. Everything howls and churns. I think we are doomed" (*TW*, 184).

Readers of *The Wanderer* who are eager to find a full description of the 45-foot boat will be disappointed. We are left with questions that cannot be answered by the text, including ones like these: What does the boat actually look like, once it is repaired? Where do Sophie, Cody, Brian and their three uncles sleep? Do they have a shower or bathtub? Does the boat smell of dead fish after they prepare their daily meals during the voyage? Does it smell of dirty people after several days of the voyage? What is sunrise and sunset like from the deck? How many stars can they see, during a clear night at sea, and how does the view compare with ones that they have when in town, at home, looking up to the sky? What kind of night noises do they hear when out on the calm ocean? How do they feel when they are covered with sea spray after a rain or storm?

These questions notwithstanding, the primary setting is actually the sea itself, not the boat, and it is unique among Creech's novels.

There is one connection in terms of story setting that readers of Creech's previous novels will be sure to notice, however: Sophie has moved, with her adoptive parents, from the coast of Virginia to the woods of Kentucky. She describes the Ohio River area where her mother had grown up, and that she has been drawn back to, as one that people "sure love," then adds that she does not know why they do. Sophie misses Virginia, where she lived on the coast, and is surprised that her new classmates can even enjoy the river, which has "no crabs or jellyfish living in it" (*TW*, 9). She recognizes that the kids with whom she goes to school treat the Ohio River as if it is a "paradise," a place where they fish, swim, raft, and relax (*TW*, 9). Nevertheless, Sophie longs to have adventures on the sea. Her friends question why she would want to travel on the ocean when she could stay home and explore the Ohio River, and one suggests that she will be a prisoner on a boat while crossing the Atlantic, a thought that provokes Sophie to respond with a romantic description of rolling waves calling gently to her, and of herself as being as free as a bird while she is on the ocean. Her friends reject the vision with warnings that the trip could be disastrous, that she could die at sea. Sophie concludes that they would never understand her reasons for taking such an extreme adventure, her reasons for going on the sailboat with her cousins and uncles, at all.

A SENSE OF HOPE

Creech concludes the pounding story with a strong sense of hope, a sense that the pieces of life, even when fractured like Sophie's was through her parents' death and her time as a foster child, can be put back together again to form a whole. As readers, we know that Sophie is strong in terms of her physical stature and her temperament. We are not as sure, though, that she is emotionally strong; her past is caught in a mental mist, she has a terrible recurring nightmare, and she is incapable of acknowledging her tragic past, even as it relates to her current place in life. However, during the story, she becomes stronger emotionally at the same that that she endures the physical challenges of living at sea and battling a ferocious storm while on a sailboat. The gentleness and soft guidance that three characters show her help Sophie develop confidence and self-awareness, and eventually she is able to accept her own story and move forward from it. Dock shows her that he trusts her physical abilities by assigning her chores on the ship that the other uncles would reserve for males, and he treads lightly across questions about her past experiences, helping her sort out her story only when she is fully ready to do so. Cody demonstrates that she can trust him with her fears; he becomes the person with whom she talks deeply about life, and also the person with whom she celebrates her enthusiasm for the natural beauty that surrounds them, knowing he shares it. Bompie "remembers" the granddaughter whom he has never met, upon their first encounter, even when he confuses the identities of his own sons.

None of the characters is completely cured of his or her problems by the time the novel ends, but each has discovered that he or she can rely on others as a source of help, and that each has a hand in shaping his or her own future.

FINGERPRINTS OF CREECH, THE ARTIST, CREECH THE TEACHER IN *THE WANDERER*

As readers, we find the distinct sets of Creech's fingerprints marking *The Wanderer* that we have learned to associate with the author and former teacher: the importance of writing as a mode of thinking, the introduction of vocabulary words that enhance our enjoyment of the story and give us insider status, and the use of literary references to add layers of interpretive possibility to the novel.

The Teacher's Fingerprints: Journal Writing, Vocabulary Lessons, and Literary Allusions in The Wanderer

Just as we, as readers, learn about the events of their individual stories from Mary Lou's journal in *Absolutely Normal Chaos*, Sal's trip narrative and storytelling in *Walk Two Moons*, Zinny's firsthand account of her trail-building summer in *Chasing Redbird*, and Dinnie's narration paired with her dreams in *Bloomability*, we come to know about the boat, *The Wanderer*, through the perspectives of Sophie, who is thirteen, and her cousin, Cody. In *The Wanderer*, both Sophie and her cousin Cody keep journals, and their entries become the vehicle through which the story is told. Each chapter alternates from Sophie to Cody, so that in this novel, readers are offered two narrative points of view.

We also find distinct vocabulary lessons in *The Wanderer*. The new words that Creech introduces us to, through Sophie, Cody, and the others who sail with them, including cousin Brian and uncles Mo, Dock, and Stew, relate to sailing and to the sea. These lessons are necessary for readers who are unacquainted with the language of sailing, since the story is set primarily in a 45-foot sailboat that is traveling across the Atlantic Ocean.

When we read closely, we see Creech's fingerprints in the use of literary references, as well. Though few, they are squeezed into the story like a sink and stove are tucked into a sailboat galley. When the group of six spots an island at the end of their long and arduous journey from the United States, the unflappable Uncle Dock celebrates by immediately breaking into lines from "The Rime of the Ancient Mariner" (*TW*, 246). In another nod to literary allusions, this story is, in itself, a representative of the archetypal journey. In it, Sophie, Cody, Brian, and the three uncles journey across the ocean; they must face and conquer severe obstacles, such as broken equipment, close quarters, a terrible storm, injury, and intolerance toward each other's behaviors, before they can attain their individual and group goals. The ultimate goal, finding Bompie, is coupled with a goal that emerges as they travel: learning the truth about Sophie's previous life and her connection to Bompie, whom she refers to as her grandfather, and whose stories she tells.

Subtle but Distinctive Fingerprints

We can also lift copies of the subtler fingerprints that Creech, author and former teacher, leaves on her novels in *The Wanderer*: exquisite use of figurative language, natural imagery, dialectal language, and rhythmic syntax.

Figurative Language, Natural Imagery, Comfortable Dialect, and Rhythmic Syntax

We are enchanted by Creech's use of figurative language, especially in powerful lines of personification, such as Sophie's observation that the ocean is "moody, oh so moody" (*TW*, 133), and that "The fog shrinks the ocean" (*TW*, 93), and with anthropomorphism, such as the description of storm waves as "drooling monsters" (*TW*, 235). We identify her fingerprints in the use of natural imagery, particularly as it reflects Sophie's state of mind, such as when Sophie celebrates the first night that the six sailors take *The Wanderer* out for a test run: "I thought my heart would leap out into the sky. ... The smell of the sea, the feel of the wind on your face and your arms, the flapping of the sails—oh, it was magic!" (*TW*, p. 23). We hear hints of dialect that make use of the language in the novel comfortable, familiar, for readers; occasionally, the language makes us laugh, as when we listen to Cody's tendency to twist nautical terms and bellow orders that make no sense: "Winch the mast and hoist the boom" (*TW*, 39), and when we overhear him use "darlings" as a pet names for dolphins (*TW*, 56). Readers spot clear, clean sets of Creech's fingerprints in her expert use of rhythmic syntax in this novel.

Creech chooses to begin several of the chapters with lines that rock her readers with the motion of the boat itself, using phrases that move gently, such as these chapter-opening lines: "The sea, the sea, the sea. It rolled and rolled and called to me" (*TW*, 1), and then repeats those lines, with the tense changed to the present, as an indication of the unfathomable way that time passes for Sophie while she is on the boat: "The sea... It rolls and rolls and calls to me" (*TW*, 100, 123). The rhythmic syntax that draws our attention to the opening of several chapters serves to warn us of trouble when the weather is threatening: "The sea, the sea, the sea. It heaves and rolls and rumbles at me" (*TW*, 182) and later, when the situation is desperate, "The sea, the sea the sea. It thunders and rolls and unsettles me; it unsettles all of us" (*TW*, 217). The break in rhythm with the last clause of this sentence, "it unsettles all of us," reflects the broken rhythm of the waves that have grown fierce and unpredictable in their fury.

SPECIAL NARRATIVE FEATURES OF *THE WANDERER*: FORESHADOWING, FLASHBACKS, AND A DREAM OF THE WAVE

The characteristics that Creech has used so well to establish herself as one of the premier contemporary writers for adolescents are abundant in *The Wanderer*. Nevertheless, what sets this novel apart from the body of her literary work is the intensity with which the story is told, and Creech's use of layers of meaning that readers must unravel then reassemble in order to piece together Sophie's story. Even the ocean, as the primary setting, and the weather seem to work in sympathy with Sophie and her struggle to understand herself and her history: the more frequently the flashbacks occur that evoke stories about "the little kid," the harsher the nightmare becomes that fills her with dread about the giant black wave. The more nervous Sophie gets about meeting Bompie, the worse the weather at sea gets. Finally, it becomes violent and life threatening. The passages in which the storm is described are almost literally exhausting. The efforts that we, as readers, must exert in order to solve the mysteries of Sophie's identity are continuous, intriguing, and finally fulfilling. We cannot rush the unraveling and piecing together of Sophie's story, since details that contribute to our knowledge are revealed one moment at a time, often through flashbacks and foreshadowing. Creech demands a lot from us as readers of this unique, powerful, dark yet uplifting novel, but we are rewarded with treasures that we uncover in many places as we move through the pages.

Multi-layers of Foreshadowing, Flashbacks, and the Wave Dream

As noted earlier, the first hint of foreshadowing comes in the opening pages of the novel, in which Sophie, as the initial narrator, reveals her dream to sail across the sea, and yet mentions the contents of the nightmare about the black wave, too. We continue to assemble pieces of information about Sophie but have to learn that we need to examine that information through our own filters, since Sophie's memory is hazy and her recollections are distorted.

Early in the novel, Creech foregrounds one of Sophie's foggy flash-backs to begin to raise questions for her readers in regard to Sophie's past when Sophie reports the following in her journal, after visiting Block Island with the crew. She recalls walking along a flower-dappled hill there, going clamming on the shore at night, but she is unsure about who was with her, and wonders whether it had been her parents and grandfather. The incomplete memories leave her with a sense of connection, but with questions and loss too, a loss that is enhanced by her knowledge that, although she had longed to return to Block Island every summer after that first trip, "There wasn't time" (*TW*, 27).

In this reflective episode, Sophie first asks herself whether she had been with her parents and grandfather, but then, before she completes the recall of the scene, she has convinced herself that it was indeed her grandfather, claiming that he gave her a captain's cap. Later, we realize that Sophie has sealed away memories of her first set of parents, perhaps as an unconscious vehicle for protecting herself from the pain of recalling the truth about their death. Apparently, she is able to craft memories to make them match her new sense of reality, as she does with this image of a grandfather. As readers, we cannot be sure who she is remembering as the person who gave her the cap, but suspect, when reflecting on this episode, that the person must have been a composite figure—a relative of her first, biological parents, and the man she refers to as her grandfather now: Bompie.

A less direct example of the weaving of foreshadowing to point us toward what will be revealed about Sophie, with the use of flashback to help us piece together events of Sophie's past occurs when Uncle Stew casually refers to Sophie as "the orphan" (*TW*, 28). His son, Brian, eventually picks up this label for his cousin, too. However, Cody is disturbed by his own miscue when he accidentally brings up the idea of an orphan with Sophie.

He reports on an episode with Sophie in his journal, revealing some of his emotional growth while revealing Sophie's vulnerability.

He first notes in the journal entry that he enjoys being with Sophie when others are not around, since she make no demands on anyone, and has a habit of "smiling at the wind and the sun and the waves" (*TW*, p. 5). He then acknowledges that he almost ruined a peaceful moment that the two shared by referring to an apparently abandoned chick that they found on in the bushes as "an orphan," a term that clearly made

Sophie uncomfortable. She reacted by quickly picking up the chick and returning it to a nest they had seen, and she left Brian wishing that he had not used the word "orphan" in his cousin's presence.

During the climax of the story, the storm at sea, Creech unites the foreshadowing and flashbacks, so that within Sophie's nascent yet still shadowy memory of the wave that killed her parents in the past is illuminated, partially, by the wave that threatens the sailboat and the crew in the frightening present. When Sophie describes the worst of the storm, we understand that she has suffered through a tempest before:

> … this wave was unlike any other. It had a curl, a distinct high curl… and then it curled over *The Wanderer*, thousands of gallons of water, white and lashing.
>
> …I was inside the wave, floating, spinning, thrown this way and that. I remember …wondering if my breath would last. Such intense force was pushing me; it didn't seem like it could possibly be water—soft, gentle water—that was doing this.
> ………
> Was this the ocean? Was I over the side and in the sea? Was I four years old? In my head, a child's voice was screaming, "Mommy! Daddy!"
>
> And then I heard, "Sophie!"
>
> I think I will be sick now, writing about it. (*TW*, 208–209)

After the storm and when the six-person crew is beginning to heal from scrapes, bruises, gashes, and terror, Sophie reports that they "are all quieter than usual, thinking about being alive, and how fragile a line there is between being alive and not being alive" (*TW*, 223). Later, Sophie reflects on the lasting impact of the storm and the giant wave. The positive impact is that it has helped strengthen her bond with Cody, since they are the only two who actually saw the wave before it lashed the boat. She also thinks about the way the actual wave was so similar to the one in her repeated nightmares, except that the present wave was white, while the one in her memory is black. She begins to realize, too, that the experience at sea has unleashed painful memories of an earlier, and very real, wave—one that pulled her out to sea and set her afloat on an uncertain course that she is still trying to navigate (*TW*, 235–236).

Creech does not assume that the pieces of Sophie's story that surface during the violent storm scene will complete the puzzle for us as readers. She offers us a glimpse beneath another layer of the story through Cody's retelling of one of Sophie's "little kid" flashback stories. He relates the tale, which Sophie told him, of the "little kid" whom well-meaning adults try to comfort by saying that her parents have gone to a beautiful place called heaven. That information leaves the child to wonder why her parents didn't take her with them, if heaven is such a beautiful place. The kid, as Sophie reports to Cody, is constantly asked what she remembers about the parents who left her when they went to heaven, but the kid does not want to remember anything. She wants, instead, to move forward in the present and the future; it is too hurtful for her to look back into the past (*TW*, 231).

Realizing that Sophie is either unaware of her role as the "little kid" of her story, or that she is unwilling to admit her role, Cody does not know how to respond to Sophie. As readers, however, we have examined enough layers and put together enough pieces to understand, at this point, that Sophie is the "little kid" whose parents were killed in a storm on the ocean, and that she has chosen to refuse others' demands that she revisit her agonizing past. The physical intensity of the storm, which Creech depicts as an exhausting surge of energy, coupled with the emotional agony of Sophie's story, which she reveals in a measured, controlled way, as if protecting her character from having to face any sudden, jarring revelations, provide irrefutable evidence of Creech's artistic talent and range.

Even after the climatic storm, Sophie continues to have trouble separating her memory from her present, and her imagination from her reality. That difficulty is reinforced when the six sailors arrive at Bompie's home in England, and he graciously yet unexpectedly extends his arms and his warmth to Sophie. The bond between Bompie and Sophie surprises Bompie's sons and grandsons, who know that Sophie—a member of the family for only three years—has never met Bompie. Like Bompie's sons and grandsons, we do not yet know that Bompie has reached out to Sophie through a series of letters as a way to welcome her as the newest member of the family. We first have to eavesdrop on a conversation between Sophie and Bompie, during which she entertains him by retelling the stories that he wrote in the "twenty or thirty letters... addressed 'To My Sophie' and...all signed 'From your Bompie'" (*TW*, 284). She begins retelling each of his stories accurately, and Bompie nods as he remembers. But Sophie also changes his stories, incorporating her fear of water and storms into them.

It is Cody who points out to us that Bompie verified that she was telling his stories, and that he remembered almost everything she described, except for parts that involved struggling in the water (*TW*, 282). It isn't until this scene that we realize that she has not only changed his stories to include her fear of water, but that she has transformed her own story into one of his, too. In a poignant moment that brings the story full circle, Sophie urges her Bompie to "remember" a time when, as a child, he was sailing with his parents, and a storm arose on the sea. During the storm, according to Sophie's account, his parents wrapped him up in a blanket and placed him in a dinghy just before a giant wave covered him and left him floating, alone. As she tells this tale, thinking it is Bompie's story, he realizes that she is actually reporting her own excruciatingly painful experience. He does not remember being the child in the story since it was she, not him, who was caught in a storm, placed in a dinghy, and rescued as the sole survivor of the ordeal. After she tries to talk him through "his" story, Bompie gently whispers to her, "Sophie... That's your story, honey." With his words, the truth is finally released. Sophie responds by putting her head on his chest and crying, long and hard (*TW*, 283–284).

The resolution of Sophie's story is achieved artistically through the combination of flashbacks, foreshadowing, and attention to the wave dream. This matrix of layers gives shape to Sophie's story, and guides our interpretation of it. Creech's skill in navigating the turbulent water of confused and repressed memories, of a character's gradual awakening to her own past history, is stunning here, in this late part of the novel.

CONCLUSION: THE SURFACE AND WHAT LIES BENEATH

When sunshine reflects on ocean water, the color of the water seems to change its hues. The result is a kind of kaleidoscope that intrigues viewers with its colors, shades, and shifts. Reading Creech's *The Wanderer* is similar to looking at light reflected on the ocean. Meanings change hues;

they shift and form intriguing, kaleidoscopic patterns. It is a multi-layered book that has rich treasures beneath the surface.

We realize on page 28 at the beginning of a chapter titled "Slugs and Bananas," that 13-year-old Sophie will be joined, as narrator of *The Wanderer*, by her male cousin, Cody. At once, we sense that this novel will be different from the novels that Sharon Creech wrote prior to its 2000 publication: each of the earlier novels features a single adolescent female protagonist, one with a strong voice, strong sense of self, and a clear direction. Sophie, who alternates the role of narrator with Cody, is a conundrum: she is strong but has extreme weaknesses, is driven to action but is also afraid to move. Her cousin is an antidote; he is confident, kind, and direct. Cody knows what he wants and moves toward his goals in a straight line.

Treasures within *The Wanderer* are revealed as we dive beneath the surface of the simple linear plot, in which six relatives travel on a sailboat from the northeast United States to England, where they visit the old man who is their father and grandfather, and survive a tempest. In order to uncover the treasures, we must examine many layers of meaning, moving back and forth through the passages, attending to cues and clues about how events that are reported fit together, chronologically and psychologically. The treasure hunt is a rewarding adventure in itself. It showcases a strong cast of realistic, memorable adult and adolescent characters. We are reminded, through the reading experience, that when people cooperate with and support each other, great goals can be reached. Each time we approach this novel, we are likely to find new jewels tucked into its pages, shimmering with meaning and significance.

Sophie boarded *The Wanderer* knowing only that she longed to be on the open sea. During the voyage, she learned to depend on others and trust her fears, as well as her joy, with her relatives. She found enough clues to allow her to accept the painful events of her past, and experienced enough support to allow her to move forward with a new family. Cody believed at the start of the voyage that he and his father were worlds apart in spirit and attitude. He learned during the trip that both he and his father could develop emotional depth and grow closer together.

As readers, we are left with many questions raised by the voyage and the characters who participate in it: How will Sophie's relationship with her adoptive parents change, now that the facts of her earlier life have been dredged up and she has been forced to associate them with her own experience? How has the trip changed both Cody and his father, Mo? Does each find more value in the other, now that each has had an opportunity to reveal his depths of talent and his vulnerability of feelings to the other? Will Stew pursue a new career in a line of work that he enjoys, or will he return to doing a job that requires him to hone his skills of organization at the sacrifice of satisfaction? What will the impact of the trip be on Brian? When he recounts his summer adventure for his friends, how will he portray himself and the others who participated? What about Bompie and Dock? Will Bompie die soon, or will he continue to live for years in his partially aware state, happy to be on his home soil again? Will Rosalie return to Dock after she takes care of her prior obligations, or is that chapter of Dock's life finally closed permanently? Will the six ever travel together again?

This novel, in which Sharon Creech's characteristic themes, her artistic and teacherly fingerprints, and special narrative features are present, generates questions for readers long after we finish its last pages, and even after we return to key passages to revisit them in light of revelations that come later. Based on and dedicated to her daughter Karin, who took a similar dangerous trip after her college graduation, Creech's novel is a beautiful vessel that sails on currents and breezes, intriguing, challenging, and rewarding its readers.

CHAPTER EIGHT

POETRY AND A PUPPY: SHARON CREECH'S *LOVE THAT DOG*

T HIS LITTLE BOOK—we can read its 86 brief pages in one sitting—is tricky. It is a novel with the kind of features that will hold our attention when we take it to our favorite reading spot and spend some time with it: a plot that moves us through the beginning, middle, and end of the story; characters in whom we become interested and with whom we sympathize; themes that provoke thought and challenge us to respond; settings that we can envision; and conflicts that fuel psychological or physical action, or both. But it is not a novel, really. Or maybe it is, but it is not like most novels, in which the words fill the page from top to bottom, side to side. The pages of this book are sparse; few are more than half-filled with words. The words are arranged in lines that change lengths, too, suggesting that the words form poems, not the standard narrative text of a book like Sharon Creech's *The Wanderer*, or one of J. K. Rowling's thick Harry Potter books. Another distinction is that almost every page has a date on it; the first page of the book is labeled September 13; the last is June 6. These are dates that correspond, for teens in many schools across the United States, with the school year.

So this book is tricky. How can we make sense of what it says if we can't decide what it is? There are other books that we can turn to for help. Karen Hesse's Newbery Medal book *Out of the Dust* (1997) and Jacqueline Woodson's wonderfully poignant *Locomotion* (2003) also look like collections of poems, but each tells a story. Helen Frost's Michael Printz Honor book *Keesha's House* (2003) and her amazing *The Braid* (2006) are two others that use poems to introduce compelling characters and tell their stories. These books, like Creech's *Love that Dog*, are usually categorized as "novels in verse," or sometimes as "poetic fiction."

As a novel in verse, *Love that Dog* includes many of the artistic characteristics that readers associate with Creech. The first of these is that she gives undivided attention to the voice and words of a young person. In this book, that person is the young student, Jack. The story is narrated totally through what Jack includes in his poetry journal, so that we get to read his unpolished accounts of conversations with his teacher and his reflections of what happens in and outside of school, as well as his polished poems—recollections of his treasured pet, Sky, and his communications with his literary hero, Mr. Walter Dean Myers. As readers, we get the sense of overhearing only Jack's side of the telephone conversation, but we can infer what Miss Stretchberry says to him through his poetic replies. In a second artistic characteristic, Creech presents a setting that we quickly recognize and in which we feel familiar. In *Love that Dog*, the setting is a classroom, and although Jack's poetic journal entries allow us to glimpse the sights and sounds of the neighborhood streets, we never actually leave the classroom in this slim book. The third artistic characteristic that we have learned to associate with Creech, the creation of a main character about whom we grow to care deeply, is also present in this novel through Jack. When he writes about his loss of Sky, we want to cry with him. When he is jubilant about Myers' visit, we want to celebrate with him. We also want to cheer for Miss Stretchberry, a teacher whom many of us wish we could have had when we were in elementary or middle school. Finally, this novel exhibits the fourth artistic characteristic that is common in Creech's books: it offers us a gift of hope. Even though we know that Jack will continue to miss his Sky, we sense that he will recover from his loss, because he has learned to express his grief. He has learned to trust his feelings to his classmates, his teacher, even a famous poet, and has grown stronger with each attempt that he has made to reach out and connect with others through his sincere, heartfelt words about Sky. The story may leave us in tears, but they are tears touched with joy.

In addition to her artistic characteristics, we see Creech's teacherly fingerprints within the book. Her lessons about writing as a mode of thinking are apparent in Jack's compositions; he learns that he can use poems to express his awkwardness, confusion, grief, happiness, and strength. Creech's teacherly tendency to teach vocabulary words in her literary works is apparent in *Love that Dog*: Jack questions the meaning of "anonymous" (*LTD*, 11) when Miss Stretchberry uses it in reference to his unsigned poems, and the phrase "Inspired by" so that Jack can signify his reliance on Walter Dean Myers' "Love that Boy" when he imitates it for his "Love that Dog" (*LTD*, 50). Often in this book, though, Creech combines her customary interest in introducing vocabulary words with an interest in teaching literature to her readers through her perfectly chosen placement of literary allusions. For example, in the first quarter of *Love that Dog*, we read along as Jack is introduced to William Carlos Williams' "The Red Wheelbarrow," and uses it as a model for his own poem (*LTD*, 3), and as he becomes acquainted with Robert Frost's "Stopping By Woods on a Snowy Evening" and "The Pasture" (*LTD*, 6, 21), and William Blake's "Tiger, Tiger," from his "Songs of Experience" (*LTD*, 8). Jack learns about shape poems, and experiments with them, too, creating "My Yellow Dog" so that the poem resembles the profile of a dog (*LTD*, 37).

Although it is short, this book is wonderfully representative of the best of Sharon Creech's literary contributions: it carries her signature artistic features of a commitment that the voices of young people are featured and that their concerns are treated as significant; it has a setting that is comfortable enough to invite a visit, and it is uplifting, truly filled with a sense of the goodness of people, both the young and old. In its brief pages, it also reflects Creech's teacherly past, with its attention to the generative and healing power of writing and literature.

LOVE THAT DOG (HARPERCOLLINS, 2001): THE PLOT, CHARACTERS, AND SETTING

The plot of this book is simple yet profound, in the way that many books of novels in verse, or poetic fiction, are profound: a boy learns about poetry; he begins to write poetry as a way to memorialize, celebrate, and grieve the loss of his beloved dog, Sky. He becomes so enchanted with the poem of one writer, Walter Dean Myers, that his teacher encourages him to invite Myers to the school. Myers accepts the invitation and is a hit as a classroom guest.

The simplicity of the plot belies the tenderness of the story itself. Jack is the student; he is in Miss Stretchberry's class, apparently in an elementary or middle school. She introduces the class to poetry and asks them to write poems. Jack resists, writing these lines as his first poetry journal entry: "I don't want to/because boys/don't write poetry.//Girls do" (LTD, 1). He also initially resists reading and studying poetry, because he thinks that he is expected to understand every word and line. Once he learns to relax as a reader, he is able to make sense of others' poems. When he understands that he can write about subjects that matter to him, Jack's attitude toward writing poetry changes, too.

The subject about which Jack writes, continually, is his yellow dog, Sky. Early in the book, Creech provides ominous foreshadowing related to Sky. We read one of Jack's poems, about a speeding blue car, then overhear Jack's side of a conversation with Miss Stretchberry, who had asked him to explain why "so much depends up a blue car" (LTD, 5). We slowly suspect that Jack's beloved dog Sky has been run over by a car and killed. Jack's constant focus on his dog becomes comprehensible to us once Jack confirms Sky's death in the elegiac "My Sky," the poem that appears as a May 14th journal entry (LTD, 86–71).

This revelation provides readers with one pivot point in the story. The other pivot is provided by Walter Dean Myers' "Love that Boy," a poem that Jack reads and clings to, using it as a model when he writes a celebration of Sky. The poem speaks so distinctly to Jack that he wants to meet its author, and Miss Stretchberry suggests that Jack write Mr. Myers to invite him for a visit to the school. To Jack's astonishment, Mr. Myers agrees to come to the school. He reads and responds to Jack's imitative poem with pleasure and compliments, assuring Jack that he is flattered that Jack borrowed some of his words for the poem about Sky, and that he especially appreciates the fact that Jack added to his poem, "inspired by/Walter Dean Myers" (LTD, 84). When we read the poetic letter that Jack writes to thank Myers for the visit, and Jack's poem, "Love that Dog," which occupies the last page of the novel (LTD, 86), we begin to understand how significant the visit was for the young poet Jack and for his classmates.

Creech encourages readers to use poems as models for their own writing, to move with Jack beyond the stage of resistance to reading and writing poetry, as we experience the text. As an appendix to the story, Creech includes full copies of several of the poems that Jack models, including Williams's, Frost's, and Blake's, and Arnold Adoff's, and she adds, as the penultimate entry in the book, a shape poem of her own: "The Apple," by S. C.

Rigg. The book's final page is devoted to a copy of stanza one of Myers' "Love that Boy." The book becomes, then, a resource for emerging teen poets, as well as a treasure for teen and adult readers.

TONE AND POINT OF VIEW AS A SPECIAL FEATURES OF *LOVE THAT DOG*

Noting that she has "been fortunate in that all [of her] books have found good homes with readers," Sharon Creech acknowledges that *Love that Dog*, which made its way to the *New York Times* Bestseller list, and her Newbery Medal winner, *Walk Two Moons*, are the two books of her collection that "have generated the most and strongest response" (personal communication, January 3, 2007). The strong response to this touching novel in verse is not surprising. Creech has demonstrated artistic genius in the tone and point of view that she uses in this novel; it is difficult to imagine reading the book and being unaffected by it. Had she chosen too sentimental an approach to Jack's story, however, the book could have been sappy and sickeningly sweet. Had she chosen a different narrative point of view, having several of Jack's classmates report on their reactions to his focus on Sky, for example, we would have heard snickering and taunts from those kids in the group who wished to appear unmoved by the overwhelming evidence of Jack's devotion to his pet, and by the poem that recounts Sky's death. Instead, Creech's tone and point of view are perfectly matched so that as we read, our compassion for Jack, and admiration for Jack and his teacher, grow.

Finely Tuned Tone in Love that Dog

"Tone" refers to the ways that an author expresses an attitude toward the topic of and toward the reader; we pay attention to tone as the author's intonation because it subtly expresses an author's intended meanings. Think of the difference between an episode of the cartoon *South Park* and one of the animated *Peanuts* specials. Each has its own tone: generally, we expect *South Park* to be sarcastic and cynical and *Peanuts* to be wholesome and sweet. Creech's tone, we have learned, is characteristically respectful of teenagers and youth and is positive and hopeful. In this delicate book, she has to work extraordinarily carefully to create a tone that is not overpowering, not too obvious. The positive lessons that Jack learns—lessons about using poetry to express his grief and celebrations, and lessons about how adults can be reliable heroes—must grow out of Jack's experiences.

We see Jack as a dispirited kid who grows determined to use what he is learning about reading and writing poetry as a way to honor his dog. Early in the novel, he is reluctant to let anyone know that he is using words as an outlet. In his fourth journal entry, recorded October 4th, Jack gives Miss Stretchberry a poem, his response to Williams' "Red Wheelbarrow," but begs his teacher, "Do you promise/not to read it/out loud?/ Do you promise/not to put it/on the board?" then turns it over to her, adding, "Okay, here it is,/but I don't like it" (*LTD*, 4).

His confidence as a reader and writer of poetry has increased by January 10th, when he writes a strong reaction against Frost's "The Pasture":

I really really really
did NOT get
the pasture poem
you read today.
I mean:
somebody's going out

...and he isn't going
to be gone long
and he wants YOU
(who is YOU?)
to come too.
I mean REALLY.
...
I think Mr. Robert Frost
has a little
too
much
time
on his
hands. (*LTD* 20–21)

Then we hear his jubilant excitement in the poignantly simple stanza of his May 25th journal entry, and the first stanza of a poem that follows shortly thereafter, in the May 29th entry, when the news of Myers' visit is announced:

> Wow!
> Wow wow wow wow wow!
> That was the best best BEST
> News
> Ever
> I can't believe it (*LTD*, 75)

> I can't wait.
> I can't sleep. (*LTD*, 79)

The tone of *Love that Dog* resonates with us as readers. It helps us develop a positive image of Jack, a young boy who is struggling to deal with the death of his beloved Sky and who finds joy in an unlikely place: the words and presence of a poet, Walter Dean Myers. Creech's use of tone, which includes a legitimate sadness along with a sense of strength, confidence, and exuberance, avoiding sugary sentimentality, is finely tuned for this novel in verse. Instead of telling us about Miss Stretch-berry's lessons on poetry with a heavy, pedantic tone, and instead of giving us a transcript of Walter Dean Myer's school visit talk, with an accurate expository tone, for example, we "hear" about each and experience it for ourselves through Jack's responses to Miss Stretchberry and Myers. That is, the poetry assignments and Myers' classroom visit are filtered through Jack's mind, and the result is that the tone of this novel in verse is filled with what we associate with the essence of a young boy's yearning mind and spirit. It is a delightfully tender yet serious, searching yet ultimately satisfied, tone. There is some self-doubt, early in the novel; there is no sarcasm or cynicism. The tone is characteristic of Creech: positive, uplifting.

Precisely the Right Point of View for Love that Dog

Point of view refers to the perspective, the angle, from which a story is told. In this case, the narrator is Jack, who is also the protagonist. We rely on Jack to tell us everything that is revealed about Miss Stretchberry's classroom and about his own life. Jack presents his narration in first person, using "I," so we get the impression that there is little distance between him, as the narrator, and us, as the readers or listeners. We feel as if we are in the same room with Jack as he tells his story. The only problem with a first-person narrator is this: if Jack misinterprets some-thing—if he puts too much stock in someone's insignificant words, for example—we will read or hear a distortion of the objective truth, since our narrator is wrong. Jack seems trustworthy, but he is a sensitive young boy, so as we read, we have to keep in mind that his interpretations of the truth might not always correspond with reality. Because she fre-quently uses first-person narrators who are teenagers, Creech recognizes this potential problem: in *Love that Dog*, she skillfully builds in elements of believability so that we trust Jack fully. He tells us, for instance, that he can't write poetry when he tries the first time: "Can't do it. Brain's empty" (*LTD*, 2) and we not only believe him, but we also understand his feeling, since we have felt that same kind of block when trying to do some kind of writing that is difficult for us, too. We recognize, too, his reluctant pride and fear of embarrassment when Miss Stretchberry wants to put one of his poems on the board, and he responds by writing that she can put it on the board if she wishes to, but that he does not want her to put his name on it, for fear that his classmates will fail to recog-nize that it is a poem (*LTD*, 17). Later, we hear Jack beginning to gain confidence, because he is writing about Sky and using the shape poem format, when he tells his teacher, "..maybe/it would look/really really good/on yellow paper. Maybe you could/put my name on it./But only if you want to./Only if you think it/looks/good enough (*LTD*, 38). The use of Jack's point of view helps us, as readers, participate in the excitement of inviting Mr. Walter Dean Myers to Miss Stretchberry's class; part of the five-page invitation that Jack writes him, authentically, unguardedly includes these lines:

> You probably don't want to hear from me
> Because I am only a boy
> And not a teacher
> And I don't use
> Big words
> And you probably won't read this
> Or even if you do read it

You probably are way too busy
To answer it
Let alone do the thing
I am going to ask you
And I want you to know
That's okay.
...
If you ever get time
To leave your house
And if you ever feel
Like visiting a school
Where there might be some kids
Who like your poems
Would you ever maybe
Think about maybe
Coming
Maybe
To our school
Which is a clean place
With mostly nice
people in it... (*LTD*, p. 55–57)

This is not the invitation that a teacher would have written, but it tells us so much about Jack and his enthusiasm for having Mr. Myers visit. In the other lines of the invitation, Jack acknowledges his awareness of all of the chores that poets must do—"writing their words," answering telephones, paying bills, getting sick, shopping for groceries, fixing cars, doing laundry, cleaning floors—and he apologizes that reading his letter has taken up some of his time, too. These lines are endearing, and make us hope, with Jack, that Mr. Myers is able to fulfill Jack's dream of coming to the school so that Jack and his classmates can hear some of his poems and see his face, which Jack assures him, "I bet/is a friendly face" (*LTD*, 59).

When Jack writes Myers a thank you letter-poem following the visit, his enthusiasm has not dimmed. He remarks on Myers' "best best BEST/ voice/low and deep and friendly and warm/like it was reaching out and/

wrapping us all up/in a big squeeze" and the poet's "best best BEST/
laugh…/like it was coming from way down deep/and bubbling up and/
rolling and tumbling/out into the air" (*LTD*, 83). Jack also comments on
Myer's own obvious pleasure at the visit, by noting that the author was
"smile-smile-smiling/all over the place" (*LTD*, 83). These words, expressions, and exclamations, coming from the perspective of a young boy,
carry the sincere enthusiasm that balance the sadness of the death of
Sky and create an overwhelmingly positive sense in *Love that Dog*.
Creech's choice to have Jack serve as the first-person narrator was the
perfect one.

Jack is shy, but he is not a pushover; we get to know him best
through the words he uses, words that show us his deep caring, sadness,
and concern, and words that erupt into ebullience at the thought of
Myers' visit. This shy and sensitive boy, one who doesn't want his classmates to know that he is a poet, and who doesn't want to make anyone
cry by posting the sad poem of Sky's death on the board, captures our
spirits. We want him to be happy. The tone, which invites compassion,
and the point of view, which allows us to see the world as Jack does and
to experience Jack's blend of emotions, subtly but steadily guide our
responses to this beautifully balanced, exquisitely crafted book.

CONCLUSION

On her Web site (www.sharoncreech.com), Sharon Creech acknowledges
that she had only met Walter Dean Myers one time when she decided to
write him into this novel. The poem, "Love that Boy," not the man himself, was the initial inspiration for the novel; she had a copy of the poem
hung over her computer desk, and began wondering about "what that boy
might love," until she decided to write from his perspective. She admits
that she "tried to get Walter Dean Myers out of the story," but could not,
because "his absence left a big, empty hole. The whole story pivots on his
poem and his influence on Jack." (www.sharoncreech.com/novels/01.asp,
retrieved December 1, 2006). Fortunately for us as readers, Creech
trusted her instincts and allowed Myers to stay.

Since that time, Creech has joyfully become part of an authors'
readers' theater group (www.authorsreaderstheatre.com) that includes
Walter Dean Myers, Avi, Sarah Weeks, and sometimes Richard Peck, in

a venture that "brings books alive." The four or five authors rehearse and then travel across the United States, presenting scenes and readings from a few of their books. Their schedule calls for eight events in 2007. Creech says that she "loves the spirit of this venture," and that "the audience response has been rejuvenating" in their appreciation and responsiveness.

CHAPTER NINE

RUN AND SHOUT IN SHARON CREECH'S RUBY HOLLER

ACCOLADES AND APPRECIATION FOR RUBY HOLLER

RUBY HOLLER IS A FUN NOVEL that is filled with a sense of hopefulness and possibilities. Despite the fact that it revolves around orphaned twins who, as young teens, have been shuffled from home to home and have no permanent family, it is uplifting and, in places, humorous. When we first meet the twins, Dallas and Florida Carter, they are being kept in the spirit-zapping orphanage, Boxton Creek Home for Children, by two strict operators of the home: Mr. and Mrs. Trepid. The Trepids use Dallas and Florida, who are the oldest residents of the Home, as slaves. The nasty couple seems to delight in punishing the two young teens, whom they label the "trouble twins," with extra work and excessive time in the "Thinking Corner," which is "the damp, dark, cobwebbed corner of the basement" (*RH*, 7). Visions of Charles Dickens's *Oliver Twist* emerge for us, as readers, when we adjust our eyesight to the dark and dingy Home of the Trepids.

Although *Ruby Holler* is firmly set in rural North America, it is a book that has universal appeal. British author Philip Pullman, whose own *His Dark Materials* trilogy has made him one of today's most popular writers for young adults, reviewed *Ruby Holler*. His review appeared in the Saturday, July 6, 2002, issue of *The Guardian*, a British newspaper with a reputation that is as weighty as the reputation of the *New York Times* across the United States. In the review, Pullman refers to Creech's "absolute certainty of tone," her talent for "putting the camera in the right place," and her ability to "distribute attention equally among the adults and children" in *Ruby Holler*. He adds that "The effect is to give the reader a sense of deep security: we're confident in the authority of the storyteller" ("Philip Pullman applauds a novel of unobtrusive crafts-manship," at books.guardian.co.uk/reviews/story/0.12084,749907,00.html, retrieved December 3, 2006). When asked to respond to Pullman's high praise, Creech offers a response that points to her respect for her teen readers:

> To receive a review like that from a colleague, especially one as highly-regarded as Philip Pullman, is indeed heartwarming and I was honored by his review. However, I'm not writing for reviewers or critics; I'm writing for readers; it means as much to me when young readers love a book.

She hesitantly adds further insight into her reaction to others' reviews of her work:

> I'm always a little puzzled, too, that I tend not to remember these glowing reviews: the ones that I remember best are the negative ones! I don't want to remember them, but I do. And if I receive a stack of 100 fan letters, and 99 are glowing but one is negative, it is hard to forget that one negative letter. (personal correspondence, January 2, 2007)

What Pullman fails to note in his positive review is that Creech was presented with England's most prestigious award for children's or young adults' book, the CILIP Carnegie Medal, for *Ruby Holler*. Given to the "outstanding book for children and young people" by CILIP (the acronym for the Chartered Institute of Library and Information Professionals), the award is the British equivalent of the Newbery Award in the United States. Each represents its country's highest professional honor for a book for children or youth. First given in 1936 to Arthur Ransome, the Carnegie Medal has honored such notables as C. S. Lewis and Philip Pullman himself. Sharon Creech could start a new club, however, with her Carnegie Medal: when it was presented to her for *Ruby Holler* at a special noon ceremony held at the British Library, London (June 11, 2002), Creech became the only author to have been awarded both the Newbery, which she received for *Walk Two Moons* in 1994, and the CILIP Carnegie Medal.

When asked about her reaction to receiving this major award and her status as the only writer to have both the Newbery Medal and the Carnegie Medal, Creech replies with humility and honesty:

> The Newbery Medal made me feel so humbled and it also gave me a huge boost of affirmation. I felt as if I'd been given a golden blessing by my home country. Receiving the Carnegie Medal was a second blessing, especially poignant to me because I'd lived there for nineteen years and considered England my second home. I feel deeply, deeply honored to be in the company of other writers who have received these medals.
>
> But it was not easy to adjust to how others perceived me after receiving the Newbery, the first of the awards. Even though I knew I was a writer, and hoped I was a good one, suddenly that was publicly acknowledged. I felt uneasy. I was not sure I could live up to the expectations that accompany this award. I am now more comfortable in this skin I'm in: I do the best I can do and feel extremely grateful that I can work at something I love so much. (personal correspondence, January 2, 2007)

SYNOPSIS OF *RUBY HOLLER* (HARPERCOLLINS, 2002)

Dallas and Florida Carter are 13-year-old twins who were abandoned, as babies, on the doorstep of the Boxton Creek Home for Children. Although they have been sent to different couples throughout the years, they have always returned to the Home, redeposited there by unhappy adults as if they are damaged merchandise or shoes that don't fit well enough to keep.

The twins depend on each other for understanding, fun, and the strength to endure life as teenaged orphans. As the omniscient third-person narrator tells us, Florida cannot imagine life apart from Dallas, and it is their connection that has kept the twins from becoming "cowardly wimps or juvenile delinquents" (RH, 33).

Their lives change for the better when a long-married old couple, Tiller and Sairy Morey, show up at the Home. Tiller and Sairy have decided that they will go on separate vacations, leaving their home in beautiful but remote Ruby Holler and separating from each other for the first time in years. Tiller has difficulty envisioning himself on a trip without his life's partner, an uneasiness that mirrors the trouble that the twins have in conceiving themselves separated from one another. However, the adults realize that in order to accomplish their goals—Tiller longs to take his boat down the Rutabago River and its tributaries, and his wife, Sairy, has her heart set on flying to Kangadoon to track a rare bird—they need the help of two strong, smart teens.

The owners of Boxton Creek Home, Mr. and Mrs. Trepid, are happy to be rid of the "trouble twins," even for the short time that Sairy says they will spend in Ruby Holler and with them on their trips. Tiller and Sairy have raised four children of their own in Ruby Holler, and they don't anticipate quickly growing to love the twins. However, Dallas and Florida are so deeply in need of affection, kindness, and positive attention that the old couple soon realizes that they want to provide a kind and warm home for them.

Dallas and Florida have been betrayed by adults so often that they are suspicious of Tiller and Sairy at first. They decide they need to run away from the cabin and Ruby Holler before the old couple grows hateful, like they assume adults always do, and send them back to the Home. They try to leave a couple of times, only to find that they cannot successfully hike out of the holler at night, and to realize that that they don't want to be far from their new family and Ruby Holler, anyway. They learn to depend on and appreciate the big breakfasts, soft feather beds, storytelling, and laughter at the Morey's cabin home. When Tiller and Sairy decide to do a rehearsal for the trips, Tiller takes Florida with him down the river, and Sairy takes Dallas on a short camping trip. An adventure, with a rush of danger, awaits them on their rehearsal trips. While they are hiking near the cabin, Dallas senses that Florida is in grave danger; ironically, Sairy feels the same kind of intuitive fear for Tiller. Both trust their intuitions, and move quickly to try to find their partners, their best friends (RH, 243). Dallas's and Sairy's fears are legitimate; Florida has been thrown from the boat and is being taken by the current down the river, and Tiller is fighting for his life in the river, too. While Dallas and Sairy flag down a neighbor, Z, who helps them search for their beloved partners, Florida is able to save herself, then she rescues Tiller. The terrifying episode causes him to have a mild heart attack.

While the foursome is off on their practice adventures, the cabin is empty. This offers Mr. Trepid the perfect opportunity to enact his greedy, criminal scheme. After he learns from Dallas, by tricking the teen into conversation, that the Morey's keep their money hidden under stones on their property (the "understone funds"), Mr. Trepid hatches a plan to rob them. He hires the lanky, quiet Z, who appears to be a harmless nobody, to survey the land and map the stones. He does not tell Z what he is after, and Z does not tell Mr. Trepid that he is in fact the neighbor and friend of Sairy and Tiller. Z reports Mr. Trepid's plan to Tiller, and the family, including Dallas and Florida, move into action, replacing the couple's money boxes with bags of crawly insects, thorny weeds, and other items that Mr. Trepid does not expect to find as he digs in for the understone funds. They also plant fake jewels, and readers have the opportunity to laugh at Mr. Trepid as he tries to sell the worthless bag of colored glass to a jeweler, thinking he has unearthed a bag of almost priceless gems.

In the meantime, Z begins to realize that the twins are the age of the babies that his wife, who left him, delivered thirteen years ago. Similarities in the appearances of Z and Dallas, both of whom stand "in a sort of loose-limbed way" with "feet splayed out" (RH, 24), foreshadow the possibility that the twins are Z's biological children. Although Z vows to himself that he will clean up his own shack and himself in order to be a suitable father, if the kids or Tiller and Sairy should need him to assume that role, the novel ends with Dallas and Florida happy to be at home with his neighbors, Sairy and Tiller.

CREECH'S ARTISTIC CHARACTERISTICS IN *RUBY HOLLER*: ADULTS WHO MAKE A DIFFERENCE IN TEENS' WORLDS

A characteristic of Creech's books for young adults and adolescents is her portrayal of adults who fill important roles in the lives of teenage protagonists. Unlike some authors of young adult and adolescent literature, Creech neither removes adults from her stories, nor vilifies all of them as unconcerned or unaware of what is going on in the lives of the teenagers around them. In *Ruby Holler*, she portrays adults who span a continuum of personal traits, from the wicked Trepids, to the ineffectual Z, and the wonderful Tiller and Sairy. The despicably greedy and cruel Trepids are exaggerated to the point that, as managers of the Boxton Creek Home for

Children, they emerge from the story like caricatures. Z is a loyal friend to Tiller and Sairy Morey, but he is incapable of tending to his own needs very well, and he is totally ill-prepared to assume responsibility for children. These seedy characters are contrasted with the wise, gentle, adventurous older couple, Tiller and Sairy Morey. Although the old couple has charming eccentricities and foibles, they instinctively understand what the orphaned twins Dallas and Florida need most—love, trust, confidence—and provide it for them in abundance. Due to Tiller's and Sairy's influence on their lives, Dallas and Florida no longer have to believe that "an adult [is] someone to escape" (*RH*, 10).

As Philip Pullman notes in his review of *Ruby Holler*, Creech deftly balances attention to her teenaged protagonists and the adults with whom those teenagers interact in this novel. Frequently, Creech draws on the unspoken connections that link teens and the elderly when she creates allies for teen protagonists. In *Walk Two Moons* (1994), it is Gramps and Gram who take Sal Hiddle on a trip that traces her deceased mother's final journey, and who help her begin to understand her own place in the family and the world. In *The Wanderer* (2000), it is Sophie's constant yet secret communications with her adoptive grandfather, Bompie, and her desire to meet him in person, that gives Sophie the lifeline she needs after enduring a childhood marked by the tragic death of her parents. In *Ruby Holler*, the old couple Tiller and Sairy Morey, whose own children are grown, demonstrate to Dallas and Florida that adults can be relied upon and trusted, that they can love without conditions.

Tiller and Sairy

It is Tiller and Sairy Morey, who live deep in Ruby Holler and carve wooden animals to earn money from curious tourists, who rescue Dallas and Florida from the oppressive drudgery of life as the oldest children at the Boxton Creek Home. The old couple's own four children have grown up and moved away from Ruby Holler, and the pair miss the liveliness of having young people in Ruby Holler, though they are reluctant to admit their regrets to each other. Sairy and Tiller have a gentle way of encouraging the twins to develop their trust in adults and to increase their estimation of their own qualities. When, for example, the twins cut a hole in the barn in a effort to give it more light after Tiller complains of its darkness, they don't get mad at the twins or punish them; instead, after they catch their breath and collect their thoughts, Sairy tells them that it is a brilliant idea to add a window to the barn, and comments warmly on how thoughtful the twins were for starting the project for them (*RH*, 84–85). When the twins decide that they must run away, before what they assume will be their inevitable return to the Home, they don't actually make it out of Ruby Holler; Tiller and Sairy find them and pretend to believe that the two were merely testing out the new sleeping bags that they had gotten to use on the adventures (*RH*, 152–154).

Z

The strange man named only "Z" is described by the narrator as "a shiftless man, slipping in and out of town like a slithery possum" (*RH*, 145). Slowly, however, he evolves into a caring creature. He helps Dallas and Sairy rescue Florida and Tiller, and begins to believe that he could be the twins' biological father. Z tries to talk himself into cleaning up—getting rid of the fleas in his shack, shaving his scraggly whiskers, and putting on clean clothes, in order to appear to be a responsible adult who could raise teenagers. Ultimately, though, he is defeated by his habits, and we as readers understand that Dallas and Florida will not go to live with him, even if they are his progeny, since they are much better off with Tiller and Sairy. When he goes inside his own cabin and looks around, the mess bothers him. He tells himself that he ought to start cleaning and shopping for groceries, and doing the things that other adults do to make places habitable, but the thoughts seem to exhaust him, and he retires to his bed before making even the tiniest improvement (*RH*, 305).

AN ACTION-FILLED PLOT AND INTRIGUING SUBPLOTS

Although Tiller and Sairy seem destined to become Dallas's and Florida's adoptive parents, they do not realize when they go to the Boxton Creek Home to ask Mr. and Mrs. Trepid for their help that they will adopt two new kids. Their intention initially is to ask the kids to help them as they prepare for and take separate journeys: Tiller down the Rutabago River on his own boat, and Sairy to Kangadoon, where she hopes to spot a rare bird. The novel is propelled by the question of whether or not Florida and Dallas will be able to stay permanently with Sairy and Tiller. The odds seemed stacked against the possibility, since Dallas and Florida are initially invited to spend only a short time with the couple, and because they attempt to run away from Tiller and Sairy and from Ruby Holler, twice, out of fear that if they don't leave on their own, they will be forced against their wills to return to the Boxton Creek Home. Eventually, it is not physical action, but consistency in love and care that draws Dallas and Florida to Tiller and Sairy and allows the twins to trust their unlikely adoptive parents.

Subplots focus on two different events. One is the river trip rehearsal during which Tiller and Florida almost lose their lives after being tossed from the boat in a swollen and raging river. Dallas and Sairy intuitively know that something is wrong with the two people who mean the most in the world to them and start a rescue operation. The second subplot involves the conniving of Mr. Trepid, who tries to steal Tiller and Sairy's money once Dallas and Florida innocently tell him that the Moreys don't use a bank, but that they bury their money under stones on their property, and call the burial sites their "understone funds." This subplot introduces the possibility that one of Tiller and Sairy's neighbors, a man known only as Z, might be the biological father of the twins. The intrigue added by Z's presence adds texture to the subplot, since Mr. Trepid asks Z to help him as he prepares to steal the couple's money, and his presence adds richness to the main plot, too, since questions of the twin's parentage and of their future are threaded throughout the novel.

CONTRASTS IN SETTINGS

Another constant across Creech's body of literature, her *oeuvre*, is the depiction of a setting that is attractive not only to the teen protagonists, but that is inviting to her readers. This novel is named for the primary setting, Ruby Holler, which is a lush valley tucked into mountains. Remote and undeveloped, it provides Dallas and Florida with opportunities to explore, run, shout, and spread their wings. The first setting that we find as readers, though, contrasts sharply with Ruby Holler. It is the Boxton Creek Home for Children.

Prior to their lives with Tiller and Sairy, the twins had experienced the dirty, dark, overcrowded Boxton Creek Home, a "misfit" institution that had lost most of its funding and all of its professional staff of social workers, doctors, and even the secretary over the years. The place is in need of repair and paint, and the additions that have been added on haphazardly at the back of the main house only increase its ugliness. Sadly, though, the dilapidated place, which looks to Dallas like a string of derailed train cars and which reminds Florida of "a dragon, with its huge mouth at the front door, waiting to swallow up children who entered it" is the only home that Florida and Dallas really know until they meet Tiller and Sairy Morey (*RH*, 8–9).

The Home's oldest residents, Dallas and Florida, were forced to share space in the very back of the house, where "two cubicles huddled side by side" (*RH*, 10). Each twin had one old bed, a single-exposed light bulb hanging from the middle of the room, and a closet. As meager as the rooms are, Florida and Dallas had known only a series of foster homes in which they were locked in cellars, accused of stealing, or teased and abused by other children except for their place there. They have no reason to expect that life can be good—until they leave the Home with Tiller and Sairy.

When we see them enter Ruby Holler and the warmth of Sairy and Tiller's cabin, follow them upstairs as they first explore the loft bedroom with its soft feather beds, and sit with them as they eat at Sairy's table, loaded with meals like their first one there: "sliced ham, warm applesauce sprinkled with cinnamon, hot corn bread, and green beans," (*RH*, 39), we understand that the place itself provides encouragement for the twins. The Ruby Holler setting takes on the force of another character in the novel, offering a source of energy and optimism. After only a few weeks in the holler, they "had run up and down its hills and shouted across its streams and thrown mud at each other and scrambled over bushes and up trees and spit in a hundred places and dug up worms near the damp creek bank…" (*RH*, 103).

Like a person, though, even the idyllic Ruby Holler has different personalities. When the twins decide that it is time to run away, they try to find their way across the hills and streams at night and discover that the holler can be an unfriendly host. When bats dive at them, Florida and Dallas begin to worry that rats and other "whiskery disgusting things"—creatures they had seen in the cellar of the Home—will gnaw on them as they sleep in their sleeping bags. Fear pushes them to go deeper into the woods than they have traveled in daylight, and they find themselves "stumbling, tripping, falling, scrambling" across a creek, up and down hills, and through thick brush (*RH*, 137). Florida shouts, in frustration, "We don't have any danged idea where we are, do we?…We might be in the lost wilderness—in the lost, lost lost wilderness where …nobody's going to get out alive" (*RH*, 137–138). The twins' fears vanish when, after spending a sleepless night in the woods of the holler, tucked deep inside their sleeping bag, they awake to the familiar smell of bacon cooking, and realize that, somehow, Tiller and Sairy have found them and are nearby. The twins are stunned when Tiller and Sairy cook a campfire breakfast for them instead of punishing them. They don't realize that when Sairy exclaims, "You two are about the smartest kids I ever met…Coming up with such a good idea, to try out our equipment before we set off on our trips" (*RH*, 151), that she is providing the runaways with an easy alibi, a reason for finding them out in the woods of the holler in the early morning. In daylight, the personality of the holler reflects the kindness that Dallas and Florida experience in the presence of Tiller and Sairy.

HOPEFULNESS IN THE FACE OF ADVERSITIES

Creech writes novels that include physical and emotional challenges that teen protagonists must face, but she also provides, through good-hearted characters, a sense of hopefulness, an assurance that the teens will be better people for having gone through the experiences that they endure. This novel is no exception. It is triumphant because it shows that Dallas and Florida can prove that the moniker given them by the Trepids, "trouble twins," is inaccurate, and that despite their horrible background, they are still able to respond to love and care. Although Tiller and Sairy pick up the twins at the Boxton Creek Home for what Mrs. Trepid calls a "very temporary—foster arrangement" (*RH*, 27), they grow unable to imagine sending the twins back to the home after only a few weeks. Sairy explains to Tiller her attachment to them when he reconsiders whether the twins should accompany them on their separate trips. She exclaims to her husband that they "can't send them back as if they're a pair of boots that don't fit right," then explains that, first, the twins are no more trouble than any other kids, and second, that she has noticed that Tiller is beginning to enjoy spending time in the holler with them, whether he is willing to admit it or not (*RH*, 77).

In this scene, we sense great hope for the twins; they are being protected by Sairy's maternal instincts and actions, and we suspect that her affection for them will grow, and that it will last. What is less obvious as a sign of hope in the story is also present in the same scene: the twins bring new enthusiasm for life and for their home to Tiller and Sairy. Their presence is a salve to the old couple, who miss their own children, all four of whom have grown up and left the holler.

Characteristics common in Creech's literary art: her attention to the voices of teen protagonists, her use of intriguing settings, and the presence of hope are clearly evident in this Carnegie Medal novel. Creech's fingerprints as a former teacher, and special features of her talent as a novelist, are also apparent. Readers familiar with Creech's work will find them easy to identify.

CREECH'S TEACHERLY FINGERPRINTS ON *RUBY HOLLER*

The fingerprints that we have noticed in the previous novels of Sharon Creech are not all apparent on the surface of *Ruby Holler*—no character uses writing as a mode of thinking, thus the story is told in third-person omniscient voice. The use of third-person narrative is a change of perspective for Creech, who writes most often using first person through a teen protagonist's voice, as she did in *Absolutely Normal Chaos,* narrated by Mary Lou Finney; *Walk Two Moons*, narrated by Sal Hiddle; *Bloomability*, narrated by Dinnie Doone; *The Wanderer*, narrated in alternating parts by Sophie and Cody; and *Love that Dog*, narrated by young Jack. The omniscient perspective is particularly effective in *Ruby Holler*, because it allows readers to see the actions that the twins would not see if they told the story themselves, including the attitudes and concerns of Sairy and Tiller.

Few vocabulary words are introduced to readers at the very moment that they are introduced to the characters. We have to look more diligently for Creech's teacherly fingerprints on the pages of this novel, but our search pays off. We find evidence of her presence as an artist and a former teacher in her use of teenaged humor and in the deeply descriptive language that she uses to paint the settings of glorious Ruby Holler and, in contrast, the worn out edifice and surroundings of the Boxton Creek Home for Children.

Humor for Teen Readers

Creech delights in adding childhood humor along with the adventure and intrigue of the novel. Often, the humor is delivered through Florida's direct, unpolished, less-than-polite language. Her favorite descriptor is "putrid," a word she uses to describe the Boxton Creek home, her room there, and the Trepids themselves. When she talks about a couple with whom the twins had lived prior to Tiller and Sairy's arrival, she refers to them as "that slimeball slave driver and his twitchy wife" (*RH*, 32). When Dallas expresses delight about the bedroom loft that Sairy and Tiller provide for the twins, and exclaims that lying on the bed is "like floating on a cloud," Florida notes, with trademark candor and skepticism, that the bed is sure to have bugs in it, then asks her brother to consider the old couple's motive, and raises the question, "Are they going to fatten us up like Hansel and Gretel and stick us in the oven?" (*RH*, 38).

Creech also creates a dark kind of humor by contrasting Dallas's dreamy attitude with Florida's caustic realism. For example, when he is sent to the dark, damp basement to spend time alone in the "Thinking Corner," Dallas is able to talk himself into imagining that he is not in the cellar, but instead is someplace "green and sunny," a place where he can act like a boy by throwing rocks and running through trails, without ever getting in trouble.

Florida, on the other hand, refuses to enter the cellar quietly; she stomps across the floor as she chimes, with false bravado, "My turn" to Dallas. Instead of imagining herself in a pleasant setting, she refuses to think at all, forcing her mind to become an empty slate (*RH*, 23).

Deeply Descriptive Language

Creech also provides lush descriptions of Ruby Holler, the old couple's home place. The setting is given such a strong presence in the novel that we are prepared when it assumes the importance of a character within the story. For example, Dallas passes on to Florida what he has learned about how the maple leaves in the woods earned Ruby Holler its name:

> … in the fall all those … red leaves look like a million bazillion rubies dangling on the trees. …in the summer, right after a rain, [they] look like a bazillion shimmery emeralds, and in the winter, after an ice storm, it looks like a bazillion gazillion sparkly diamonds in the trees. (*RH*, 78)

In other parts of the novel, an omniscient narrator, one who sees the entire picture and knows each of the characters' actions and thoughts, provides details about Ruby Holler. For example, the narrator describes the nighttime, when there is a full moon, as filled with the purest silver light [that] makes everything above and below look soft and rich, like velvet," and in this light, all of the creatures move gently, "as if their feet are padded with cotton" (*RH*, 306).

This description contrasts with the image of Ruby Holler on a moonless night, which is described as a creepy place into which unwary trespassers risk falling into holes or tripping over roots, a place "full of shadows and silence" that erupts with animals' darting movements and their deep groans, snorts, and cries (*RH*, 133).

Although Creech allows readers to creep through the holler at nighttime with Dallas and Florida, so that we experience it from their perspective, she relies on the narrator to use the perspective of its long-time residents, Tiller and Sairy, to provide a detailed description, which she presents in rhythmic language, referring to the couple's long-held knowledge of "every twist and turn in it, every path, every foxhole and beehive…where the stream was wide and where it was narrow, where shallow and where deep" (*RH*, 101–102).

The narrator explains that, although Sairy and Tiller do not use scientific names for the flora and geographic features of the holler, they have developed their own lexicon for the local area, referring, for example, to the "picnic tree" and the "tickle violets" near it—flowers that had made their daughter giggle when she touched them (*RH*, 101–102).

While attention to teenage humor and to richly descriptive language are fingerprints that we expect to find in Creech's novels if we have read more than one, there are also special features in *Ruby Holler* that push it to the top of a list of her most successful literary works. Two of them are her use of natural imagery as symbols of freedom, hope, and wholeness, and a compelling journey motif.

SPECIAL ARTISTIC FEATURES OF *RUBY HOLLER*
Natural Imagery as Symbols of Freedom, Hope, and Wholeness

The orphanage is contrasted with the wild hills and valleys that surround Ruby Holler, where Dallas and Florida get to live, at least temporarily, after they are selected by an older couple who need the help of young, energetic teens. The natural imagery through which Creech paints much of the setting of Ruby Holler becomes symbolic in the novel. The most vital of the symbols is that of a wild, beautiful bird. The novel opens with an image of a silver bird swooping over the alleys, train tracks, and dried up creek of small-town Boxton. Thirteen-year-old Dallas Carter watches it from his closet bedroom window at the Boxton Creek Home for Children. The image of the bird, and the freedom, beauty, and hope that it symbolizes, is juxtaposed against Dallas' ugly reality: his reverie is broken by Mr. Trepid's rough shout, "Get out of that window!…Get out of that window, or you're going to join your sister down here pulling weeds" (*RH*, 2).

As if to remind her readers of the benefit of continuing to look skyward, toward our dreams, Creech brings the bird dream back three times in the novel. First, after they are selected to go with Sairy and Tiller, to help the couple as each prepares for and completes his and her trips, Dallas has a mysterious, tantalizing dream in which he is alongside a stream that is so clear he could see each tiny fish swimming along the bottom, and where a "spectacular silver bird" strutted along the stream bank, then stopped, turned its head toward Dallas, and said,

> "There is a place where you can go, where everything is___"
> "Is what?" Dallas asked. "Where everything is—what?"
> But the bird never finished its sentence. (*RH*, 79–80)

Second, Sairy chooses Dallas to accompany her on a quest to find a rare bird in exotic Kangadoon. Third, Creech closes the novel with the silver bird, as well. Dallas again dreams of the bird, seeing it flutter from the sky to tell him that there is a place where he is welcome to go, and this time the bird finishes the sentence with "where everything is magic" (*RH*, 309). When the teen awakens, it is with a new truth: he and his sister, Florida, get to experience the magic of being welcomed to a real and permanent home by the odd old couple, Tiller and Sairy Morey, in beautiful Ruby Holler.

In the most poignant chapter of the novel, Creech provides us with an image that we cannot shake as we contrast the treatment that Florida and Dallas have come to expect from adults with the limitless possibilities they enjoy with Tiller and Sairy. The chapter is called, simply, "The Egg." In it, Dallas brings Florida a bird's egg that he has found in the woods. She takes it upstairs and snuggles it under her pillow, hoping to keep it warm, but she squeezes it too hard and breaks it. Suddenly, her memory is jarred to a terrible scene from years earlier, when she was playing on the kitchen floor in someone's house. She was smashing eggs and watching the "lovely yellow goo" seep from the shells, while spreading peanut butter into the cracks of the wooden floor. Suddenly, she recalls what followed her moment of play: her memory recalls abuse and produces a repeat of her original sense of humiliation:

> Slap, slap, slap. Someone was slapping her arm. "I didn't mean it," Florida whimpered. Someone screaming at her. Slap, slap, slap. Stinging on her arm and face.
>
> Who was that slapping person? Florida wondered. One of those trouble grown-ups? One of those people who sent me and Dallas back, as if we were clothing that didn't fit? (*RH*, 46–47)

The recalled memory unsettles Florida and causes her to fling the egg that she had accidentally broken, along with the pillows from her bed, against that wall of her room and say, in self-protective disgust, "Putrid egg" (*RH*, 47).

Florida is a believable character whose sassiness and strength are built on a strong survival instinct. Through "The Egg," we are given a glimpse of the forces that have shaped her, and better understand her desperation to find a good, permanent place in the world for herself—and for her twin.

THE JOURNEY MOTIF IN *RUBY HOLLER*
Travel-tinged Names

The unquenchable energy of this book is generated, in at least three ways, by the notion of travel. First, Florida explains that the twins' names are derived from the papers on which they lay when they were abandoned on the porch of the Boxton Creek Home for Children: She had been placed in a box, wrapped in a white blanket, atop a travel brochure that advertised "Fly to Florida!" while her brother had been wrapped in a blanket and set atop a brochure that proclaimed, "Destination Dallas!" The place names are the ones that the Trepids agreed to give the twins (*RH*, 210). Never does Florida indicate that she knows anything about the state for which she is named—its beaches and amusement parks as popular vacation destinations, or about the city for which her twin is named, with its money, power, and size. Until the Moreys come to take them from the Boxton Creek Home, their worlds are restricted to the views of the homes where they had been sent and from which they had been returned, like clothing that is the wrong size or food that has spoiled, and the view of the dilapidated orphanage. The place disturbs Sairy, who sees the tilting house in the midst of a field that is speckled with junk car parts and garbage (*RH*, 115).

Under the sinister eyes of the Trepids, Dallas and Florida have been expected to be quiet and to move slowly. Once they move in with Tiller and Sairy, they are able to run and play, to shout and tumble, to be kids. Before leaving the Home with Tiller and Sairy, Dallas dreams of exactly the kind of life he would find in Ruby Holler:

> [He] imagined a broad field rimmed with trees, and in that imaginary field he ran and shouted and threw sticks and mud, and when he was tired, he lay down in the green grass and felt himself getting smaller and smaller until he was a little baby lying in the grass, and someone with a sweet face leaned down and wrapped him in a white blanket. (*RH*, 6)

His ability to drift into dreamy places is off set by Florida's attachment to the world in which she finds herself living. She will not allow herself to dream. Instead, she resists the rules of the Home where she spent her childhood years, thumbing her nose at it by arguing with the Trepids whenever she is corrected, in order to exert the only power she can—an emotional detachment from the pain the she suffers there (*RH*, 7).

Sairy, who has raised four children who love the holler, although they have moved from it, understands what freedom means to Dallas and Florida. Although she is torn about whether or not she and Tiller are too old to adopt the twins, and she wonders whether her desire to adopt them is a selfish one, one that emerges as an answer to the emptiness of their lonely cabin, she has no doubts about what their preference would be: she knows that they love the holler and the freedom to run, play, shout that they have found amid its streams, hills, rocks, and trees (*RH*, 303).

Planning Travel

Second, the novel's main plot involves the preparation for real journeys. The twins are taken from the Boxton Creek Home for Children by Tiller

and Sairy because the old couple need capable, strong, young companions to help them with the adventure that each has dreamed of and is
now planning: Sairy plans to fly to Kangadoon, to search for a rare bird,
while Tiller wants to navigate the Rutabago River in his own boat. Tiller
secretly wishes that Sairy would agree to accompany him on the boat trip,
but he respects her independent spirit and does not force the point, since
he knows she wants to fly to the island to find the bird so badly that she
will leave him and Ruby Holler for a while in order to do it. The couple
agrees to take the twins for the duration of their trips, only, and plans to
return them to the Home after their trips end. Yet soon they become en-
amored with the twins and can't imagine sending them back to the terrible Trepids and the Boxton Creek Home for Children. Nor can they
imagine their own lives in Ruby Holler without the renewed presence of
children's laughter, running, and shouting. This sense of longing for
children's sounds is captured in a scene in which Tiller is reflecting on
the two secrets he and Sairy had kept from each other for so many years:
one was the location of their individual "understone funds"—the buried
money boxes that both Sairy and Tiller planted somewhere on their vast
property in Ruby Holler, and the other, the question of why neither had
admitted that how much it bothered him/her that their own children had
left the holler when they grew up (*RH*, 103). The journey that each plans
to take is preceded by a rehearsal trip—a long hike and camp out for
Sairy and her helper, Dallas, and a boat ride down a nearby portion of
the Rutabago River for Tiller and his crew, Florida. The rehearsal trips
substitute, in the end, for the extended adventures that Tiller and Sairy
imagine when the novel begins, because the old couple, like the twins,
realizes that a large part of the joy of life comes from experiencing it together, not separated from one another.

Inward Travel

Third, the novel maps out internal journeys for Dallas and Florida, and
also for Tiller and Sairy. The twins learn, as they move through the world
of the novel, of better life possibilities than those they have experienced.
They lived with the Cranbeps, whose daughter spit on the twins (*RH*,
124) then complained when Dallas punched her. They lived temporarily
with the Burgertons; Mrs. Burgerton insisted that the twins sleep on their

stomachs, and became angry when they turned over, even in their sleep. The three Burgerton boys caused mischief, breaking windows and setting a fire to a neighbor's house, then blamed Dallas and Florida in order to get the twins into trouble and assure that they were returned to the Home (*RH*, 142–144). Dallas and Florida were also forced to stay a few days with the "scary, toothless lunatic" Mr. Dreep, who locked them in his dark cellar at night and had them dig a well during the day (*RH*, 134).

What the twins learn from Tiller and Sairy transcends lessons about rebuilding boats, using a compass, or preparing "welcome home bacon" after a long night of sleeping in the woods. The gentle old couple teach Dallas and Florida that self-confidence grows when they are able to honor the trust that others, like Sairy and Tiller, extend to them. When Dallas and Florida assume that they will be punished for breaking a glass or a wooden carving, Tiller and Sairy assure them that there is no need for punishment. When the twins sneak out of the cabin and try to run away, only to be discovered by Tiller and Sairy and welcomed back, Sairy provides an excuse that the twins quickly accept and use. She tells them that they were brilliant for deciding to go out at night to try out the camping equipment, and that when she and Tiller had discovered that they were camping nearby, the two adults decided they would join them for breakfast, and brought along food and a skillet. She extends the fib by asking the twins, simply, "Ready to eat?" as if her story had been the most reasonable one ever told, and without giving the twins time to explain that she had made an error in her account (*RH*, 152).

When Florida concedes that they should have told Tiller and Sairy where they were going, Sairy continues with her fib, and reveals her child-rearing philosophy, too:

> No call to do that....I can see what you were thinking. You were thinking, *Let's not disturb Tiller and Sairy. Let's just try out this stuff without bothering anybody.* Kids ought to have a little choice, that's what I think. (*RH*, 153)

The twins begin to realize that they are equipped with good sense and brains, and that their greatest treasure is not money, but having a sibling to depend on, for life. They learn to respect their own intelligence and common sense; they prove to themselves that they can make good choices, even when under pressure, and they finally realize that the characteristics that Tiller and Sairy notice about them are real: they are smart and caring and capable.

Tiller and Sairy experience more than physical journeys in *Ruby Holler*, too. They learn to further trust their instincts as parents, and to treasure interactions with the young twins whom others had deemed "trouble." They reverently and thoughtfully celebrate the teens' small triumphs, such as Florida's first experience with seeing a rocking chair. The teen is embarrassed when she realizes that Tiller is surprised that she does not know what a rocking chair is, and responds when he asks her if she has never seen one before with a gruff, "Well, criminy, I might've seen a picture of one, but I haven't ever seen a real one," and when he invites her to sit in it and rock, she refuses, stating that she would probably just break it. However, the next morning, Tiller hears a creaking coming from his and Sairy's bedroom, and when it looks inside, he sees Florida in the chair, and her softly whispering comfort to two carved birds that she held in her lap. The scene has a strong impact on Tiller, who steps away and reflects on the difference in his own childhood, and his children's, and the lives that Florida and Dallas have lived. He wonders, with sadness, "what it would be like never to have been rocked" (*RH*, 88–89).

This poignant scene of reminiscence, of the comforting memories of family connections, and of the despair in recognition of the depravations that Florida and Dallas have suffered, helps Tiller determine that he and Sairy still have plenty of room—in their cabin, in the holler, and in their hearts—for the twins to take up residence as part of their family there.

CONCLUSION: THE BRIGHT PROMISES OF *RUBY HOLLER*

The eponymous Ruby Holler (the name gives the book its title) is a fictionalized portrayal of a real setting—the place where Sharon Creech's father spent part of his childhood. Creech writes on her Web site (www.sharoncreech.com/novels/11.asp) about the genesis for the novel, explaining that an aunt, one of her father's sisters, told her about the "holler" where they had lived and played as children, piquing the author's instincts for the stories about her father's childhood that the aunt might share. After learning that he was a mischievous kid who enjoyed playing outside, running through the woods of the holler, she began to imagine the characters who became Dallas and Florida. The book demonstrates her delight not only in the stories about her father, but for the landscape of the hollers of the southeast. Creech explains in her own words:

> My father's family lived in southern Ohio and in northern Kentucky, and we visited there often. For me, a suburban Cleveland [Ohio] girl, those hills and trees and creeks were heaven! I loved the cows, the horses, the chickens, the fields, the barns all of it. I loved climbing hills and trees and swimming in the creek. I don't know exactly why, but I have always been—and still am—drawn to rural locations and feel calmed by them.

In this novel, Creech combines her characteristic attention to teenage protagonists' voices, to adults who play important and supportive roles in the lives of teens, and to a pervasive sense of hope, despite seemingly dire circumstances. She also demonstrates artistic talent and a teacher's love of humor and richly descriptive language, and a sensitivity to figurative, symbolic language, and is thus able to capture for readers the very feeling of a young person, joyfully playing in the beauty of a mountain holler that is painted with the ruby red of maple trees. The journey motif carries the novel further into the territory of emotions, providing the characters and readers with opportunities to stop and examine where they have been, and where they might be going. The novel is an accomplishment of exceptional and lasting beauty, one that will surely become one of the "new classics" of adolescent and young adult literature.

CHAPTER TEN

THE RHYTHMS OF SHARON CREECH'S *HEARTBEAT*

H EARTBEAT (2004) SURGES with the regular and sometimes erratic rhythms of life. Written as a series of free-verse poems in the voice of 12-year-old Annie, the simple story pumps steadily, with rushes of anxiety, sadness, fear, and joy. Creech demonstrates, in *Heartbeat*, that short, uncluttered lines of poetry can deliver glimpses into complex human truths. Among those truths are contradictions that we learn about as we move through life: birth and death, joy and pain, clarity and confusion, winning and losing, taking and giving. These are some of the contradictions that provide this profound little book with its substance and rhythm.

Sharon Creech wrote this book after she became a grandmother, a time when she was exploring the relationship between mothers and their daughters, and the relationship between a grandparent and grandchild. Creech notes how finding answers for protagonist Annie's questions directed her writing in this book:

> As I was writing this book, I felt as if I were taking the pulse of this young girl, Annie, who is trying to place herself on this spectrum of life. Where does she fit in? She wonders what it would be like to be old, and what it would be like to be an infant, and how she became who she is, and who exactly is she, and why is she here?
>
> These are questions I had when I was Annie's age, when my grandparents were aging, and when my mother was expecting my youngest brother. I felt as if I were balancing on the cusp of some important life thread, and it was essential to try to understand where I was, in the larger scheme of things. (www.Sharon creech.com/novels/13asp, retrieved January 21, 2007)

In *Heartbeat*, Annie tries to determine who she is meant to be, and where she fits in the family and in the world. When her English teacher has all the students in her class list the things that they fear and that they love, Annie writes about her fear of murders and war, and her sense that the cycle of killing that is fueled by revenge will eventually wipe out the human population (*H*, 32). She writes more extensively about what she loves most: running, with attention to the air, trees, and grass around her and the ground beneath her feet; drawing, "because it feels like running/ in your mind/and on a blank page/a picture appears/straight out of your mind/a phantom treasure"; laughing, with a focus on the sound of freedom that it brings (*H*, 33–34). When she compares her lists of fears and loves with her classmates', she realizes that her items suddenly seem "too big," and she wonders if she would be more normal if she had listed items that sounded more like her friends' lists: that she fears math and that she "loves candy and television/weekends and sleeping" (*H*, 34). We learn a lot about Annie's confidence and independence when she concludes her self-reflective questioning by stating, to herself, that even if she has done the assignment incorrectly, she is "feeling stubborn" and will not erase her lists to compose more insipid ones (*H*, 36). "Who am I?" and "Where do I fit?" are crucial questions for Annie and for all teens. Creech addresses the questions, and those who ask them, with uncommon respect and care in *Heartbeat*.

PLOT SUMMARY OF *HEARTBEAT* (HARPERCOLLINS, 2004)

Annie is a runner. She runs barefooted as far as her legs and lungs will carry her, and in doing so, carries forward her grandfather's love for the sport. She likes running best when her lifelong friend Max joins her. Max is a strange 13-year-old who seems to understand, as Annie does, the language of footfalls and breath intake. Friends since they were young children, neither needs to rely on words, when running, to communicate with the other.

When we meet Annie, she is at a critical point in her life: almost a teenager, she is witnessing her mother's pregnancy, and preparing for a shift from being the only child to becoming a sister. Her mother's pregnancy both amazes and concerns Annie. At the same time, she is watching her maternal grandpa, who lives at the family's home, slip further and further into memory loss and dementia, a process that confuses and saddens her. During this time in which her family is experiencing such change, Annie is able to focus her attention on two individual pursuits: her running, and her art project.

Annie is a strong, fast runner, but she refuses to compete, despite the track coach's urging. She insists that she is not interested in "watching people/worry about fast and faster and fastest/and about/winning and losing" (H, 83) and tells the track coach, who continues to beg her to join the team, that she is not interested. She raises important questions for adults to consider when she responds to the track coach's plea that she reconsider her stance and join the team when she asks, rhetorically, why adults don't seem to listen when a teenager says, "No," and why they think that teenagers are "too stupid/or too young/to understand" or "too shy/to reply" (H, 69). As readers, we note, though, that she does seem to shy to tell the coach all of her reasons for avoiding the team; Annie quietly rejects the coach's pleas, but never gives the coach any help in understanding her feelings.

Annie's grandpa, in lucid moments, listens to her objection to joining the school team and supports her choice, telling her that when he stopped racing, everyone told him he would regret it, but that he never did, "Not for one tiny moment" (H, 85). He quit competing when he was fifteen, after winning the national title, for reasons that, as readers, we are not told. He did not run again until his daughter, Annie's mother, was old enough to run with him. Jogs with his young daughter became, for him, "...the only kind of running/he would ever do/because it was the best kind of running/and the only kind of running/that made any sense to him at all" (H, 10).

Annie's enthusiasm for the joy of feeling free and strong while running is contradicted by the attitude of her lifelong friend, Max. For "Moody Max" (H, 3), running does not provide a pleasant release of energy; instead, it is an escape. Max wants to leave behind the small town where they live, and where he has memories of his life being shattered when his father left and his grandfather died. He tells Annie, with conviction, "These feet are my tickets/out of here" (H, 18). Max is compelled to join the track team and to compete. When he loses a big race, he feels as if he has lost his ticket out of town, his escape. After the disappointment of losing the race, though, Annie's grandpa reminds him of great runners' secret of success: "Run for the pleasure of running" (H, 172). That simple advice allows Max to release his anger and resentment, to focus on the freedom instead of the self-established *competition, to begin to run for joy instead of for escape. Grandpa gives Max lenses through which to view the world more positively.*

Annie's other pursuit is her art project. The teacher has given an assignment that Creech borrowed from the actual experience of her daughter: students are to draw the same apple every day for one hundred days (H, 59–61) (www.sharoncreech.com/novels/tidbits.asp). At first Annie doesn't see much change in the apple, but slowly she learns to pay close attention to its subtle changes. As it ages, the apple loses it sheen. Because he doesn't understand that that apple is part of her art project, Grandpa takes a bite from it. After he does, the apple begins to turn brown and shrink; its decay accelerates. Annie's final drawing, completed on day one hundred of the project, captures the apple's single remaining feature: its brown oval seed. This drawing represents the conflicts that are at the heart of the poetic story: the apple's seed is a symbol of beginnings and endings, and of "both old and the new" (H, 180).

Annie's increased attention to the apple transfers to her attention to the people around her, especially Grandpa, whose splotchy and withered skin she begins to notice as if the markings of age have come on suddenly. One afternoon she looks at him, noticing how the muscles in his face relax to become "slack" as he sleeps, and asks herself:

> *Has that brown spot on his cheek*
> *always been that large?*
> *Has it always been the shape*
> *of a pear? (H, 85)*

The conflict of old and new is also emphasized in a scene in which Annie and Grandpa are looking together through a family photograph album. Annie reflects on the experience and comments to herself that it is difficult to reconcile the image of her grandfather now, a man who is growing feeble, with the smooth-skinned, dark-haired, long-legged boy in decades-old family photographs. Then she makes a wonderfully astute observation: as her grandfather stares at his own photograph from the time he was a teen, she notices that he, too, has troubling making the connection, and knows that he must wonder "how that young boy/turned into an old grandpa" (H, 75–76), how he deals with the rhythm of days and years passing.

Annie is beginning to explore the rhythm of aging, of old and new, and accepts them as part of life. Everyone around Annie seems to be changing.

Annie's mother comes closer to delivery of the baby. Grandpa is slowly sink-ing into dementia. One day he recognizes himself in a photograph taken when he was a young track star, and another day, he accuses the person in the photograph of staring at him in a challenging way, and insists that the photograph be taken down. Although he can remember a strawberry dessert that Annie's daughter served at a dinner ten years earlier (H, 41), he panics when he realizes that he cannot recall how to make fried chicken (H, 39), a dish that he prepared every week for forty years. Annie sees the signs of dete-rioration, and gently accepts them because she loves her grandfather. She does not flinch when he seems confused; she does not apologize to Max when Grandpa doesn't recognize him as her lifelong friend. Max is changing, too. No longer the steady, amiable friend, he is getting more focused on running a big race with the hopes of establishing himself as a track star. He grows more and more intent on using his athletic skill as a way out of town.

In glaring contrast to the scenes that focus on Grandpa's aging, and as a counterpoint to Max's discontent, Creech presents images of new life. If Annie's attention to Grandpa's aging is like a musical downbeat, her atten-tion to her mother's pregnancy provides the upbeat, thus providing balance for the rhythm of life that she is beginning to feel and move to as she learns to pay more attention to those around her. The family—Dad, Mom, and Annie—visit a birthing center where a midwife will soon deliver the baby, and all three family members view videos about childbirth. Annie and her father are frightened but excited. In a fluke of timing, it is during Max's big race, which he desperately wants Annie to watch, that Annie's mother goes into labor. The family rushes to the birthing center where, after a protracted time, baby Joey is delivered. Immediately following its birth, the baby is unable to breath on its own. The time between delivery and his first breath seems to be an eternity, but after the midwife gives him a single puff of oxy-gen, he begins to wail healthily, "and the relief rustles/through the room—/ you can see it, feel it, hear it. //Everyone bursts into tears/mother, father, me, midwife" (H, 153).

Grandpa does not make the trip to the birthing center, but stays at the house under the care of a neighbor, to whom he proudly claims, "we're hav-ing a baby today!" (H, p. 141). Again, Creech emphasizes here the tenuous balance between beginnings and endings, between life and death. Baby Joey's birth is difficult; he is gray, still, and silent when delivered, and requires the help of a midwife with an oxygen tube to take his first breath. Once he does inhale and exhale, he releases a hearty wail, an indication that his future has begun. Joey will have a lifetime, it seems, to compile knowledge and memories, continuing the cycle that his grandfather has participated in throughout a lifetime, and is now beginning to relinquish.

When Annie comments on the baby's dependence on his family for food, clothing, safety, and love, she could be describing her elderly and fragile grandpa, as well as the baby, thus reflecting that tenuous line that separates the two: He needs us to love him/And it makes me worry/About all the babies in the world/Who might not be warm or fed/Or protected or loved (H, 158–159).

The novel ends without fanfare, but with the beautifully quiet scene in which Grandpa is holding Joey and looking through Annie's 100 days of apple drawings, ending with the drawing of the naked seed, the symbol of beginnings and endings, of "old and new" (H, 180) and of not-yet-revealed treasures. Max has learned to run for joy instead of escape; baby Joey is thriving, and Grandpa is still well enough to help care for Joey by holding him, singing to him, comforting him. Annie begins to consider some older girls' questions about Max, and the nature of their relationship; she realizes that their unshakable friendship might grow into another kind of relationship, especially after Max gives her an extremely thoughtful gift, anonymously: a set of colored pencils for her drawing. As readers, we sense the possibility for a deeper connection in the future for Max and Annie.

CREECH'S ART IN HEARTBEAT
Adults in Adolescents' Lives

Like her other books for young people, this short novel in verse addresses the relationship between teens and an older generation, and does so by giving prominent attention to the adolescent protagonist's perspective. Annie watches helplessly as her grandfather is "evaporating/or shrinking/disappearing—/little pieces vanishing each day" (*H*, 24). In a lesson about grace, Creech portrays Annie's responses to him as gentle and kind. When he frets because he cannot remember something, she softly touches his hand and then goes to find an answer for him, instead of treating him as though he is a child who can't know the answer to the question he is asking, the one that makes him fretful. Annie compares the baby that is yet to be born with her grandfather, and wonders about what each knows and thinks. She connects those thoughts to herself, too, asking "And what did I think/when I was small/and why did I forget? // And what else will I forget/when I grow older? //And if you forget/is it as if/it never happened? //Will none of the things/you saw or thought or dreamed/matter?" (*H*, 43–44). We sense that Annie is developing compassion that she will carry with her throughout life. She understands that living with an aging grandfather is an opportunity to learn from him, even when he no longer is aware that he is teaching her.

Annie's parents are understandably preoccupied with the imminent birth of the new baby, their second child, born twelve years after Annie. Her father talks directly to the baby, calling it "pumpkin alien baby," and consults a baby book so that he will know which stage the new baby is going through each month of development (*H*, 37). Beyond their attention to the baby, we learn little about Annie's parents. They appear to be happy and to provide a good life for Annie. The single exception is a scene in which Annie's mother has to acknowledge the painful strangeness of Grandpa's memory loss: he is unable to recall how he made fried chicken, which he did every week for forty years, yet he vividly remembers a strawberry dessert, and the apartment she lived in when she prepared it, once, ten years earlier. Annie records only that her mother "bites her lip" in acknowledgement of her sorrow (*H*, 42).

Unlike Annie, Max does not have a stable, supportive family life. His odd behavior and his continual withdrawal seem related to his home life. We do not learn about Max's parents, except that his father has left the family and he is unhappy, eager to leave the town that he finds "too small" and where he there are too many "boys with nothing" (*H*, 25, 31).

There are other adults who also have an impact on Annie in *Heartbeat*. The teacher who assigns the art project, Miss Freely, seems to be tuned into young teenagers' need to find and celebrate what is unique in their own worlds. Miss Freely tells her students that they will draw apples, and tempts them to try to prove her wrong by claiming, "No apple is ordinary/You'll see" (*H*, 99). Annie is immediately captured by the assignment, and though her classmates finish their first drawing at school, she takes hers home to complete it. She is disappointed with the result, saying "It seemed a bit stiff/too much like a drawing of an apple/with none of the feeling of an apple" (*H*, 65). These words provide a clue about the assignment and about Miss Freely's intention: She wants her students to learn to portray the apple with the kind of attention to details that will bring it to life. When Annie applies these same lenses to looking at her grandfather, even as he sleeps, she recognizes his nobility and uniqueness, instead of seeing a wrinkled old man.

Mr. Welling, the English teacher, also has a positive impact on Annie. Like Miss Freely, who teaches her to notice the world around her, Mr. Welling teaches her to acknowledge what she finds. In one lesson, his influence on Annie is particularly strong. He prompts Annie and her classmates to list their fears and loves, and the results lead Annie to wonder how she is like and unlike her classmates, and to consider what her differences say about who she is. With Mr. Welling's guidance, Annie begins to use writing as she does drawing—a kind of "running/in your mind/and on a blank page" (*H*, 34).

THE TEACHERLY FINGERPRINTS OF CREECH

Teachers play influential roles in the life of the protagonist in *Heartbeat*. As readers who are familiar with Creech's art, we know that we can look for the author's own fingerprints as a former teacher on the book, too. We discover that Creech's teacherly fingerprints are abundant in this novel in verse. The most obvious are found in the book's form—a free-verse poem that captures the voice of a 12-year-old, and that distills Annie's thoughts so that we can focus on the most significant ones. The controlled yet free-verse form suggests that Annie's perspective has been shaped by someone who is older and more experienced than is Annie, someone who has spent significant amounts of time with adolescents.

There are other direct fingerprints, including a focus on Annie's vocabulary, her use of prohibited words such as "Like" and "Well" at the start of a sentence, her use of footnotes, and her enthusiasm for using a thesaurus. When Max begs her to be at his big race, Annie describes her feeling as "confused/baffled/bewildered/disarranged/decomposed/disoriented/embarrassed/flustered/mortified/muddled/and perplexed" and adds the footnote that her descriptors are "Courtesy of the thesaurus" (*H*, 130). She continues to refine her use of adjectives, defining baby Joey's birth as a "miracle," then extending the definition by qualifying the miracle as "a marvel—an astonishing/astounding/fabulous/incredible/phenomenal/prodigious/stupendous/wonderous/*miracle*" (*H*, 154–155).

A more subtle teacherly fingerprint is found in the letters that Grandpa leaves as a gift for Annie. He has written and bound a letter in white thread on each of Annie's birthdays, starting with the day she was born. He keeps the letters and will not allow her to read them until after his death. This act of writing and collecting letters for Annie is indicative of a deep, profound sense of connection between Annie and her grandfather. Like Bompie in Creech's *The Wanderer* (2000), who writes letters to welcome Sophie into the family that she has been adopted into, Grandpa shows Annie that she is incredibly important to him through his collection of letters. As readers, we are left to imagine the contents of those letters.

CONCLUSION: CREECH'S ARTISTIC STYLE BEATS WITH THE RHYTHM OF LIFE

As noted in the introduction, this little book is filled with contradictions. The contradictory pairs—life and death, new and old, experienced and inexperienced, and so on, are represented in symbols throughout the novel. The most compelling symbol is the one of the gradual withering of the apple. It reflects Grandpa's slow decline, his withering and shrinking, and can represent life and death, beginnings and ends, fruitfulness and decay. But the apple does not isolate life from death; it denotes the cycle of life and death, and is therefore both sad and comforting. The last of Annie's drawings of the apple is of a single, tear-shaped, brown apple seed. This picture is one that Grandpa turns to while he is holding the infant Joey in his arms. The image of grandfather and newborn baby, seated before a picture of an apple seed, is a powerful visual image of the rhythm of life.

Creech also reinforces the sense of the rhythm of life in the style that she chooses for the poetic lines of *Heartbeat*. Often, words and phrase structures are repeated to imitate the sound of a runner's heartbeat, as in the opening lines of the book:

Thump-thump, thump-thump
Bare feet hitting the grass

> As I run run run
> in the air and like the air
> weaving through the trees
> skimming over the ground. (*H*, 1)

Not only are the words "thump" and "run" repeated here, but the pattern of a present participle (the –ing words) followed by a prepositional phrase, in "Weaving through the trees/skimming over the ground" is also repeated. This pattern lends a sense of movement, of forward motion, which is another important idea in the book. The "thump thump thump" refers to Annie's feet as they hit the ground during a long run; as we learn later in the novel, it also resonates with her grandfather's fading heart-beat, and her baby brother's strengthening one.

Syntactic patterns (the way that the sentences are structured) are repeated in portions of the book throughout the short text. Each repetition denotes something that is meaningful. For example, prior to Joey's birth, Annie tries to convince herself "I am going to be there/and I will have a sister or brother/and I will not be afraid" (*H*, 95). The repeated "I will" emphasizes her determination to handle the baby's birth well, and to perform properly as a big sister. Later, when Grandpa expresses to Annie his fears about a boy in a photograph who "wouldn't stop staring" at him, a photograph that is actually of Grandpa, taken when he was a boy, Annie reflects on the contrasts of Grandpa as he is now with the way she thinks of him from the past:

> I do not like to see my grandpa like this.
> Always he was so busy
> so wise
> so comforting.
> Always he was the grandpa
> the one who knew everything
> the one who would laugh with me
> And run with me.

The repetition of "always" and "so" reinforce the sense of loss related to the changes in her grandfather. She can no longer use the word "always" to describe him in the present, since he is changing, deteriorating, so quickly. She cannot use the qualifier "so" to refer to his wisdom and ability to comfort any longer, since his mind is no longer stable. The repetition of the phrase "the one who" highlights the immensely important role that Grandpa has filled in Annie's life; he has been "the one" for her, but is no longer able to satisfy many of the demands of that role.

With the symbol of the apple and seed at its center, and the structure of the novel, with its bold, short lines that feature repeated words and phrases, Creech has achieved a special artistic accomplishment in *Heartbeat.* In this book, the form and structure beautifully reinforce and underscore one of the book's essential themes of hope for young and old, beginnings and endings, past and future. It is a powerful and profound book, one of those that we can read in an hour but that stays in our memory for years. This is a book that leaves all readers, young and old, moving to Creech's beat, and appreciating her attention to the wonderfully varied rhythms of life.

CHAPTER ELEVEN

PLAY IT AGAIN IN SHARON CREECH'S *REPLAY*

YOUNG LEO IN THE SPOTLIGHT

ANY READER WHO HAS ever dreamed big dreams will be drawn immediately to Leo, the young protagonist of *Replay* who withdraws to his own imagination when he wants to feel special, to stand out, to be noticed. In his family, Leo is the second oldest of four children; he feels invisible in the loud family, so he dreams of occasions in which he is a star, a hero, a wonder. When *Replay* opens, he has just rescued a neighborhood woman whom he finds lying unconscious on the sidewalk. His fantasizing is abruptly interrupted by the shrill call of his older sister, "Hey, sardine! Fog boy! What the heck are you doing? Mom is looking all over for you...." (R, p. 2). Undeterred by the clash of his imagined and real worlds, Leo presses on, in his imagination: "Trouble? Maybe someone needs him. He dashes for home. Maybe he will get there just in time" (R, 2). Moments after getting home, he shifts his attention to another dream. In this one, he is on national television, "tapping up a storm." The audience is erupting into applause and the television show host exclaims, "Have you ever seen anything like it?" while Leo continues to perform, spinning wildly, and leaping over a chair as he continues to tap (R, 6).

Throughout the novel, he puts himself in roles that exaggerate his courage, talent, and popularity. Leo's internal life is much more exciting than his real life, and he appeals to all young teen readers who feel that they, too, suffer mundane lives. Yet as the novel progresses, Leo faces some exciting changes in his real life.

For one thing, he discovers in the attic of his home an *Autobiography of Giorgio, Age Thirteen*, and realizes that the book was painstakingly written decades earlier by his own father. In the box where he finds the autobiography, he also finds a pair of tap shoes, shoes that his father danced in when he was a happy kid (*R*, 56). Leo tries on the tap shoes, which fit perfectly, and falls in love with the freedom he feels as he slides across the attic floor, tapping his feet. Tap dancing becomes a secret pleasure for Leo, and one through which he imagines a connection with his father. When his large family is gone from the crowded house, he risks bringing the tap shoes down stairs, where he taps throughout the house.

A parent's autobiography and tap shoes that appear in the novel apparently had been hidden away in the corner of Creech's mind, waiting to be dusted off and used. In 1995, when describing her home office, where there are "dozens of pictures of my family, so that everywhere I look, someone is looking back at me," the author mentioned an actual composition that eventually is transformed into the fictitious autobiography:

> On the bulletin board nearest my desk are two quotes....
> One quote tacked nearby is from Ernie Pyle's Second World War correspondence. It reads simply: "The human spirit is just like a cork." I love that line. The second quote is from an autobiographical essay that my mother wrote in 1933. She was fifteen years old: it was the middle of the Depression; her life was not an easy one. But she says, in the middle of this essay, "Whenever I feel especially happy, I tap dance." And I love that line, too. (Creech, 1995, 423–424)

The autobiography also prompts a second major change for Leo; in it, his father mentions Rosaria, the youngest sister. Leo recognizes all of his other aunts' names, but he has never heard of this youngest, Rosaria. Determining who she is or was, and why no one has ever spoken of her, becomes a mission for Leo. Clearly, the family has been hurt by Rosaria, but neither Leo nor we, as readers, can know whether she is alive or now dead at this point. The uncertainty and secrets fuel Leo's dreams of being a hero: he vows that he will solve the mystery of Rosaria.

The third major change is that this year, Leo has an opportunity to act out in real life his fantasy of being an actor. His teacher has written a play, "Rumpopo's Porch," and Leo is determined to land a role in it. When he learns that he has been assigned a small role as an "old crone," he is disappointed, but still committed to showing his family, friends, and the world his talents. Leo settles for the part of the old woman, despite being teased by his friends and family about it. His goal is to prove his talent for acting. He also hopes to recover the dignity he lost in his dramatic debut, a school play during which he uttered his only line, "Is he hurt?" loudly, boldly, as "Is he glurt?" (*R*, p. 16). Leo blends his imagined life with his real one when he rehearses his few lines while he taps in his father's old shoes:

> OLD CRONE: I will find out (*tappety tap*) what that old Rumpopo (*tappety tap*) is up to (*tappety tap leap*). (*R*, 56)

THE PLOT OF *REPLAY* (HARPERCOLLINS, 2005)

Life is not simple in a family filled with growing children. Leo spends his days away from school sneaking off into quiet corners, or perching on the roof top or in a tree in order to delve into his father's autobiography, a treasure that he keeps protectively to himself. At school, he is focused wholly on "Rumpopo's Porch," and the potential for success or disaster of the play, which includes a live dog and in which his best friend, Ruby, plays a wise donkey. Leo would rather read or act than play sports, so a distance grows between him and his closest brother, Pietro, who is an accomplished athlete. Instead of spending time with Pietro, Leo hangs around with his friend Ruby. She has suffered what is, for Leo, almost unimaginable: her younger brother Johnny died of an illness. A stoic balance to his dreamy demeanor, Ruby becomes Leo's sounding board. She helps him understand how fortunate he is to live in a large family, even on days that he complains of feeling "invisible" in the midst of three demanding siblings and a host of aunts and uncles.

Meanwhile, his family's life goes on around him. In the middle of the novel, three chapters start with similar scenes: In "Crash, Smash, Crumple" (R, 116–119), Pietro is late for a football game and anticipates that his coach will kill him. Youngest child Nunzio has lost his shoes (which he calls "thothes," since he has a prominent lisp and it is so cute that no one attempts to teach him how to pronounce Ss). Pietro suffers a broken leg during the game, and is rushed off the field on a stretcher and taken to the hospital.

In "Splat," (R, 120–124) the oldest sibling, Contento, is late for her soccer game and worried that her coach will kill her. Nunzio has lost his shoes, and slows down the family's progress. During the game, Contento "slips in the mud," and loses control of her legs; she is suspended above the field for a tense moment, then "splat, she comes down hard, and she lies there, writhing and moaning" (R, 122). She is carried off on a stretcher and taken to the hospital, where she is treated for a dislocated knee.

"Agony," (R, 125–130) occurs later the same week. Nunzio is ready for his musical performance, but Pietro and Contento are having trouble hurrying on their crutches. Nunzio is sure his teacher will be angry. However, the performance, including Nunzio's angelic solo, goes well until the end. During the applause, the boys on the highest riser topple forward, crashing down on top of the smaller boys in front. Only two boys are taken away on stretchers; one is Nunzio, who is taken to the hospital, unconscious. He has to stay several days at the hospital, and during that time, Grandma stays with the other children at home.

It is while Nunzio is in the hospital, and Leo is terribly worried about him, that Grandma decides to reveal the story about the unknown aunt, Rosaria. She explains that Rosaria is still alive, but that the errant daughter and sister has had no contact with her parents or siblings for years. The reasons for the separation are not convincing to Leo, who doesn't understand why she has been excommunicated from the family just because she ran away and got married, years earlier, at a time when she was angry with her parents. Because his close friendship with Ruby helps Leo understand how devastating the loss of a sibling can be, he finds it impossible to accept the adults' lack of effort to restore Rosaria to her place in the family as his grandfather's favorite child. He imagines several scenes in which he brings Rosaria back home and is a hero within the family. The reconnection and repair of feelings, or rapprochement, is initiated when Grandma phones Rosaria's home and leaves a message on the answering machine, but a reunion does not occur before the novel ends.

What Leo is able to accomplish by the end of the novel is an acting performance that makes even his father proud. More important, he has learned more about his family and himself. He is now old enough to be trusted with the truth, and he is able to accept the fact that every family has to deal with loss—some permanent, as his friend Ruby does in the death of *her younger brother, and some that are possibly temporary, as the family acknowledges the hope that Rosaria will return home some day. Grandma has gotten her phone number and left a message. The next step will be Rosaria's. For Leo, though, the future begins to look more promising: "He can't help it, off he goes, feeling so full of his family and the play, as if he is standing on the porch of his life, like his father stands in that last photo in his book"; when Pieto complains of noise in the attic, his father yells so that the entire household can hear: "Zitti! It's Leo. Leave him alone. He's just trying to grow up" (R, 180).*

CENTRAL THEME: FINDING ANSWERS TO TEENAGERS' QUESTIONS, "WHO AM I?" AND "WHERE DO I FIT IN THE WORLD?"

This novel examines the central teen questions, "Who am I?" and "Where do I fit in the world?" from at least four entertaining and intriguing angles. Twelve-year-old Leonardo is the central focus. As we follow Leo through the novel, we learn that he is a dreamer who imagines himself fulfilling wonderful roles: he is a rescue squad hero (R, 1), a Nobel prize winning author being interviewed on the *Today* show (R, 12), a famous tap dancer (R, 6), a knight on a quest (R, 26), a family healer (R, 141). But Leo's reality is not nearly so glamorous as the life he imagines for himself. To his older sister, two younger brothers, and even his parents, he is known as "Sardine," a stinky nickname he inherited when the house was filled with relatives, and he complained, "I'm just a little sardine, squashed in a tin" (R, 3). Leo's other nickname is "fog boy" (R, 2); he earns this hazy moniker by keeping his head in the clouds rather than concentrating on what is going on around him.

Leo's place in the family is reminiscent of Mary Lou's, in Creech's *Absolutely Normal Chaos* (1990). Mary Lou is thirteen and the second oldest of five children; she is "waiting to find out" who she is and what she will become (ANC, 5). Leo's place in the family is also similar to Zinny Taylor's in Creech's *Chasing Redbird* (1997). Zinny, thirteen, lives among a "slew of brothers and sisters and [her] parents" (CR, 2) and next door to Aunt Jessie and Uncle Nate. Uncle Nate is befuddled by the presence of so many children, so he simply "called all the boys *tadpole*— and all the girls *pumpkin*" (CR, 21). The story is not only about Leo and how he finds his own identity, however. As readers, we are able to watch a second iteration of the "Who am I?" question unfold, as Leo learns about his father, Giorgio, through the autobiography that his father wrote when he was just a year older than Leo is now. Leo is surprised to discover that his gloomy, careful accountant father once loved to tap dance, swim, and sing. When he begins to reflect on who his father really is, his knowledge propels Leo to remember the few times—prior to Giorgio's heart attack—that he and his father laughed and played together. One day he is playing outside and has a vision, one that is rooted in his memory; the memory is of Leo and his father, holding hands while running around the yard, playing. His father has on a yellow, happy shirt, and is barefoot, carefree, laughing (R, 27).

Later, he reflects on what he does and doesn't know about his own father:

> So, there is this whole other person who is Leo's father, before he was Leo's father, and Leo doesn't know him.... When he finishes Papa's book, will he know all about this other person? Leo doesn't think so... (R, 81)

Questions about his father's full identity lead Leo to wonder why people change into the people they become, when they start out so differently. These questions may remind Creech's readers of the ones that Cody raises in *The Wanderer*, as he also begins to realize how little he actually knows about his father. In a third iteration of the "Who am I?" question, Leo expresses fear that his brother Pietro has already lost the part of himself that held Leo in esteem as the older brother. There had been a time when Pietro, a year younger than Leo, would not let his brother out of his sight. He even habitually snuck out of bed to sleep with Leo. He would crawl in the bed with his brother and insist, "Leo, need you"; when Leo told him, "You're supposed to be in your own bed, Papa says," little Pietro would look up at him and reply, "Not.... Not doing." Leo finds himself longing for the young, innocent "bear cub" Pietro when he looks at his athletic brother, a brother who talks and dreams only about football and who thinks girls are "yukky," and Leo wonders whether or not he, too, "has changed from a cute cub into something revolting, and he wonders if anyone misses the younger him" (R, 34). Leo worries, too, that the family's baby, Nunzio, will also lose his respect for his older brother as he grows up:

Nunzio, the baby of the family, four years younger than Leo, was born with a mass of soft black hair, like a velvety halo all around his head, … and ebony eyes so dark you felt as if you could fall into them and disappear.

When Nunzio learned to speak, it was with an endearing lisp;
NUNZIO: Thardine? You help me?
NUNZIO: Thardine, Lithen to me. Lithen to thith thong.

It is easy for Leo to see the connections between Nunzio-then and Nunzio-now. Nunzio is still a happy, singing, lisping kid. But Nunzio is only eight, and Leo hopes he won't change like Pietro did (*R*, 38).

While reading his dad's autobiography, Leo makes the other discovery, a list that raises questions that are more shocking even than the fact that his father loved to tap dance as a kid. He father had written in his book:

Angela	My oldest sister, temperamental
Maddalena	My sister, loud
Carmella	My sister, jealous
Rosaria	My youngest sister, happy (*R*, 25)

So Leo realizes that somewhere he has, or had, an Aunt Rosaria. He is baffled that no one in the large, loud family, including Giorgio's other sisters, has ever mentioned her. The mystery associated with Aunt Rosaria, and why she has never been mentioned, consumes Leo. This fourth version of the "Who am I?" question is a matter of family identity. Leo reads his father's list of his sisters in *Autobiography of Giorgio, Age of Thirteen,* and the list leaves him confused—not only about the aunts, but about what else his family may be hiding from him.

Leo is determined to find out about the missing Aunt Rosaria, so he asks his grandmother about her one evening when the entire family is gathered around the dinner table. The response he gets from Grandmother Navy (so named because she and her husband wear only navy blue) is a shriek of pain before she runs from the dinner table and then leaves the room. His father is angry, and asks Leo where or from whom he heard about Rosaria, before demanding, "Do not ever mention Rosaria again, you hear me?" (R, 63–64). During the next family gathering, Leo approaches the topic of Rosaria more cautiously. He has noticed a family photo in which she is sitting with a white dog, and asks, innocently enough, "Auntie Carmella, did you and Papa and everybody ever have a dog?" Again the response is unexpected. She gasps, Leo's father yells at him, and Grandma Navy "rushes off to the bathroom," crying, "Oh, oh oh!" (R, 113). Leo's eagerness to solve the mystery of Rosaria's identity, which flies in the face of his father's attempts to conceal it, raises the "Who am I?" and "Where do I fit?" question to a new level. Unless he solves the mystery of who his relative is and why no one wants to talk about her, he cannot feel that he knows his family or himself.

The mystery is finally solved when Grandma decides it is time to talk, again, about Rosaria. She starts by telling Leo about his aunt's "deep and hearty ha ha ha" and her penetrating stare. These remarks about her personal qualities intrigue Leo. When Grandma adds, "And how she loved to dance!…Her little feet, tapping all the time…And sing! Oh, she loved to sing, too!" Leo's imagination soars; he imagines his happy young father tap dancing with the beautiful little sister. Grandma reinforces his vision when she points to a photo of Rosaria; the moment of recollection is magical for Leo, but it is almost overwhelming for Grandma:

> "She's acting out a little play with your papa. That's his hat she's wearing."
> Leo leans toward the photograph. "Papa? Doing plays?"
> Grandma says, "Oh yes, your papa loved to do plays. He turned everything into a play."
> "Papa?"
> Why didn't Papa write about this in his autobiography?…
> Grandma returns to the first photograph. … "And Rosaria loved that little dog, how she loved—" Her voice catches, and she stops. Grandpa turns from his place at the window and comes to her. He takes the album gently, as if it might dissolve in his hands, and he stares at the picture. (R, 136–137)

Grandma continues after a few moments, saying that Rosaria has left home and the family, and that they have no contact with her. Leo, fearing that

Rosaria had died, like his friend Ruby's younger brother had, was relieved. He is baffled, nevertheless. Grandma explains how extremely close Rosaria and her father had been, but that they got into one huge fight and without warning, she ran away from home with her boyfriend. The fight, Grandma explains, occurred at a bad time for Rosaria; she was inconsolably grieving the death of her beloved constant companion: the little white dog that Leo spotted in the old family photos. With this explanation, Grandma hints that Rosaria had not been thinking clearly when she left home with the boyfriend. Yet Leo questions Grandma about why no one begged Rosaria to come home, why they treated her as a criminal when she ran away. The couple married, but their marriage lasted only a short while. As a result of those events, though, Rosaria, the once-happy sister, was forever changed. She returned home only one time, and the visit ended in anger and Rosaria's accusations that her parents didn't even know her any longer.

Leo feels sympathy for Rosaria, since he believes that no one, including his parents, know him, either. In one of his dreamy scenes, he imagines trudging through the snow in dense woods, where he finds Rosaria, bundled up under wool blankets, sitting in a small, cold hut. In his mind, he rescues her, brings her home, and initiates actions that heal the family. But Leo's imagination is not strong enough to take him to Rosaria, or to heal the family's pain. The differences in how he interprets the situation and how his grandparents did suggests a breach of understanding across generations that is rare in a Creech novel.

With his help, Grandma is able to find her current telephone number and calls it, but she does not connect with Rosaria. She leaves a message on the voice mail. The mystery of Rosaria is solved, in terms of who and where she is, but the bigger question, "Where does she fit in the world?" remains open for Leo, his family, and for Creech's readers.

SPECIAL ARTISTIC FEATURES: LEO'S DREAMS AND DRAMATIC EMBELLISHMENTS

Creech deviates from straightforward narrative text in this book in two important ways. One is through the use of Leo's dreams. They appear almost like flashbacks…scenes that occur out of time and out of place in terms of the novel's setting. Quickly we realize that Leo spends much of his time dreaming, and his fantastic stories reflect internal, mental adventures, not actual ones. The novel opens with one dream scene: Leo imagines himself saving a neighborhood woman who has fallen on the sidewalk, and being praised by members of a rescue team who show up after he has done his good deed. Readers will enjoy tracking Leo's dreams, and many will recognize his tendency to put himself in starring roles within his own private fantasies. They include these:

> Leo as hero who rescues an old woman (page 2)
> Leo as tap dancing television star (page 6)
> Leo as a genius novelist who is asked to appear on the *Today* show (page 12)
> Leo as a knight on a quest (page 26)
> Leo as the one who finds Rosaria and brings her home (page 141)

We also enjoy reading along as Leo learns more about his father, whom he affectionately calls "Papa," by reading his father's autobiography. Particularly poignant scenes occur at these points:

> Rosaria is first mentioned in the autobiography (page 24).
> A photograph captures the image of Leo's father at age twelve, sitting on a front porch and smiling; Leo imagines his father playing on the porch with Rosaria, and with his own children, too (page 27).
> Papa recounts a "no sisters allowed" camping trip on which his father, Leo's grandfather, took the boys of the family; Leo's dad writes about knowing his quiet father was happy, at that time, and Leo wonders whether his own dad is ever happy (pages 45–46).
> Papa writes about finding the old tap shoes and asking a man who was throwing them away if he could take them. He says that he let Rosaria try on the shoes after he did, and that although they were too big, she put on three pairs of socks the "tapped all around the room, around and around and around," then concludes the autobiographical entry with "When I am happy, I tap-dance" (pages 55–56). This quote becomes more

poignant when we realize that Creech lifted it directly from her own mother's autobiographical essay.

Leo contrasts his father's entry about how much he loved the weightlessness and freedom of swimming with the terrible day that he found his father lying in the dirt of the garden after having a heart attack (pages 65–67).

Papa explains that he got a scar (which Leo knows is still visible) when a bully burned him with a hot coal poker, and Leo is in awe that his father "does not tell if he cried, if he hurt," and thinks, "maybe the fact that the does *not* say that he cried or hurt says a lot about him" (pages 80–82).

Papa lists his interests and goals for high school and for life, noting items including "to be on the honor roll" and "to be captain of the gymnastics team" and, for life goals, to be a singer, a dancer, and a writer (R, 87). Leo is concerned, upon reading the lists, that Papa did not include "be a father" on any of his lists, but the lists inspire Leo to record his own interests and ambitions, and he finds himself setting high goals:

1. To save the sick and starving children.
2. To stop war.
3. To save the environment. (R, 89)

Then he stops. He thinks of all the amazing things a person could try to do, but they seem too big, all those things, and so he scratches them out and writes:

1. To be a father. (pages 86 88).

Creech provides readers with a glimpse into Leo's thoughts by allowing us to read Papa's autobiography with him and to observe his responses to it. Even though Leo is not a first-person narrator, we are given plenty of help in understanding his thoughts through the narrative and plot structure of the novel.

Creech also deviates from straightforward narrative by inserting some features that give the novel the appearance of a play. When the third-person narrator records conversations that Leo has with his brothers, Creech sets those conversations aside in dialogue markers. For example, in a

touching scene that follows the death of the boys' pet parakeet, Leo and
the lisping Nunzio have a talk; Creech records it this way:

> LEO: What are you looking for, Nunzio-bunzio?
> NUNZIO: Petie.
> LEO: The parakeet? Is this where Papa buried him?
> NUNZIO: Yeth, I think.
> ...
> NUNZIO: I want to see if he'th thill there.
> LEO: Where else would he be?
> NUNZIO: Heaven, of courth. (R, 72)

Hints of a stage production appear in the book's physical layout, too.
The names of the characters who people the book are listed as if they are
characters in a play, on pages that precede the opening chapter. Leo is
listed there as "Leonardo....Sardine and fog boy, 12" in a reflection of
how most everyone views him. His mother is listed as "Mom.....(Mariana)
Frazzled mother," and father as "Papa....frazzled father" (R, iii) in a
reflection of how Leo views his parents.

Finally, this novel is uncommon because after "the curtain closes"
(R, 181), readers find the complete text of "Rumpopo's Porch," the play
that Creech has created to include in the novel. She directly encourages
readers to read or perform it, pretending it is the English teacher Mr.
Beeber's work. The play is a simple story of an old man who cares for lost,
homeless children in his home in the woods. When he tells stories, he
becomes young again, and when he wishes hard enough, he can perform
magic. He turns green feathers into an emerald table, for instance. His
talents make the villagers fearful that he is using wizardry and witchcraft,
and that he will be a danger to the children who are attracted to him, his
stories, and his magic. In the end, though, they realize that what he offers
is happiness and hope, and nothing they need fear.

It may be reasonable to wonder whether or not the play that she created for the novel, "Rumpopo's Porch," is Creech's vehicle for asking
readers to consider their own reactions to others' stories, to be less quick
to judge them as "dangerous" and unacceptable and more eager to listen
to them with open minds and hearts. Regardless of her intention, the play
does allow readers to consider contemporary questions about how readers

respond to fantasy tales, with an eye toward the wonder produced by the stories instead of any potentially hazardous ideas about magical powers that they might promote.

CONCLUSION

This fun novel is more like *Absolutely Normal Chaos* in its tone and energy than the novels that have come between the two. Its appeal is probably greatest among young teenagers. Both have a cast of rambunctious family members, with the protagonist as the next oldest child—the birth order that Creech herself held. Both have a protagonist who uses imagination to transcend the everyday world. In *Absolutely Normal Chaos*, Mary Lou draws on the language of *The Odyssey* to lend an air of drama to her fairly ordinary life. In *Replay*, Leo fantasizes, putting himself in lead roles, and observes his family and friends, involved in their daily routines, from that lofty perspective. And both novels feature the artistic characteristics that we associate with Creech: the author respectfully presents adolescents' perspectives—Mary Lou's and Carl Ray's in *Absolutely Normal Chaos* and Leo's in *Replay*. She gives attention to the supportive roles that adults provide for the teenagers, especially through her portrayals of Mr. and Mrs. Finney in *Absolutely Normal Chaos*, and through Leo's parents and grandparents in *Replay*. At the same time she demonstrates that adults are fallible, just like teens are—even when they are family members—through characters like Carl Ray's stubborn father and Leo's quarrelsome aunties.

Most important in these two books, as in her entire body of fiction for adolescents and young adults, Creech provides teen characters, as well as teen readers, with a sense of hope. In *Absolutely Normal Chaos*, Mary Lou looks forward to a new school year with more challenges as a writer and with a developing relationship with Ben; Carl Ray begins a new phase of life, one without secrets about his parentage and with great potential for him to make something of himself. Leo better understands his own family and his place within it; he recognizes that his father's demeanor has been shaped more by fear of aging and bad health than disinterest, he has helped initiate the renewal of contact with Rosaria, and he has had a successful, confidence-building experience with the school play.

Creech's fingerprints as a former teacher of English are also clear to readers of *Replay*. Creech draws attention to her own penchant for drama when she uses a drama production as the centerpiece for the story's main plot. Readers who are interested in her connection to plays will want to follow Creech's Web site for news about her participation in an authors' readers' theatre group. Creech, along with Avi, Walter Dean Myers, Sarah Weeks, and Richard Peck, have formed a group that travels to present readings from their novels, in dramatic fashion (personal communication, January 2, 2007). Those who are familiar with Creech's biography will also recall that she wrote a play, *The Center of the Universe: Waiting for the Girl*, which was produced off-off Broadway in the early 1990s (www.edupaperback.org, retrieved December 3, 2006), and worked at the Federal Theatre Project Archives in Fairfax, Virginia, while completing graduate school at George Mason University (www.ohiocenterfortheboo-k.org). Perhaps the addition of "Rumpopo's Porch" as a plot feature as well as a full text element is an indication that she is again attracted to exploring her talents as a writer of drama.

Other fingerprints are evident in the way she joyfully plays with words and language in *Replay*. Although this book does not include the direct vocabulary lessons of some of her other novels, like *Absolutely Normal Chaos* and *Love that Dog*, Creech masterfully brings language itself to the surface for readers to examine in this one. The Italian names are full of life and energy: Leonardo, Contento, Pietro, Nunzio, Giorgia, Mariana; Aunties Carmella, Angela, Maddalena, and Rosaria; Uncles Carlo, Paulo, and Guido. The lisping talk of the youngest child, Nunzio, marks him as a spoiled and coddled family treasure. That sweet innocence is balanced against the mock-heroic language of comic book heroes that Leo adopts when he tells stories about his heroic and magnificent feats.

In *Replay*, Creech combines her love for families, theater, and positive personal connections in a way that invites readers to become part of Leo's large, loud, family for a few hours. She encourages us to take stock of our own family relationships and shows us that long-standing problems can be addressed if communications are open, even though people are not perfect. In *Replay*, as in her other novels, Creech encourages her readers to risk dreaming big dreams. That encouragement is perhaps Sharon Creech's greatest gift to teen readers.

Works Cited

Creech, Sharon. (1998). An interview with Sharon Creech. At www.achuka.co. uk/interviews/creech.phpo. Retrieved December 2, 2006.

Creech, Sharon. "Newbery Medal Acceptance," *Horn Book*, July/August, 1995, 418–425.

Creech, Sharon. Personal correspondence with Pamela S. Carroll, January 2, 2007.

Creech, Sharon. "*Walk Two Moons*," www.sharoncreech.com/novels/06.asp. Retrieved on December 1, 2004.

Creech, Sharon. www.sharoncreech.com. Retrieved December 12, 2006.

Creech, Sharon. www.sharoncreech.com/novels/11.asp. Retrieved January 19, 2007.

cummings, e.e. *Complete Poems 1904–1962*. George J. Firmage, Ed. New York: Liveright, 1991, 657.

Donelson, Kenneth L. and Nilsen, Aileen Pace. *Literature for Today's Young Adults*, 7th ed. Boston: Allyn & Bacon, 2004.

Frost, Helen. *The Braid*. New York: Farrar Straus and Giroux, 2006.

Frost, Helen. *Keesha's House*. New York: Farrar Straus and Giroux, 2003.

Hesse, Karen. *Out of the Dust*. New York: Scholastic, 1997.

Hipple, Ted and Clairborne, Jennifer. "The Best YA Books of All Time," *English Journal*. 94(3), January, 2005, 99–103.

Pullman, Philip. "Philip Pullman applauds a novel of unobtrusive craftsmanship." At books.guardian.co.uk/reviews/story/0.12084,749907,00.html. Retrieved December 3, 2006.

Rigg, Lyle D. "Sharon Creech." *Horn Book*, July/August, 1995, 426–429.

Rigg, Sharon. *The Recital*. London: Pan, 1990.

Rigg, Sharon. *Nickel Malley*. London: Pan, 1991.

Woodson, Jacqueline. *Locomotion*. New York: Putnam, 2003.

www.ala.org/ala/alsc/alscnews/news.htm. American Library Association. Retrieved January 3, 2006.

www.authorsreaderstheatre.com. Authors' Readers' Theatre. Retrieved January 15, 2007.

www.edupaperback.org/showauth.cfm?authid+51. Retrieved December 3, 2006.

www.ohiocenterforthebook.org/OhioAuthors.aspx?id=174&mode+detail. Retrieved January 30, 2007.

Bibliography of Sharon Creech's Novels that are Featured in this Book

Creech, Sharon. *Absolutely Normal Chaos*. New York: HarperCollins Trophy, 1990.

Creech, Sharon. *Walk Two Moons*. New York: HarperCollins Trophy, 1994.

Creech, Sharon. *Chasing Redbird*. New York: HarperCollins Trophy, 1997.

Creech, Sharon. *Bloomability*. New York: HarperCollins Trophy, 1998.

Creech, Sharon. *The Wanderer*. New York: HarperCollins Trophy, 2000.

Creech, Sharon. *Love that Dog*. New York: HarperCollins Trophy, 2001.

Creech, Sharon. *Ruby Holler*. New York: HarperCollins Trophy, 2002.

Creech, Sharon. *Heartbeat*. New York: HarperCollins Trophy, 2004.

Creech, Sharon. *Replay*. New York: HarperCollins Trophy, 2005.

INDEX

About the Author

PAMELA SISSI CARROLL, a former teacher of middle and high school English language arts, has devoted her attention, as a professor of English Education, to helping teachers, media specialists, and readers connect with young adult literature by studying the artistic qualities of the best books of the genre, by highlighting the ways that it can illuminate teens' social, emotional, and spiritual worlds, and by pointing to its potential for building reading skills while providing meaningful literary experiences for readers. Carroll, who has published books and articles on young adult literature, and who is the former editor of The ALAN Review, was named in 2006 as the University Distinguished Teaching Professor for Florida State University, where she has served as a faculty member since 1990. She edited Greenwood's *Using Literature to Help Troubled Teens Cope with Societal Issues* (1999).